*Creativity
and
Psychological
Health*

*To my father and my mother,
Frank and Sarah Barron,
and to my wife Nancy and
our son Francis Charles Xavier*

"*I have no doubt whatever that most people live, whether physically, intellectually or morally, in a very restricted circle of their potential being. They make use of a very small portion of their possible consciousness, and of their soul's resources in general, much like a man who, out of his whole bodily organism, should get into a habit of using and moving only his little finger. Great emergencies and crises show us how much greater our vital resources are than we had supposed.*"

> WILLIAM JAMES (in a letter to W. Lutoslawski, Cambridge, May 6, 1906; *Letters of William James*, pp. 253–254)

"*Let us love with all our might, Jennie, for who knows where our hearts go, when this world is done?*"

> EMILY DICKINSON (in a letter to Jane Humphrey, October 16, 1855; *Letters of Emily Dickinson*, Vol. II, edited by Thomas H. Johnson)

"*All creation has been committed and offered to the human spirit, that man may penetrate it and thus be able to understand more and more fully the infinite grandeur of his Creator.*"

> POPE PIUS XII (in a speech of welcome to a group of astronautical scientists meeting in Rome)

CREATIVITY AND
PSYCHOLOGICAL
HEALTH

Origins of Personal Vitality and Creative Freedom

FRANK BARRON

Research Psychologist,
Institute of Personality Assessment and Research
University of California, Berkeley

D. VAN NOSTRAND COMPANY, INC.
Princeton, New Jersey
New York   *Toronto*   *London*

D. VAN NOSTRAND COMPANY, INC.
120 Alexander St., Princeton, New Jersey (*Principal office*)
24 West 40 Street, New York 18, New York

D. VAN NOSTRAND COMPANY, LTD.
358, Kensington High Street, London, W.14, England

D. VAN NOSTRAND COMPANY (Canada), LTD.
25 Hollinger Road, Toronto 16, Canada

ACKNOWLEDGMENTS
The author and the publisher wish to express their thanks to the following:

The American Psychological Association for permission to draw upon four of the author's papers—from the *Journal of Abnormal and Social Psychology:* "Complexity-simplicity as a personality dimension," Vol. 48, 2, Apr. 1963; "The disposition toward originality," Vol. 51, 3, Nov. 1955; from the *Journal of Consulting Psychology:* "Test correlates of improvement in psychotherapy," Aug. 1953, Vol. XVII, 4, 235–241; and "An ego-strength scale which predicts response to psychotherapy," Oct. 1953, Vol. XVII, 5, 327–333.

Harper and Row for permission to reprint material from the author's "A case study of a residual" in *Clinical Studies of Personality*, edited by Arthur Burton and Robert E. Harris.

The *Journal of Personality* for permission to draw upon two of the author's papers—"Some personality correlates of independence of judgment," Vol. 21, 3, Mar. 1953, and "Originality in relation to personality and intellect," Vol. 25, 6, Dec. 1957.

C. F. MacIntyre and the University of California Press for permission to quote from Mr. MacIntyre's English translation of *Sonnets to Orpheus*, by Rainer Maria Rilke.

The Society of Authors, literary representative of the Estate of the late A. E. Housman and the Messrs. Jonathan Cape Ltd., and Holt, Rinehart and Winston, Inc. for permission to reprint "Oh, when I was in love with you" from A. E. Housman's *Collected Poems*. U.S. Copyright © 1959 by Holt, Rinehart and Winston, Inc.

The University of California Press for permission to reprint a somewhat condensed version of the author's monograph, *Personal Soundness in University Graduate Students*.

The University of Minnesota Press for material from the author's chapter entitled "Ego-strength and the management of aggression" in *Basic Readings in the MMPI in Psychology and Medicine*, edited by George S. Welsh and Grant Dahlstrom.

Preface

I HAD not intended to become a psychologist, but in the summer of 1941 psychology came and got me. A college classmate who was then planning to be a psychiatrist had taken a summer job as an attendant in a hospital for the mentally ill at Norristown, Pennsylvania. He very much wanted to have a friend on the premises, and he persuaded me to accompany him. In those days, mental hospitals were terribly understaffed, and we found ourselves working a 13-hour day, seven days out of every eight; most hours of most days I was in sole charge of a locked ward with more than one hundred patients. In that summer between my junior and senior years in college I suddenly got educated in psychology without benefit of textbook.

The first thing I learned about the mentally ill in that hospital was that they weren't nearly so different from everyone else as common opinion would have us believe. I became well acquainted with forty or fifty patients and had many long conversations with them. They remain vividly alive in my memory and imagination today. I found that I liked most of them, if not all, and a lot of them liked me. The distinction between mental health and mental illness began almost imperceptibly to soften. Questions slowly posed themselves to me, questions about the meaning of fear and of anger, of apathy, self-abasement, suicide, delinquency, the whole mysterious drift of society, and the portent of intense though aberrant feeling. On the ward there was hurt and pain so big and so deep that speech could not express it. I had been interested in philosophy, and suddenly philosophy came alive for me, for here the basic questions of human existence were not abstractions: they were embodied in human suffering.

When I returned to college in the Fall, I knew I wanted to study psychology. It was my good fortune to begin by picking out from the shelves of the Philadelphia Public Library four musty but likely-looking tomes: the two volumes of William James, *The Principles of Psychology,* and the two of F. W. H. Myers, *Human Personality and Its Survival of Bodily Death.* All the work I have done since then shows the effect of my experience that summer and my reading during the ensuing year.

World War II and combat operations with a field hospital in Europe brought further learning, both of the most personal sort and vicariously from my interviews when the war was over with several hundred combat infantrymen who had been decorated for valor. There began my special interest as a psychologist in courage, resourcefulness, flexibility, strength in meeting crises, the ability to rally from setbacks—in brief, the manifestations of personal vitality and spirit.

The themes in my work derive as well from my early instruction in the Roman Catholic faith and from my formal study of metaphysics at La Salle College. I learned much also in the methodically uncommitted (or so they said) curriculum in Moral Science at Cambridge University. Many of the actual research techniques I acquired during graduate training at the University of Minnesota. Minnesota offered more than just technique, of course; in a sense, what I learned there was how to inquire empirically into matters in the little-explored domain of ethics and values. In my experience, Herbert Fiegl's course at Minnesota in the Philosophy of Science ranked with Sir Frederic Bartlett's seminar at Cambridge on Thinking and Remembering and with Brother J. Emilian's lectures at La Salle on History of Philosophy in stirring the student, myself, to radical outward questioning and inward mental or spiritual questings.

The research upon which this book is based has been done in several different settings: the Institute of Personality Assessment and Research, Bryn Mawr College, Swarthmore College, Vassar College, the Harvard Psychological Clinic and the Center for Research in Personality at Harvard, Langley Porter Clinic and the Berkeley Mental Hygiene Clinic, and the Center for Advanced Study in the Behavioral Sciences, Palo Alto, California. I am indebted for generous support of the work and for helpfulness in matters of administration to the senior scientists in those various places: to Donald W. MacKinnon, Nevitt Sanford, Robert E. Harris, Solomon Asch, Henry A. Murray, Robert W. White, David C. McClelland, and Ralph Tyler.

To Dr. MacKinnon I am especially grateful for his loyal personal support over the years; I have learned to have confidence both in his critical scholarly judgment and in his sound sense of policy in administering the affairs of the Institute. The central core of the Institute's work owes much to his wisdom.

My research associates have been many, and I shall mention only those who helped directly as interviewers, observers, or experimenters: Jack Block, Donald Brown, Richard S. Crutchfield, Erik Erikson, Harrison G. Gough, Wallace B. Hall, Eugenia Hanfman, Ravenna Helson, Timothy F. Leary, John Perry, Harriet Podell, Harold Renaud, and George S. Welsh. My thanks for other assistance in the research goes to these psychologists: Elizabeth R. Kalis, Joseph Kamiya, John Loehlin, Arnold Mordkoff, Jean Shimek, and James R. Yandell. For secretarial help I am most deeply indebted to Judith Benjamin, Judi Danner, and Elizabeth Urquhart.

It is a pleasure as well to acknowledge the support that my work has received from the U.S. Public Health Service, the Ford Foundation, the Carnegie Corporation, and the Rockefeller Foundation. I am especially grateful to the Ford Foundation for the unencumbered and exceptionally exciting year I spent at the Center for Advanced Study in the Behavioral Sciences (1958-59) and for a grant that has enabled me since 1957 to have secretarial and clerical assistance and to have real freedom of movement because it required no "reason" for travel. Dr. Bernard Berelson of the Behavioral Sciences Division was the responsible administrator in that decision, and I am grateful to him.

I think also of my steadfast friend, Arthur Gladman, who helped immensely in all this work.

A great debt, and one that I acknowledge with deep feeling, is to the many hundreds of persons who offered themselves as subjects in these studies. All in all, more than 5,000 individuals took part in the research. Of these, nearly 1,500 participated in intensive and detailed case studies; approximately another 1,500 gave a day or two of their time to studies involving extensive group testing; and the remaining 2,000 or more served as normative groups for the initial standardization of particular single tests.

Perhaps it would not be amiss here to direct a remark or two to Kenneth Rexroth, a gentleman who is mostly a poet but who goes in for social criticism as well. Rexroth was, as he has most publicly said, a subject in a study partially reported in this volume: the study of creative writers. After taking part in the research, he wrote a piece for *The Nation* ("The Vivisection of a Poet") in which he made three salient points: (1) psychology is powerless; (2) psychology is a dangerous force; (3) psychological research is supported in luxury by the money filched or pirated by the millionaire foundation-makers from the steel workers, *et al.*

To the last point first: in 1949 I did all the work reported in two of the chapters in this book (Chapters 8 and 9) on a grant totaling $2000 for the entire year, including my full salary, from the U.S. Public Health Service. In the following year I advanced to a half-time salary of $1350 supplied by the Rockefeller Foundation, and in that year I did most of the work reported in Chapters 5 and 15. From this I marched onward and upward to a 12-month full-time salary of $3700 as a college lecturer, and in that year I did the research reported in Chapter 14.

Writers and musicians and painters—artists in general—are rewarded so abominably in worldly goods that I can feel only the most profound sympathy with Rexroth's complaint. Social scientists, including psychologists, have lately been doing much better, so there is justice to the charge that the "students of creativity" are more valued by the social organizations, if valuation is shown by monetary reward, than the creators themselves. Not long ago I was walking down a street in Berkeley and I met another subject in the study of writers, a poet also, who was making a living by typing manuscripts for undergraduates. He happened to be flat broke at the time and needed carfare back to San Francisco, so he asked me to lend him a dollar. I started to do so, but he interrupted to say that he had another idea: he could sell me a copy of one of his books of poetry, which he happened to have with him. "Oh, yes," I said, "do that," so he sold me the book, for the filthy dollar I had taken from the pockets of the steel workers, and he drew a picture in the book besides, and inscribed his name and the date there. Poetry is its own reward, but one could wish that all those whose task and pleasure it is to create beauty in the world, and who can do so if the world will only give their time back to them, might have leave to do for an ordinary living wage the work their heart desires.

As for the power of psychology, or its lack, I should say that what many people sense, psychologists and nonpsychologists alike, is the enormous potential of mind itself for the control of its own mighty destiny; and psychology as a science is the disciplined effort of mind to understand itself and to achieve self-control. The danger of extinction we face at our own hands makes more poignant the gap between our potentiality and our actuality. Hence psychology itself seems immensely powerful and yet frightfully weak.

More than that, there is a negative side to the possibility of control: *1984*, brainwashing, the inhuman workings of the totalitarian state—these are the dreadful possible outcomes that are to be feared. Each of us feels in his own soul both the hope of freedom and the fear of loss of individuality. It is easy to be bitter when such hopes are disappointed or their realization deferred. And it is tempting to escape from fear by saying that there really is no threat, that the science of mind is powerless. My own belief is that psychology has very great potential for good and for evil, and that the development of this potential as well as the account to which we turn it is strictly up to us.

FRANK BARRON

Berkeley, California
April, 1963

Contents

1

Psychological Vitality: An Attempt at Philosophical Definition

A QUICK glance at a good psychological library is sufficient to indicate that psychologists have traditionally been much more interested in psychological illness than in psychological health. Many and heavy are the books on mental illness, but few and light are the books on mental health. In fact, when one looks closely at volumes whose titles suggest that they perhaps deal with mental health, they usually turn out to be much more concerned with mental illness.

Of course, this greater attention to disease and malfunction is not just an oddity of the psychological profession. Most of us pay little attention to our health when it is good, just as we pay little attention to our automobile as long as it is running well. It is when we are physically ill that our body comes to our notice, and it is usually when we are a bit upset and anxious that we become *self-conscious;* when we are just *being our natural self* we are in good health mentally. In brief, disease is more vivid and more noticeable than efficient functioning, and consequently has had more scientific attention paid to it.

This natural tendency to give more notice to the pathological resulted in a relative neglect in psychological theory of the conditions and characteristics that define psychological health. Just after World War II, however, a group of psychologists at the University of California, in reviewing what during the war they had learned at first hand of heroic human reactions to terrible stress, decided that it was high time that psychology should take a look at the positive side of human nature and concern itself with unusual vitality in human beings rather than with disease. It appeared to them that psychological health had always been defined negatively, in terms of what is present when health is absent. So they decided to attempt a definition that would state *what is present when health is present.*

It was my pleasure to participate in this enterprise with what has turned out to be a very active research group at the University during the past dozen years. The first attempt we made at defining psychological health came during the first six months of our organizational life, shortly after we had begun work as the Institute of Personality Assessment and Research. Because we intended to employ the special research method known as the living-in assessment, in which the subjects live for several days at the Institute house (a former fraternity house, incidentally), we had at our disposal a well-furnished living room equipped with soft armchairs. One of our first decisions was to sit down in the armchairs and think about psychological health in positive terms.

With some half-dozen psychologists arrayed in a circle and comfortably seated, it was natural enough that a sort of informal symposium should quickly organize itself. We listened as a group as each of us in turn presented his own ideas of what the psychologically healthy person should be like. After a bit of listening, it became clear to me that I had fallen in with a group of rather noble souls, for the traits which they uniformly ascribed to the psychologically healthy person were the sort that would earn anyone a reward in the afterlife, if indeed he had not already been amply rewarded here below. As I listened further, however, I began to realize that the catalogue of named virtues would be somewhat more appropriate to an effectively functioning person in the temperate zone than in the tropical or arctic zones. Then it came to me that the effectively functioning person had had two other rather locally determined restrictions imposed upon him; namely, like each and every staff member of the Institute, he was a man rather than a woman, and rather closer to middle age than to adolescence. At the end of those first comfortable discussions, then, we had arrived at an excellent picture of an effectively functioning and notably virtuous man in his middle years in late summer at Berkeley, California.

Several of our staff members, however, have distinguished themselves by their penetrating psychological insights into ethnocentrism, and they could not long remain unconscious of a major if essentially rather gentle exhibition of it. A happy piece of data analysis finally made the diagnosis certain. In our first official contact with subjects selected for their general effectiveness as persons, we employed an adjective checklist by means of which each staff member described each subject whom we studied during three days of living-in assessment. Our intention was to derive from these checklists a composite staff description of each subject and then to correlate the composite description with external criterion ratings (i.e., real-life judgments by nonpsychologists) of the individuals so-called *Soundness as a Person*. This indeed we did, with interesting results; but we went further, and analyzed separately the individual checklists which went to make up the composite. Thus for staff member *A*, for example, we were able to discover with what adjectives he more often characterized subjects rated high on Soundness by external public opinion than subjects rated low. The results of this analysis were impressive. It turned out that individual staff members were using quite different adjectives to describe the same person, but with great consistency they were describing highly effective people by exactly the adjectives with which in a private moment of good will toward themselves they would use to describe *themselves*. Moreover, they tended to describe clearly ineffective persons as possessing traits which in themselves they most strongly denied, i.e., possible human characteristics which they had repudiated with special vigor. Thus, one staff member noted for his simple and clear thought processes most frequently described an ineffective person as *confused;* another staff member who is especially well-behaved in matters of duty checked the adjectives *conscientious* and *responsible* most frequently in describing highly rated subjects. Our most notably non-ethnocentric staff member found effective persons more *tolerant* than anything else; another staff member who has subsequently been interested professionally in independence of judgment saw effective subjects as *independent* and *fair-minded*. Each of us, in brief, saw his own image in what he judged to be good.

There is a rather strong ethical tone to some of these preconceptions, as I have suggested. But I would urge here that we must avoid any implication that the healthy person psychologically must necessarily be a good person morally. For the most part it is probably a healthy thing to be rather well behaved, and as a rule we are in better health when we are cool and collected than when we are agitated. But there are times when it is a mark of greater health to be unruly, and a sign of greater inner resources to be able to upset one's own balance and to seek a new order of selfhood.

The ability to permit oneself to become disorganized is in my judgment quite crucial to the development of a very high level of integration. Because we are capable of reflecting upon ourselves, we are committed, willy-nilly, to an artistic enterprise in the creation of our own personality. By our very nature as intelligent beings, we are compelled to make an image of ourselves which will be coherent and of enduring recognizability, to us and to others. One judges the degree of success of this inevitable reflective act by precisely the criteria with which one judges a work of art, or a scientific theory at that level of generality where science and art alike are concerned with problems of universal validities. We are accustomed to say of a mathematical explanation or of a scientific theory that it is most elegant when with a minimum of postulates it embraces a maximum of implications. In art the analogue to this is the art product that communicates the greatest richness and depth of experience in the simplest and clearest manner. I think that some such concept as that of elegance is needed if we are to talk meaningfully of psychological health. A person may be said to be most elegant, and most healthy, when his awareness includes the broadest possible aspects of human experience, and the deepest possible comprehension of them, while at the same time he is most simple and direct in his feelings, thoughts, and actions.

Certain facts concerning temporary upset and agitation in especially healthy or potentially healthy persons can thus be explained in terms of the creative act necessary in order to achieve integration at the most complex level. A certain amount of discord and disorder must be permitted into the perceptual system if a more complex synthesis is to result. Usually, of course, some discord is brought in by new experiences that are common to all of us. Weaning is one, toilet training is another, the discovery of pleasure in the genitals is a third. Many others might be mentioned, such as the first recognition that one is dependent for one's life upon the actions and feelings of others, and that regardless of anything else that occurs, one must finally die.

At some time in life there arises also what might be called "the crisis in belief," in which it becomes necessary to re-examine the basis of one's religious or philosophical beliefs, and to come to some sort of explanation for oneself of what the universe is all about and what life itself signifies. The choice of a life work and the choice of a life mate are two other nearly universal crises.

The more energy a person has at his disposal, the more fully will he become committed to the most complex possible integration. In this connection I think it is important to remember that intelligence is a form of energy. Psychoanalysis has tended to represent the sexual drives as the most powerful and most basic source of energy in the organism, and indeed at times such drives are seen as most difficult to control, because they represent the forces of blind desire. But the capacity to symbolize, to create a valid image of reality, is the peculiarly human energy, the triumphant form of energy in the living world. In the world of living forms it is the most intelligent form, not the most instinct-dominated, which succeeds; within the human person we might expect a similar outcome. The fact is, of course, that intelligence in general does succeed in containing impulse, through the creation of an image of the self as differentiated from the surround, the interpersonal environment. The image of the self is a complicated pattern, an artistic endeavor, as I have suggested, to which we are committed whether we will or no. In psychological sickness our image of ourself blurs, the colors run, it is not integrated or beautiful. We become conscious of its existence momentarily, and hence awkwardness ensues. But in health there is no awkwardness, for the moment of health is the moment of unconscious creative synthesis, when without thinking about it at all we know that we make sense to ourselves and to others. In the most elegant of cases, this synthesis involves a tremendous interpenetration of symbols, drawn from our sexuality, our philosophy, and the meaning of our work, with complex overdetermination of actions and feelings which are themselves expressively simple.

When such simplicity amid complexity has been achieved, I think that two new and most important affects come into existence in the individual's experience. One of these is the feeling that one is free and that life and its outcome are in one's own hands. The other is a new experience of the passage of time, and a deeper sense of relaxed participation in the present moment. All of experience is consequently permanent at the very moment of its occurrence, and life ceases to be a course between birth and death and becomes instead a fully realized experience of change in which every single state is as valid and as necessary as every other.

2

Uses, and the Danger of Abuses, of Research on Creativity

Since the day on which that awesome mushroom cloud arose indifferently over Hiroshima, signaling the end of an era of unprecedented human destructiveness and the beginning of a new era of unprecedented power for destruction or construction, the minds of men in the most advanced clusters of culture (the United States, Great Britain, Europe, the Soviet Union, China) have turned intently toward the potential for creation which we human beings possess in unique degree in the world of living things.

Governments became interested because the sheer physical power and, by a very short step, political power that comes from inventiveness had suddenly become so manifest; commerce is newly interested because the increase in goods, services, and profits is most evidently dependent on new ideas; religion is interested because old meanings have been destroyed and new ones call to be created; the individual is interested because to create is to be more fully and more freely oneself. Perhaps at no other time in all of human history has there been such general recognition that to be creative in one's own everyday activity is a positive good.

Science and art, of course, have always been interested; the act of imagination is their business. A scientific theory is an imagining of the way things could really be behind their appearances, expressed formally and accompanied by a set of rules whereby the goodness of the imagining may be appraised; a work of art is an expression of individual vision couched in a form which aspires to an audience of at least one who can say, "Yes, so it is!"

Beyond these local interests, whether individual or national, is the increasing recognition by men in all parts of the globe that our capacity for creative thought and action may literally make all the difference in the world. The power of scientific discovery has suddenly increased the stakes, both for ethics and for politics; in its crassest form, science serves merely national striving for power, but in its purest it serves that aspect of power involving the spread of our form of life and intelligence throughout the universe. Human creativity may prove to be the key to success or failure in mankind's quest for knowledge, in his journey beyond the bounds of the sure and the seen, in his exploration of the unknown.

These are some of the considerations that make the psychology of human creativity so vitally important. Such considerations played a large part in the thinking of myself and some of my colleagues as we turned our attention more and more from the appraisal of personal health and stability to the appraisal of potential for creative development in the individuals whom we studied. And no doubt some similar thoughts were in the minds of those people in such organizations as the Rockefeller Foundation, the Carnegie Corporation, and the Ford Foundation who offered us support for the kind of research that we have carried on. At the risk of being too cursory and too simplistic, I should suggest that the primary motivation of both the research psychologists and those who were the focus of their social support could be summed up in this sentence: "It would be interesting and possibly very useful if we could learn more about the nature of creative activity, so that we might more readily find and foster creativity in individuals in our society, for the common good of all." With a bit of extension and modulation such a sentiment would not be much unlike the theme that Francis Bacon at the beginning of the scientific revolution voiced in the *Novum Organum:* "for the glory of the creator and the relief of man's estate."

These sentiments may be all very well for research psychologists and for the assortment of agencies representing government, industry, enlightened philanthropy, religion, and education who think it fine that human creativity be studied scientifically; but let me tell you right at the outset of this report on my own work, which included research into the sources of artistic creativity, that poets and painters and all other artists who are poets or painters in one form or another were by no means convinced. Nor was I myself much more than halfway convinced, although it must be said of myself and of all the artists who did take part in the research that we went ahead with it. Several years ago, in describing the reaction of a number of creative writers to my invitation to them to participate as subjects in this work, I wrote in *Scientific American*, September, 1958 as follows:

> We were not surprised to encounter rather spirited objections from some of the writers whom we decided to ask to make a contribution to the study. In trenchant and not particularly orderly prose, about a fifth of those who responded to our initial letter pointed out the intrinsically evil character of psychological research. The objections to such research are mainly on these counts: it is vivisection; it is an expression of the effort of organized society to encroach upon the individual and to rob him of his freedom; it is presumptuous because it seeks to describe and to understand what is intrinsically a mystery. Psychological diagnosis is, moreover, a form of name-calling; it is a way of having the last word; it does not respect the individual. Finally, it is the present seeking to impose itself upon the future and to perpetuate the *status quo* through techniques which will identify the potentially constructive deviant and permit a stultifying society to control him.
>
> Since psychological research at its worst may indeed be destructive in just such ways, socially responsible psychologists have reason to sleep almost as uneasily as socially responsible physicists. This particular study has proceeded in recognition of some of the dangers which may be inherent in it, and it has been able to proceed because most of the creative writers who have been asked to participate have been willing to trust the investigators and to accept the inevitable hazards of all efforts at increasing knowledge. Both scientists and artists have something to fear when they embark upon the unknown. In his *Life of William Blake*, Alexander Gilchrist records three lines from Samuel Palmer's account of a conversation with Blake about the latter's designs for Dante's *Inferno*:
> "He said he began them with fear and trembling.
> "I said, 'Oh, *I* have enough of fear and trembling.'
> " 'Then,' said he, 'you'll do.' "

To this I can only add that now, several years later when most of the work is done, I feel glad that I had a part in it, and I feel also that it has done no indignity either to the creative artists who participated in it, or to the mystery itself, which I think we shall have to admit has preserved itself rather well. That which is essentially mysterious cannot yield itself to scrutiny; on the other hand, whatever we can find out about nature is ours to know. Let me repeat the words of Pope Pius XII that serve as one of this volume's epigraphs: "All creation has been committed and offered to the human spirit, that man may penetrate it and thus be able to understand more and more fully the infinite grandeur of his Creator." It is in such a spirit—tempered by the reflection that, as Emerson once put it, "Proteus is a slippery fellow," and that protean reality will hardly be caught whole in our little net of psychological tests and correlation coefficients—that we approach the phenomena of psychic vitality and creativeness.

3

Assessment?

SHORTLY after a sign reading "Institute of Personality Assessment and Research" was tacked up outside the door of the former fraternity house that was to be the dwelling place of this enterprise for at least a decade or so, there ambled indifferently over the threshold a distinctly odd and unquestionably lively young man who had come there to be an object of study. He had fallen among psychologists more or less by chance. He was an advanced graduate student in one of the sciences at a time when the Institute was initiating a study of psychological health specifically among professional and scientific workers, and his name was included in a comprehensive list of Ph.D. candidates who were judged by their department chairmen to be within one year of completing work for the degree. From a list of over 400 such names, approximately 100 were selected at random and invited to serve as subjects of study. Paul was among the 70 per cent who accepted the invitation.

He did not merely accept the invitation, however. He wrote a brief note to the psychologists who were conducting the study. The note read: "Since you claim to assess, you must know value. I myself know nothing concerning the value of persons. I am interested in learning how you go about making your judgments."

Thus formidably self-announced, Paul came to be assessed. He proved to be a tall, string-beanish, round-shouldered individual. His head, which was set rather forward on his gangling body, gave an impression of being disproportionately small. He was literally low-browed as well, and the forelock of his unruly red hair fell down over the middle of his forehead. He had pale blue eyes, which were armed with a habit of staring blankly and bleakly when he was spoken to directly. He was dressed shabbily, his suit being both frayed and rumpled, his shoes down at the heels and much scuffed. His overnight bag was literally a bag; that is, he carried his extra clothes and toilet articles in a paper sack such as one uses to carry groceries. He was the last of ten subjects to arrive at the assessment house for a weekend of study, and it may be mentioned now that he was the first to leave.

A word concerning the method of study by which Paul's "value" was to be determined. It is patterned after the assessment program used by the Office of Strategic Services during World War II, and its distinctive feature is that the subjects and the psychologists are housed together for several days, during which there are certain informal social activities in addition to the more formal techniques of study conventionally employed by psychologists. The procedures include paper-and-pencil tests, interviews, group situational tests, and experiments of a kind more commonly run in the laboratory setting. The setting in this instance, as we have said, was a former fraternity house, comfortably furnished and complete with a large dining room and kitchen, living room with fireplace, sleeping quarters, and testing rooms for both individual and group procedures. There are no chambers in which judgments are made concerning the value of persons, but it must be admitted that there is a large room in which tests are scored and percentile ranks assigned.

We shall find occasion a bit later to return to Paul and his three days on trial at the Institute, but in the meantime it may be meet to consider seriously the problem he so baldly stated. "Assessment" *is* a peculiar word to use of personality. It is a particularly odd word to couple with the word "research," for scientific research is an inquiry into the true state of affairs, with description and explanation as its aims, whereas assessment is an appraisal for the purpose of attaching value. Yet both words are properly part of the name of the psychological institute which carried out this work: their presence together indicates a central perplexity which confronts the scientific investigator who would deal with problems of human personality.

His dilemma has its origins in one of the uniquely human achievements—the moral valuation of things. In the Bible, the Fall of Man (into his present human condition) is ascribed to the act of our first parents in eating the fruit of the Tree of Knowledge of Good and Evil. The psychological experience thus symbolized is at the heart of the human achievement in a material universe, for the fall from

ASSESSMENT? **13**

innocence might better be called the accession to conscience and the beginning of civilization.

Just as it is the human being alone who judges things ethically, so it is particularly *the human act* which is so judged. A research program which accepts as its central purpose the study of excellence of human functioning is thus confronted by a special difficulty: how is such knowledge to be pursued in a purely descriptive and objective spirit in a domain of experience where fact is so interlaced with value?

In the physical sciences it is still possible to hold that the description of the world is an enterprise that is not concerned with ethics. Even there, of course, eminent scientific minds, viewing the events which flow from such description, are becoming increasingly concerned with the responsibility of the scientist to his fellow men as well as to the facts. In a sense, the discovery of fact is itself an ethical act. The consequences of scientific research, it need hardly be said any longer, are sometimes for weal and sometimes for woe. Even in our description of physical relations we are not yet beyond good and evil.

Still, the *laws* that describe the functioning of the nonhuman world have nothing of ethics in them, for the events that they subsume are ethically neutral. The psychology of human personality, however, is persistently beset by the ethical character of the phenomena it takes as its domain. When one sets out to give even a tentative definition of "excellence of human functioning," one comes almost immediately to questions of ethical valuation. To say that fact is interlaced with value is not to state the matter strongly enough, or, for that matter, accurately. It is more correct to say that human values are themselves among the salient facts, and that ethics are an integral part of the phenomena with which the psychologist must deal.

Still, one might easily draw this matter too fine and lose contact with ordinary human feeling about the meetness of evaluating others. Psychological "assessment" is part and parcel of everyday life. This fact finds expression in the common phrase "sizing someone up." It is interesting in this connection that all of us use a normative approach to human functioning when we undertake such appraisal. The source of the image is that comfortably normative mart, the haberdashery shop. Psychological diagnosis could perhaps be even better vilified than it was by some of the creative writers who turned their words upon it. It is like a ready-to-wear suit and usually fits just about as

well. But the practical value of both these articles of standard manu-
facture can hardly be gainsaid. The sizing up of others and even of
ourselves is a down-to-earth practice which is not likely to vanish,
whatever the garb that man in outer space may eventually find himself
wearing.

4

An Odd Fellow

Lᴇᴛ ᴜs return to Paul.

In research employing the living-in assessment method, the subject is given ample opportunity to define himself and to communicate this self-definition to the psychologists and to his fellow subjects. The initial interview, which is really the first procedure in assessment, is nominally devoted to gathering background information about the person, but it is functionally the subject's first step in representing himself to the staff.

Paul's first interview was with one of the staff psychoanalysts, who soon conceived the notion that his interviewee was suffering from some form of mental aberration. Several minor anomalies of the subject's behavior contributed to this impression. He entered the interview room grumpily and opened the conversation by saying, "Why do you have the window open on such a cold day?" (It was late spring in California.) At a loss for a reason, the interviewer volunteered to close the window. Paul insisted on its remaining open, however, remarking, "After all, it's your room." The interview never did flow very smoothly after this, and it was marked throughout by abrupt and challenging admissions which Paul threw at the interviewer. Apparently noticing that the latter was looking at his scuffed shoes, Paul said, "I wear old clothes because I'm poor." This is a remark rather difficult to reply to while one is attempting to establish rapport. Later Paul retaliated for the attention he imagined his appearance was unjustly receiving by staring at the interviewer's hair (which was cut in a European mode) and asking, "Where did you get the Einstein haircut?"—a remark possibly prompted in part by the fact that the interviewer had a picture of Einstein on the wall of his office and might be presumed to admire that great thinker.

This heroically ill-mannered approach to his assessors (for that he did see the staff as self-appointed judges of his ultimate value there can be no doubt) had a ludicrous quality about it, like a small dog growling at a vast and threatening shape in the darkness, when after all what is there is only a tree or some other natural and unthreatening object. In a situation of great danger, such challenging behavior might be admirable. It was ludicrous in this instance only because nothing was really threatening. As Paul saw it, of course, assessment *was* a dangerous situation, and he was set to resist valiantly any attempt to devalue him. The ludicrous thing about it all is that psychologists are in reality no more qualified to judge their subjects than their subjects are to judge the psychologists. That the behavior was not really inappropriate, however, goes without saying; it was appropriate to the fact that Paul was about to assess himself through the eyes of persons whom he had defined as superior and judging individuals.

In telling of his brief service in the military forces during World War II, Paul claimed to have been discharged "for the convenience of the Army." This was brought about, he said, by his stupidity; he could not learn to march in step, and he had difficulty in caring for his equipment, in making his bed, and even in putting on his leggings properly. In seven months of training he never once passed inspection. When assigned as company fireman he let the fires go out, and when put on kitchen duty he accidentally broke dishes or held up the work because of his slowness. He finally came to the official attention of an Army board because, when assigned to a certain guard post during maneuvers, he remained there for two days when the sergeant of the guard inadvertently neglected to give him explicit instructions that he was relieved of duty because the unit was moving on to another position. "I always did my best to obey," said Paul. He was discharged after nine months of service. The interviewer asked Paul whether he had any feeling about why he had not made the grade as a soldier. Paul with his coldest and blankest stare, replied, "It pleased me not to serve."

It was such inner violence, powerfully communicated, that led the interviewer to wonder whether chance had not brought to the Institute, which was interested in the healthy and well-functioning personality, a person who instead was seriously ill and in whom psychotic processes were close to the surface. What was not at first so evident but became clearer as assessment progressed was that Paul was in many respects quite outstandingly sane, and that in fact he had an acute sense of himself in relation to social reality and knew just how far he could let himself go in his aberrations. Even his most aberrant behavior was shrewdly self-reckoned, so that, although he made a point of introducing himself in the worst possible light, he had in reserve the qualities for which others would indeed value him.

In characterizing himself on an adjective check-list consisting of some 300 personally descriptive adjectives, Paul encircled as being especially applicable to himself these five words: independent, intelligent, pessimistic, serious, and unstable. At the end of the list he wrote, and encircled, the adjectives "churlish" and "ridiculous," which are not among the words in the standard set, but which he apparently felt some need to use. He also described himself as arrogant, bitter, headstrong, imaginative, ingenious, inventive, loud, opinionated, outspoken, quarrelsome, and unfriendly.

On a questionnaire designed to elicit expressions of personal philosophy, Paul revealed something further of his own self-perception and of his values. The qualities he thinks most important for a person to have are "intelligence and seriousness" and "a concealed sensitivity." The persons whom he most admires are Gandhi, Marx, Nietzsche, William Blake, and Einstein. (This latter revelation occurred some time after the initial interview.) In a friend, Paul would like the qualities of "tolerance, sensitivity, insight, a profound futility, and cheerfulness" ("the penultimate," he added, "being necessary to the ultimate"). In answer to the question "What would make you lose your self-respect?," he replied, "The feeling that I had given in in some important way. Purely a matter of losing whatever authenticity I have been able to muster." To the question "What might give you a feeling of awe?," he replied, "I received with awe the news that an atomic bomb had been exploded at Hiroshima."

In an interview devoted to questions of personal philosophy, Paul declared himself "no longer interested" in philosophical problems. He claimed to remember having concluded at the age of six (presumably upon attaining the use of reason) that there could not possibly be a God. At about the same time, he said, he was much concerned with the problem of death, and upon learning of physical corruption after death (information gleaned from a gravedigger in the local cemetery) he decided that "dead people were dead for good." He described himself as being entirely without religious feeling: "I can't understand the words they use." Concerning free will, he said, "There simply is no such thing. Life is entirely a matter of accident . . . a series of fortuitous circumstances." His view of the world could be described in brief as empiristic, pessimistic, irreligious, materialistic, and deterministic, which is one coherent but minority type of aesthetic preference in questions of philosophy.

SOCIAL BEHAVIOR

Paul conducted himself socially in a manner that was not calculated to win friends, but that in its total impact over several days of personal association was not nearly so fearsome as single incidents might make it seem. His social technique in a group situation consisted in making absurd, extreme, and challenging statements which any reasonable man would have to disagree with, but which nevertheless expressed somehow the irrational and inexpressible but quite real feelings of the group. It was as if Paul did these absurd and extreme things in order that other people would not have to do them; or, at least, he had a kind of license which derived from his social role as an outlet for the behaviors that a well-regulated group could not countenance in itself as a whole.

An example from the group discussion that was scheduled for the after-supper hour might serve to illustrate this. The topic that was to be discussed was "the great men of the twentieth century." The ten subjects were divided into two groups of five each, and they were charged with the task of drawing up a list of the ten greatest men of the century, in separate session. After half an hour the two groups were to come together and compare their lists, with the object then of agreeing finally on a single list of ten great men. The group of which Paul was a member began its work in an awkward and embarrassed way, and one of the gentler members of the group, with a look around the room for approval from all, suggested, "I think we should start with Freud, the great psychologist." This drew a snort from Paul, who interjected, "Not Freud—you mean Ford! The greatest man of this century is Ford. It's Ford's century." He then went on to a series of disparaging remarks about both Freud (whose name he pronounced "Frood") and psychology, all of them directed actually at the listening, observing, and presumably judging assessors, but expressing nicely for the group of assessees the feelings of suppressed hostility toward psychology that are fairly inevitable in persons who have done the really magnanimous thing of allowing their privacy to be intruded upon in the interests of scientific investigation. They had mastered their ambivalences on the surface and were genuinely cooperative, but Paul correctly and probably unconsciously perceived the lingering and suppressed resentment toward the assessment procedure, and he expressed it loudly for one and all to hear. The net result, of course, was a sneaking feeling of friendship and liking for Paul in most of the other assessees, which in fact was expressed in sociometrics on the final day of work; his fellow assessees elected Paul as the kind of person who would make a very good friend, who would be an interesting companion on a vacation trip in the mountains, who would be good fun at a party, and who even, improbably enough, would make a good department chairman.

This latter nomination grew out of Paul's behavior in one of the improvisations, or role-playing situations, to which two hours were devoted during the three days of assessment. One of the roles that Paul was required to play was that of a department chairman to whom a graduate student comes protesting over a "reservation" which he had received in one of his qualifying examinations for the Ph.D. Paul in this role was able to divest himself of his bad-boy mannerisms, and with serious, dignified, and reserved demeanor he dealt with the graduate student both sympathetically and quite realistically from the point of view of a department chairman. His response to the demands of the role was certainly all that could be asked for. In another role, however, that of a man who has been sold a house which is later found to be infested with termites who have eaten away the foundation, Paul summoned his natural unruliness with great ease and resolved the situation by threatening to send the termites back to the former owner (i.e., to the former owner's new house) unless reparations were made.

Another of the group procedures called for planning the city of the future. Again, each group of planners consisted of five assessees, and there was a final session in which the two groups presented their plans to one another and sought to integrate the various ideas they had individually generated. Here Paul was elected by his group to make the presentation of the group plan to the other contingent. His election followed upon his domination, mostly because of superior productivity and more original ideas, of the initial planning session. In this, too, he was fairly obstreperous, generally replying to realistic objections to some of his fantastic notions by the dogmatic and disposing assertion, "Science will take care of that." His premise was that anything that could be imagined would eventually come into being, the net effect being to ridicule scientific pretensions to miracle-working while at the same time permitting imagination to roam freely.

Among his unsociable acts was a conspicuous desertion of the group at midnight on the first day of assessment. Everyone else, somewhat overstimulated by the intensive and close-packed schedule, gathered in the kitchen for a snack, and there got into a session of group puzzle-solving. Paul yawned loudly three times in five minutes and then asked, when everyone else had fallen silent while trying to solve a puzzle proposed by one of the group, "Say, does this go on till morning, or can a person get some sleep?" He was told that he was free to go to bed when he wanted to, whereupon he yawned again and left the group. His implied lack of interest in puzzles as well as in further conversation should be considered together with two other items of information: one, he was outstanding in his ability to solve the so-called "insight puzzles" which constituted one of the experimental procedures, and two, at dinner that evening he had solved with considerable efficiency a rather difficult puzzle which another student had offered, and which no one else at the table was able to see through.

INTELLECTUAL ABILITY

That Paul was to be an isolate on many a scattergram was indicated early by his performances on tests of intellectual ability.[1] On the Primary Mental Abilities test he scored at the 47th percentile (general population norms); on Form G of the Miller Analogies test, however, he scored at the 98th percentile (graduate student norms). One can only wonder what aberration of motive led him to decline to perform

[1] In what follows, there are many references to published psychological tests and there is frequent use of technical terminology. The non-professional reader may find it useful to refer to the *Technical Appendix* at the back of the book for an explanation of terms and for a fuller explanation of the tests. References to the test literature have been for the most part omitted from the body of the text but may be found either in the appendix or the bibliography.

on the PMA. (It may have pleased him not to serve.) Since in the identification of high intelligence false negatives are more likely to occur than false positives, it is probably a safe conclusion that Paul is of superior intelligence.

In perceptual performances Paul was generally quite good, but again a serious discrepancy in performance occurred. In this case the discrepancy is particularly worth noting and is more readily explained psychodynamically. The general perceptual task which elicited these notably inconsistent performances is that of perceiving or recognizing a figure that is masked by another figure or by a strong alternative perceptual structuring of the field. Paul made an excellent score on the Gottschaldt test, which presents simple geometrical figures masked by more complex ones; but on a similar problem he very nearly failed to recognize the masked figure within the time limit. In the latter instance, what was presented was a square of white cardboard on which was written (in script) the word "summer" and its mirror image from below, so joined that the word tends to be masked by the larger symmetrical figure, similar to a corkscrew, which is formed. Paul at last saw the word "summer." After giving the solution he commented, "All that I could see at first was the penis." The "strong alternative structuring" was in this case one which the experimenter had not had in mind. Paul's rigidity of perception was a function of sexual shock; understanding its specific psychodiagnostic import should be one aim of a psychodynamic formulation.

In several other perceptual experiments Paul performed in a manner that suggested both efficiency and flexibility. On the Street Gestalt Test, which requires the subject to perform an act of perceptual completion when an incomplete representation of a definite stimulus image is presented for identification, Paul made the twelfth highest score of 80 subjects. He ranked eighth in the ability to shift adaptation level realistically in a weight judgment experiment; and on the "line movement" apparatus devised by Hans Wallach for the study of visual movement he ranked second in the number of changes in direction of movement which he reported. In this latter experiment, a crisscross pattern of lines drawn at a 45° angle on a continuous roll of paper is exposed behind a rectangular aperture, the paper moving downwards at a constant rate. The subject is instructed to report any changes in the direction of movement of the lines. Paul reported not only rapid changes, but actually many different *scenes*, usually involving groups of people in some regular motion. While the full significance of the measure is not yet understood, it seems on the face of it to involve the ability to see things in new patterns or to restructure rapidly and variously, precisely as Paul proved able to do.

IMAGINATION AND ORIGINAL EXPRESSION

Some assessment measures were designed especially to tap originality of thinking and expression. One of these was a modification of the "Test of Productive Thinking" devised by G. K. Bennett. This test details imaginary happenings and asks the subject to list as many consequences as he can think of. Paul made the second highest score in the graduate student sample, in terms of the unusualness of his response and their originality as rated by three independent raters. His responses to one of the test problems are given below, by way of communicating something of his style of thinking as well as his preoccupations.

> PROBLEM I. The mean level of the oceans has been lowered five feet. This change has occurred at the rate of two inches a day during a period of a month and has not resulted in any significant changes in the tides. Assume that the water has simply disappeared. What have been the consequences?

Paul's responses:

> 1. The scientific staffs of all institutions interested in such phenomena are enormously frustrated at their inability to explain the amazing vanishing of such huge amounts of water.
> 2. The great harbors of the world are unable to handle major ocean transport.
> 3. Controversies have arisen among the nations of the world over who shall have rightful claim to the areas of new land.
> 4. There is panic in Texas over the possibility that Texas may no longer be the largest state in the Union. (Some coastal states may be larger if they win claim to the great expanses of exposed tidal flats.)
> 5. Bootlegging (water) operations begin.
> 6. Fish are easier to catch.
> 7. New York City becomes filled with bearded men.
> 8. *Reader's Digest* publishes an article telling us how important water is to our daily needs.
> 9. A reduction in the production of beer is ordered, and social unrest ensues.
> 10. Land values tumble in crowded residential areas on the coasts.

11. Children enjoy not taking baths.

12. Some are heard to remark that the end of the world is in sight.

13. Russian sabotage is suspected in America, and American sabotage is suspected in Russia.

His first concern was with the mental state of scientists in the face of a puzzling phenomenon. He also made it plain that he had inferred that the volume of "vanished" water would be very great, something which not all of the respondents fully appreciated. He started out conventionally enough in his first three responses, but having thought of the possibility that there would be disputes in the interest of local advantage, he immediately made the observation facetious by attributing such motives in their most extreme form to Texans. Once launched on the ridiculous as a mode of response, he continued with a series of observations designed to ignore the more cosmic consequences of this cosmic event, in favor of its incidental effects on reading matter, shaving, bathing, the consumption of beer, and so on. His final response indicated that he finds less to choose between Russians and Americans than do the people at large in both of these countries.

In another problem in this test, it is given that the average height of Americans at age 20 has risen, over a period of 20 years, to 80 inches, and the average weight has doubled. The first consequence Paul thought of was expressed by him as follows: "The country is now peopled by relative young giants who tower above their parents and older contemporaries. This new race, tending to look down on their midget parents, have assumed a dominant role in practically everything." This fantasy is one whose origins in Paul's personal history date to the same period in which he precociously concluded that there was no God; the life events that gave rise to such themes will be described later in the record.

On the Franck Drawing Completion Test, Paul showed himself uncommonly skillful at sketching, and his drawings were rated as both the most original and the least obviously symmetrical of any subject's. It emerged elsewhere that in the years from 13 to 19 he had occupied himself extensively with painting and drawing and that for a brief period he had actually been enrolled in a school of fine arts. One of his drawings on the Franck test was of a quite comic clown performing in a circus, which in fact was something of the role he was playing in the assessment.

Another test on which he expressed himself in an unusual fashion, although it was not judged to be particularly original or artistically excellent, was the Turney Designs. This is a kind of mosaic construction test, in which the subject is given several hundred 1-inch-square pieces of solid-colored cardboard, some dozen colors being represented. The instructions are to build a mosaic design in a defined area, rectangular in shape, the dimensions being 8 inches in height and 10 inches in width. Paul turned the frame around, however, so that the vertical dimension was 10 inches and the horizontal dimension 8 inches, and proceeded to construct a question mark in yellow on a light gray background. This somewhat manneristic whimsy was unusual in several respects, one of them being that no other subject sought to inject meaning into the pattern, or at least to imply meaning. It seemed more contrary than original, however, and the artists who judged these productions gave it a low rating.

Several tests of aesthetic preference and judgment were used. One of these, the Gerard Basic Good Taste Test, requires the subject to decide which of three arrangements of simple formal elements makes the best design, the test being scored in accordance with expert judgment. Paul made a near-maximum score on this test. He also made a very high score on the Art Scale of the Welsh Figure Preference Test, which consists of line drawings which must be compared with one another and is scored so as to reflect the degree of agreement between the subject and a group of artists who took the test. Briefly, Paul's opinions on such matters coincide with those of artists, which is not surprising.

The Rorschach ink blots and the Thematic Apperception Test elicit imaginal productions which, like all fancies, may be judged in terms of their originality as well as in terms of their personal meaning to the subject. When the Rorschach and the T.A.T. records of all subjects were rated for originality by three raters working independently, Paul's performances were assigned to the top quartile in the graduate student sample.

Paul is perhaps more consistently original than he is consistently anything else.

PERSONALITY STYLE AND THEMES IN FANTASY

Several tests that reveal something of personality style and of fantasy were used. These include the Minnesota Multiphasic Personality

Inventory, the Rorschach Psychodiagnostic, the Thematic Apperception Test, and several less widely known but carefully studied instruments such as the California Psychological Inventory and the Dramatic Productions Test.

On the MMPI Paul made the following scores on the commonly used clinical and validity scales: Psychopathic Deviate, 76; Schizophrenia, 74; *F*, 70; Hypomania, 68; Masculinity-Femininity, 61; *K*, 60; Paranoia, 58; Hysteria, 56; Lie, 50; Cannot Say, 50; Depression, 49; Hypochondriasis, 48; Psychasthenia, 44. On the ego-strength scale of the MMPI, his *T* score was 66.

Paul's score on *Sc* was one of the highest earned by subjects in this sample, and his score on *Pt* was one of the lowest, although the scales intercorrelated .57; again, he was a rather lonely dot on a scatterplot. He thus admits to the detachment and affective isolation expressed in the *Sc* scale, but claims not to possess the compulsive and obsessive traits which frequently go along with such defenses; at any rate, he denies being worrisome or concerned with details. He is merely, he seems to be saying, disidentified or disassociated. The rejection of common opinions and of any participation in the common cultural values is emphasized in the *F* scale; this scale, composed as it is of items with a very low probability of being answered in the scored direction (average frequencies of 10 percent in the general population) picks up eccentric and deviant points of view (although its primary purpose, of course, is to serve as a validity indicator). On this scale Paul is saying once again, as he is at pains to say everywhere and on any occasion, that he does not agree with majority opinion, that his views are not those of most people. That this cultural disidentification is not simply schizoid, but is maintained in the interests of active rebellion, is indicated by the primary elevation on *Pd*. When *Sc* and *F* are elevated without *Pd*, what is indicated is real withdrawal and the primacy of schizophrenic processes in the character; with *Pd*, however, and particularly when *Ma* is somewhat elevated as well, a quite different interpretation is indicated. What is signified by this profile is a hostile rejection of parental (which is usually equivalent to conventional moral) values and, in a person of high intelligence, the evolvement of a philosophical outlook predicated upon originality and the creation of new values. When combined with great talent, rebellion may be transmuted into creative revolution; some of the persons whom Paul listed as "admired" by him are individuals of this stamp.

Whether he himself has all of the ingredients necessary for such transformation we do not yet know.

The score on K, considered along with a T score of 66 on the ego-strength scale, deserves special comment. Although K is thought to indicate defensiveness in taking the test, actually the correlations that have been observed consistently in the assessment of normal subjects would suggest that through part of its range (from about 50 to 65) it is associated positively with genuine strength of character. The ego-strength scale has been shown to relate to effectiveness in a wide range of situations, from ability to profit from psychotherapy, through success in graduate school, to effectiveness as a fighter in infantry combat. That Paul makes high scores on both these scales indicates a greater capacity for integration and adaptability than the profile would at first suggest.

On the Rorschach Psychodiagnostic, Paul gave the following responses:

I

Initial Responses	*Replies to Inquiry*
1. A woman diving into a dark pool of water. Waves are breaking on either side of her, the water turning white at the crest of the wave.	Well-formed young woman. Plunging in with arms outstretched. Blackness is the solid dark pool, the white spots are the top of the waves.
2. Might also be two people on a merry-go-round.	Going round and round. The merry-go-round is spinning in the center. Their coats are flying in the wind.
3. The white part could be a poor stupid idiot boy with his mouth hanging open.	Just looks stupid.

II

1. Two fencers on whom colored lights are shining, alternately crimson and black, flashing on and off so rapidly that both colors seem present together.	Well, they're wearing some flimsy gym suit of something. Gossamer-thin, catches the light. They're just parrying at the moment.
2. It could also be two big brown bears, rubbing noses.	Standing up on their hind legs. Brown coats. Kind of rough.

III

1. Two men bowling.	Stooping down to pick up the bowling balls. In adjacent alleys.

2. Or two savages bent over the ashes of a fire in some primitive land long ago.

Possibly Negroes, because of the color and the shape of the face. I think of ashes of a fire because of the fine, grayish-white appearance of this part here.

IV

1. Some type of monster of the lower depths. Looks as though he might be more pathetic than ferocious. Probably the Drooping-ham monster, riding a cow.

Cow's head is here, between legs. Big-footed monster. Kind of ridiculous-looking.

V

1. A man from another planet, where men have wings and can fly by themselves.

Just standing there, his wings temporarily inactive.

2. Could be a bat, I suppose, if you stretched a point.

Crudely shaped like a bat.

VI

1. A totem pole.

Wood-carving of a penis.

VII

1. Two old women, quarreling and nagging at one another.

Old hags, jawing.

2. Or it might be two little pickaninnies, sitting on clouds, joking at one another.

Little old black boys, about four years old, taking it easy.

VIII

1. Hyena trudging through the snow at sunset.

Rays of the setting sun make its coat red; the snow is the white surroundings.

IX

1. Reminds me of one of the sequences in *Fantasia;* a Night on Bald Mountain leading into the Ave Maria. The top part looks like Moloch on the mountain-top, ringed in flame, just coming up out of the lower depths. The bottom part is beauty and serenity, symbolized by the blue. The two are bound together, or are two parts of the same thing.

X

1. The whole thing is some sort of magic garden; none of the rules of logic or reality hold. Up here at the top are two eagles who have been released at the corners of the earth and they've flown at equal speeds toward one another until they bump heads at the center of the earth and fall into the chasm. Here are two fried eggs, sunny-side up. There are lions, and deer, and sea horses. They are all fomenting around, and there is going to be trouble. It's not so much magic as chaos.

The Rorschach is of course eminently suitable as a device for observing the way in which a person structures an ambiguous perceptual field. From this record it is evident that Paul structures ambiguity in a way that is at once dynamic, differentiated, and, to use one of his own expressions, elegant. It is also human-empathic, rich in symbolism, and somewhat original.

An ambiguous perceptual field may be said to be resolved dynamically when it is seen as containing such tensions that it can be imagined as a state of flux which has been momentarily stopped by the eye of the observer, but which in another moment will flow on again. Paul's first response is an excellent example of this dynamic resolution; the woman is diving, her arms are outstretched, the waves are surging up and breaking at the top. The second response is similar: a merry-go-round, with the riders' coats flying. There are many other excellent examples throughout Paul's record of a highly dynamic kind of perceptual resolution. Really static resolutions rarely occur, the only clear instance of one being the totem pole seen on Card VI; that this may be a significant exception is suggested by the fact that in the inquiry the "totem pole" is described as a "wood-carving of a penis." In any case, the characteristic method of dealing with the ink blot is to see it in a dynamic rather than static fashion.

That the perception is differentiated, and that the solutions may properly be called elegant, are indicated by the integrated use of detail and of surface characteristics, including texture and color. The whiteness of part of the wave suggests that it is the crest; the fineness and grayish-whiteness (both textural and color features of the bottom detail on Card III) suggest the ashes of a fire; the speckling of red and black on Card II suggests gossamer clothing and rapidly alternating colored lights; the gray suggests fluffiness of clouds on Card VII; and the redness of coat of the animal on Card VIII suggests that the sun is setting and suffusing the landscape with red; the surrounding white, however, is snow. All of this bespeaks differentiated perception and a solution that seeks to take into account as much as possible in the phenomenal field and to integrate it into a single, coherent, and comprehensive or totally inclusive picture.

Perception is human-empathic, or vitally human, when the concrete images evoked are of people in motion, or of human-like animals engaged in characteristically human activity. Almost every perception has for Paul some such human content. Even the big brown bears on Card II are standing up on their hind legs, the "more pathetic than ferocious" (a self-description?) monster on Card IV becomes "the Droopingham monster" (a former associate of L'il Abner's), and the usual bat on Card V is a bat only if one stretches a point; actually, it is a man (whose wings are temporarily inactive—another instance of stasis which may well be overdetermined).

Certainly the symbolism occurs throughout the record, but is most manifest, and also most schizoid, on Cards IX and X. The theme of evil and good ("bound together—parts of the same thing") is expressed both by the color and by an association with music; the "eagles who have been released at the corners of the earth" are somewhat obscure, but what seems to be implied is the conjunction of forces that arose from disparate and far-off sources, forces that meet exactly at some predetermined point—there to produce death and to disappear into a chasm. The magic, which is at first held to explain the disconnectedness of parts on Card X, finally becomes chaos, as troubling elements in the perception cannot be rationalized. One feels also that the woman diving into the dark pool and the man from another planet where men have wings and can fly by themselves have important symbolic meanings in the unconscious; certainly they would be easy enough to speculate about. The most striking impression produced by all of this is that Paul has a poetic imagination of the highest quality, facile in the production of symbols, integrated and complex in expression, and faithful to reality at some level of meaning—a derivative and sublimated level, of course, at many removes from the most obvious forms suggested by the ink blots.

From the point of view of personality structure, one would expect such a person to be primarily introversive in bent, and to be much occupied with inner fantasy, though not in an obsessive or repetitive way. This is certainly consistent with the high Sc and the low Pt score on the MMPI; Paul is detached and is concerned chiefly with his inner experience, but he is not psychasthenic. In so far as he is compulsive, his compulsions will be integrated wholes; a repetition compulsion dominating the entire life would not be surprising in such a case. The use of color is largely incidental; it is either light playing on moving forms or a characteristic of small elements in the magic garden—a magic garden which can readily become chaos. Still, it is subtle and realistic color, and in symbolic form (as on Card IX) it endues philosophical problems with emotional meaning. It is almost like the "concealed sensitivity" that Paul says he would want in a friend.

It remains only to be said that there is great *energy* in this record. We are dealing with an organism that will interact with experience in an extremely involved and involving way, so that at the least one would expect its life to be eventful and its personality to make its mark. Considering Paul's impact over the three days of assessment, this is probably a moderate-enough generalization.

On the Thematic Apperception Test, Paul turned facetious again. He makes the test into an opportunity for mocking what he thinks of as psychological theory. On Card 6BM, for example, he tells this story:

> Frankly, this oedipal situation is likely to cause the young man considerable difficulty. He has come to tell his mother that he wishes to marry the town whore rather than to continue living at home and competing with his father, who owns the local bank. The mother (and this needn't be true of all mothers—my own, for your information) would really like to go to bed with the son, but she feels that he would probably be better off after all with the town whore, who could support him in the style to which he is accustomed, and instead of being involved in a triangle he would now be just a point in n-dimensional space. So with an insipid mien she agrees to the life plan he has decided upon, and all ends happily.

On Card 7BM, the story is as follows:

> This situation shows a young man being beseeched to some action by either his father (in the living room) or by a chance (bistro) acquaint-

ance whom he has recently met. The latter is, of course, our new (Kinsey-era) old friend: the pederast or invert. Thus a dramatic situation unfolds, which culminates in the pederast's finally unmasking himself as the true father. Naturally, this upsets the young man, and he pleads another engagement. His final action, as he leaves our scene, is to shrug his shoulders and reflect upon the extreme variety of the human animal and the Kafkaesque nature of life.

Behind the facetiousness is undoubtedly a good deal of anxiety over the unconscious themes evoked. The choice of material is too apt to be funny, and there is considerable disorganization in the stories as well, particularly in the second one, in which the single character in the picture becomes, first, the actor in two different stories, and finally, two apparently different persons who are really only one. The story does not say specifically what action the young man is "being beseeched to," but the chance acquaintance is a pederast . . . and is also revealed in the end as the young man's father.

This is the story on Card I:

This boy, bred to the stablehand and the barkeep's daughter, is staring at the violin in the hope of obtaining, by some mystic process, the ability to seize the bow and play the instrument. Poor chap will probably cause it some unintentional harm and as a result will be boxed about the ears by its owner (currently attempting to seduce the mother). All, however, turns out well; he grows up and becomes an insipid bore, marries, has several children whom he sends off for lessons in meat-cutting, and lives amiably without ever having heard of Freud.

The theme here may be interpreted as the infantile desire for potency ("seizing the bow") and for possession of the mother (the violin to be played). The owner of the violin, who is presumably the father but who is made into an alien seducer, will avenge any harm that comes to the instrument, however; he will do so by "boxing the ears," i.e., castrating, the boy. None of this is to be taken seriously, of course; it is all a kind of joke Paul has made up.

Following this story, Paul turns from psychology to international politics. On Card 17BM, which was fourth in the order of presentation in this assessment, he made up a story concerning G. Vasolinsky, "the South Georgian hero," who is portrayed as scaling a hawser, in reverse, after having leaped through a porthole to catch a band of international capitalistic spies making off with a bushel of barley from the dockside. The T.A.T. card is actually a tinplate which hangs in all Soviet homes, and which has become a national symbol. The next story in the series involves the great South Californian hero, Dumphrey Hogart, who has interrupted one of his heroic exploits to ask for a refreshing glass of milk. The remainder of the stories tell of various heroic contentions between Vasolinsky and Hogart, who finally, however, become fast friends, and in company with Miss America and Miss Russia go off to the South Sea Isles to start a new race of heroes based on a Hegelian synthesis of capitalistic and communistic techniques of love-making. So much for the T.A.T.

One other test calling for imaginal production was employed. This is the Dramatic Productions Test developed by Erikson. In it the subject is shown a small-scale model of a stage and is offered a highly varied collection of props with which to create the scene of a play. The props include many human figures, furniture, machinery, blocks of wood, and so on. The subject is asked to make up a story to go with the scene he creates.

Paul told a simple story, using only four props. He placed an airplane in the middle of the stage, which he designated as a runway at the airport. Some distance from the plane, and blocking the way to it, he placed a policeman with upraised arm. In front of the policeman he placed the figures of two cowboys armed with six-shooters. The story he told is this: "These outlaws have stolen an extremely valuable jewel. They are now going to seize this plane and escape. The policeman is trying to stop them, to get the jewel back for its rightful owner. The outlaws will shoot the policeman if they have to, but probably the policeman won't make that necessary."

The word "seize" reminds one of the T.A.T. story in which the young boy is going to "seize the bow." The theme, indeed, is generically similar, if one interprets the jewel as signifying something sexually precious. Without bethinking himself to be facetious, Paul has told us the same story again, and it is a story of infant desires and violence against the usurper, who is also the law.

LIFE-HISTORY FACTORS

Paul is the son of the president and chief stockholder of a large corporation, a man who served as an officer in the U.S. Army in World War I and who during World War II served the government as a civilian in a position of some importance. His highly successful career was marred, however, by a period of financial and personal disaster during the late 1920's, when he lost all of his financial holdings and then attempted suicide by hanging. Paul was then five years old. The events surrounding his father's collapse were extremely traumatic, as Paul himself saw his father being removed from the house and later learned from a playmate (innocent cruelty of childhood!) that his father had been found with the rope around his neck.

The father was subsequently treated in a private sanitarium, and after about six months he was discharged as cured. He returned to commerce and public affairs, but did not make any substantial recouping of his fortunes until late in the 1930's, so that through some six or seven years he was in his own eyes and in those of his family a real failure. Even as a failure, however, he was treasurer of a small manufacturing concern, and the family was comparatively well off financially. Paul's poverty was strictly a personal achievement; he grew up in a shiny milieu, and he was shabby deliberately by contrast. That it was his pleasure not to serve (in the Army) was perhaps another expression of the same contrariness. His father served prominently and variously in civic and state affairs and held rank in the Army; Paul declined it all and remained an exceptionally private private.

Paul reported little concerning his early development, but did speak of the fact that his mother was "laid up for some time" as a result of his birth, which entailed a long and difficult labor. Although he did not elaborate on the matter, it seems possible that the "unintentional harm" referred to in the T.A.T. story may bear some relation to his fantasy concerning the mother's illness following his birth. (This is not to say that the fantasy is not without foundation in reality; but it is not old realities which are important so much as it is present realities, or fantasies, concerning them.)

The record we have of Paul's life history is quite sketchy, so that it is not possible from a study such as this to obtain a detailed understanding of his development. From what we do know, however, a schematic interpretation is easily enough made in terms of psychoanalytic theory concerning the Oedipus complex. No doubt the misfortunes of the house of Thebes are invoked much too mechanically as explanatory constructs these days, but in Paul's case one does not exactly have to search for such explanations. We have from the T.A.T. story and the Dramatic Productions Test the fantasy of seizing the phallus (the bow, or the airplane) and taking possession of the mother (making music on the violin which belongs to someone else, or escaping with the stolen jewel). There is fear of damaging the mother, however, and this one may do quite unintentionally when one is inside her; the father may then exact a frightful retribution. But the father himself is both a usurper of the mother (perhaps upon his return from the hospital) and a pederast, who will seduce the son ("beseech the young man to some action"). The son pleads another engagement, and so escapes this second threat to his masculinity, which is perhaps made more dangerous by his actual wish to have, one way or another, the father's penis. Of this latter possibility we cannot be sure, but the unusual static response to Card VI of the Rorschach and the preservation of perception in the masked-figure test suggests strong cathexis of the penis and consequent immobility in ego functions when the penis is present. The collapse of the father at a time when, according to theory, he is both seen as dangerous and wished dead, insures the continuing cathexis of the entire situation; and on theoretical grounds we would expect that the father's being taken away, on a stretcher, would create a strong sense of loss accompanying some triumph at the defeat of the threatening but beloved and needed figure of the father. The boy then, at the age of six, "decides" that there cannot be a God, and a little later he comes to the conclusion that "dead people stay dead," perhaps in reassurance that he did not actually kill the father, who returns well. When there is no father, there is no God; dead the dead must stay, and he who rises was never dead; the worst thing would be to give in; life is a series of fortuitous circumstances, and no such thing as free will exists. Certainly the resemblance to the character structure that Freud attributes to Dostoevski (in "Dostoevski and Parricide"), and through him to the unconscious criminal Oedipus, is striking.

We may recognize as much without thinking that we know more, however. There is a great deal that is unexplained about Paul, even though we may have learned the facts that are the core of the repetition compulsion and that generate much of the form of his life. But just as every significant act is overdetermined, we may expect that a personality, to a much greater extent and in a much more complex way, is overdetermined. Because we know a few of the determinants, we have some understanding of the whole, but a deeper appreciation of the personality certainly cannot be obtained without intensive study by a means other than three-day assessment.

One further note concerning life history events: The expectation that Paul would complete requirements for his Ph.D. within the year was not realized. He submitted his dissertation in rough draft to the chairman of his thesis committee and was told that it would require certain specified and extensive revisions. These he declined to make. There followed a severe intermission of work and progress toward the Ph.D., during which Paul withdrew entirely from the university and moved away from the area. When, some time later, department ratings were obtained on the "professional promise" of these assessed students, Paul was generally rated quite low. One of the faculty raters commented on the rating sheet, however, that Paul had "performed brilliantly" in his early days in the department, but had "unaccountably" failed to live up to his promise.

The work intermission is certainly not "unaccountable" in the light of the dynamics to which the testing points. The doctoral degree has for many graduate students the significance of acquiring (or seizing) potency, and it involves "sticking one's neck out" in attempting to do research that will merit for the student "entrance into the distinguished company of scholars." It is the academic, somewhat belated, equivalent of assuming the toga. It involves the risk of rejection, and to a certain extent it inevitably involves the student in competition with his adviser, whose position is defined by custom and function as the superior one. Symbolically, the aspirant is the son; the supervisor of research, the father.

In this situation Paul was exposed to what he most feared: the danger of castration, followed by a state of dependence and relative helplessness and vulnerability in relation to the faculty member who supervised his work. Whether or not he evoked an oedipal reaction from the adviser is not known; but in any event his thesis was found to be unacceptable in its first form, and he refused to perform the act of submission which revising the work would have seemed to him to be.

Some two years after the assessment one of the psychologists on the Institute staff was taking a winter vacation in Death Valley, Nevada. As with several companions he rode down a trail near an abandoned mine, he saw a solitary figure approaching on foot, leading a pack mule. He had almost passed by when he recognized the man as Paul. He stopped and hailed Paul, who had some difficulty remembering where they had met before. The word "assessment" brought it all back to him, however, and he immediately inquired what his value had been found to be. But he did not really seem much interested, and he accepted without comment the psychologist's evasion that the purpose of the study had been research rather than evaluation. When asked what he was doing, he replied, "Prospecting." "For uranium?" was the next question. No, said Paul, he was out after the baser metals —silver and gold. "Old ways are best ways," he added sententiously; "I'm for the tried and the true: silver and gold." The psychologist shortly went his way, and Paul trudged on in search of treasure.

The story does not end there, however. Paul did not find silver or gold, but the following year he returned to graduate work with a new thesis plan, one involving considerable mathematical work which he had completed during his years of absence from the university. It also involved working with a different faculty member. And while there is no ending to this sort of story, this particular chapter can have a happy ending: Paul did finally perform the daring act of obtaining the Ph.D. He has also turned his talents to good account in the years since then, but we cannot tell you in detail in what way he did so. Suffice it to say, it was in an odd way.

5

Personal Soundness in University Graduate Students

THE STUDY of which Paul was a part had, as we have said, the basic aim of describing excellence of functioning in human beings. The focus of investigation was the harmonious integration and unity of the systems of behavior which are conventionally distinguished as physiological, intellective, emotional, and social, and which eventuate, in the best instances of their integration, in mature, original, healthy, happy, and socially productive living.

In this chapter we shall deal with only one aspect, and that a very limited one, of this broad pattern of felicities in human functioning. We shall be concerned with the judgments of professors about the relative personal soundness of some 80 advanced graduate students, most of them doctoral candidates in the sciences.

As we have already indicated, we were well aware of the ethical content of the material that we were seeking to make the object of scientific inquiry. This ethical content had become abundantly clear to us when, in early planning meetings, each staff member took his turn at presenting his view of what constituted that very good thing we wished to study, known variously as effective human functioning, creative maturity, and generative integrity. It had soon become evident that the individual psychologist, like the individual nonpsychologist, spoke always of his personal ideals when he began to talk of maturity. He did not say merely what he thought maturity as a developmental stage *is* like; he said instead what he believed persons in that stage of development *should be* like.

There was, of course, a substantial core of agreement about the qualities that a creatively mature person should possess. These included self-respect and good sense; personal courage, independence, and a sense of humor; good taste; a certain innocence of vision and spontaneity of action; honesty of thought and behavior; social responsibility; and democracy in interpersonal relations. These mature ones should be persons who assumed responsibility for themselves, who treated others decently, and who felt friendly with their own past and unafraid of their future. Finally, they should be able in their own lives to contribute something of human love to the world.

A Greek philosopher, considering such a compendium of qualities, would not hesitate to name it *virtue*. To make the study of such qualities the central aim of a research project is approaching dangerously close to psychological piety. For a researcher to say what he thinks is good, and then to study instances of this goodness in order to determine what conditions generated it, is not in itself, certainly, an unscientific quest. If the human being is thought of as a natural system which possesses the greatest functional efficiency only in the presence of certain determining conditions, and if the research is aimed at describing effectiveness of function and its determinants, then the enterprise is entirely scientific in intent. Nevertheless, such a study could easily become a turning away from scientific inquiry. The inherent dangers are precisely those which scientific method is meant to guard against: the tendency of observation to jump with preconceptions, or the tendency of perception to serve one's autistic wishes at the cost of one's appreciation of reality.

The moral is that the psychologist must be particularly conscious of his ideals, and especially so when the subject matter that he is studying is so intimately concerned with human values. He must take care to arrange his studies so that the method itself guards him against prejudging the results or biasing them. If possible, he must do this without sacrificing thereby the complexity or organic quality of the phenomena to be studied, and without undue strictures on the method of observation to be employed.

Such considerations as these led this research staff to take as the measure of its central criterion variables *the social consensus*, or the averaged judgments of a number of nonpsychologists, concerning the manifestations of various kinds of human excellences.

The particular variable upon which this report focuses, *personal soundness*, is therefore more comprehensively and accurately described as "personal soundness as it is judged by university professors to be present in graduate students in the sciences and professions." Personal soundness is here taken to mean integrity, stability, and coherence of the individual personality, as those qualities show themselves socially. The actual definition of personal soundness given on the rating sheets used by the professors to express their judgments was as follows: "All-round Soundness as a Person: This refers to the soundness, balance, and degree of maturity which the individual shows in his relations with other people."

The emphasis on balance and maturity should be noted: complex living systems are usually unstable and immature at an early stage in their development, and certainly we may speak of a person who is immature and unstable but basically sound. Under certain circumstances, in fact, instability may be the most appropriate condition for a sound adult. What was being rated in this study, however, was not simply soundness as a person, but soundness in a context of maturity and balance.

It should also be noted that the "relations with other people" that were observable by the raters were as a rule scientific and professional work relations, as seen from the point of view of a person whose professional status was superior to that of the subject. This sort of personal soundness, on the face of it, is more a public fact than a private one; what is being judged is the personality that an individual projects publicly in his contacts with many people, only a few of whom are his intimates. Inner soundness is being identified only so far as it shows itself in the rather specialized sort of social interaction which obtains among graduate students and between graduate students and professors.

A further limitation of the criterion variable is that scholars and scientists are not (or at least are widely thought not to be) representative of the general population, so that they will have to be considered a special class until proved otherwise. Also, these subjects are men, and men (it is widely thought) are very different from women, so that the conclusions cannot serve as the basis for statements about personal soundness in women; and these are young men, for the most part, not middle-aged or old men; and in addition they are Americans, products of Western culture, living in the last half of the twentieth century, and attending the University of California, all of which things are unusual, considering the breadth of the variable "personal soundness" and the protean forms it has assumed historically and is presently assuming in other parts of the world.

Having noted the relatively limited character of the central dependent variable, we may note as well that it has the virtue of anchoring the study in social reality. The academic milieu is one kind of culturally coherent social matrix in which valued forms of personal integrity may develop; the marks of personal soundness as a scientist and scholar are known; there are social expectations which are transmitted from one generation of scholars to another, and which have a long tradition. One way of being personally sound, then, is to be a sound scientist and scholar.

As we have suggested, the anchoring in social reality is crucially important to a research program that seeks to study excellence of functioning. Soundness as a fact of life is always dependent on the avenues to soundness that are offered by a given cultural pattern. If personal soundness is to be studied at all, it must be studied in its concrete manifestations in a particular cultural group, and in terms of the congruence of actual behavior with the behavioral patterns that the group structure has generated as realizable roads to integrity and personal fulfillment. Indeed, the imperfections of the social pattern itself may become most evident from a study of the individuals whose behavior is most congruent with the group-endorsed way of life, and who have, actually, become as sound, balanced, and mature as their identity will let them.

The acceptance of such a *social consensus* regarding behavior that in a given milieu is considered sound thus gives one aspect of reality its due. At the same time it permits the study of what might be called the *psychological consensus* as expressive of another point of view deriving from a less culture-specific view of human functioning.

The research situation is essentially this: the psychologist is in ignorance of the social consensus concerning the relative soundness of the individual he is studying, and his aim is simply to give the best possible description (the most accurate and the most comprehensive he can) of the person's functioning. While he is giving this description, he is no doubt (whether consciously or unconsciously) *evaluating* the individual as well, in terms of what might be called the psychological ethic. However, since it is a critical feature of the research design that the psychologist is kept from knowing how the subject is rated by nonpsychologists, the description that is given is thus kept free of whatever contaminating influences would have been introduced had the social consensus been known to the assessor.

This feature of the research design, since it has achieved a reasonable safeguard against the possible contaminating influence of psychological preconceptions upon the descriptive correlates of personal soundness as that quality is seen by nonpsychologists, now permits the frank introduction of a psychological evaluation as the final step in description. Such an evaluation would be based upon the psychologist's notion of what should characterize the individual who possesses *inner* soundness. Moreover, it then permits an analysis of the agreements and the discrepancies in two kinds of judgments, which are arrived at independently of one another: (1) the social consensus, or a particular sort of public opinion regarding an individual's degree of personal soundness; and (2) the psychological consensus, based on information more private in nature and on a formulation that might be called "psychodynamic" in its foundation.

As a matter of convention in reporting, the ratings on Personal Soundness given each subject by the faculty members in his department will be referred to as Department Soundness; the ratings given by the psychological assessment staff will be referred to as Staff Soundness.

SAMPLING AND RATING

The population from which this sample was drawn consisted of all the male graduate students who were within one year of obtaining their final degree (generally the Ph.D.) in the following departments of the University of California: Anthropology, Astronomy, Biochemistry, Botany, Business Administration, Chemistry, Economics, Entomology, History, Jurisprudence, Music, Physics, Plant Biochemistry, Political Science, and Zoölogy.

Most of the doctoral candidates in the final years of work for the degree had passed the written and preliminary oral qualifying examinations but had not yet completed the thesis requirement. In the School of Jurisprudence, those in the final year were in the senior class. In Business Administration, the final year of work was the second year of graduate study. In Music, the final year was usually the second or third after the student was admitted to graduate work. The chairman of the department concerned was the judge of whether a student was in his final year of work.

The ratings were obtained by asking all department staff members who held academic rank—from assistant professor to professor—to evaluate each final-year student in terms of personal soundness. Each rater was asked to rate only those students whom he, in his opinion, knew well enough for him to make a confident estimate of their degrees of soundness. A nine-point rating scale was used. All subjects who were included in the total rated population from which the sample was finally drawn were rated by at least three raters; the average number of raters per subject was six.

The reliability of the ratings was determined by taking all the subjects who had been rated by at least six raters, and randomly dividing the sets of ratings into two groups, for which an average was then determined. The two averaged values were then correlated with each other. Statistics descriptive of the ratings, broken down by departments, are given in Table 5.1. As the table shows, the total distribution of ratings has a mean of 4.96, which is slightly higher than the mean of 4.5 which would have been obtained had the raters adhered to the normal curve frequencies specified for the nine-point scale. The distribution is slightly skewed negatively, but approximates the normal curve fairly closely. The reliabilities are high enough to be satisfac-

TABLE 5.1   *Department Ratings of Personal Soundness*

Department	N	Mean	SD	Ru
Anthropology	13	5.06	1.58	*
Astronomy	4	4.96	1.25	*
Biochemistry	11	4.83	1.19	*
Botany	9	5.50	.94	*
Business Administration	66	4.94	1.27	.67
Chemistry	63	4.89	1.29	.61
Economics	22	5.30	1.28	.82
Entomology	43	4.93	1.17	.83
History	40	4.90	1.15	.72
Jurisprudence	23	4.95	1.33	.87
Music	42	4.98	1.29	.69
Physics	62	4.76	1.20	.61
Plant Biochemistry	5	4.64	.82	*
Political Science	13	4.98	1.45	*
Zoölogy	17	5.32	1.40	.97
Total population	433	4.96	1.27	.68

* Values not computed because of fewer than six rates per subject.

tory; the over-all reliability of .68 is close to the reliability one generally finds for personality measures.

From this population of 433 rated subjects, a sample of 80 was drawn. Sampling was fairly even throughout the total range of ratings, as Figure 5.1 shows. The subjects who were asked to participate in the study were chosen randomly from the rated population. At a luncheon at the Institute house, to which they were invited by letter, the purpose and nature of the research were explained. Of the first 40 who were invited to the luncheon, 8 declined the invitation, most of these pleading pressure of work as their chief reason for not wishing to participate. Of the remaining 32 who came to the luncheon, 28

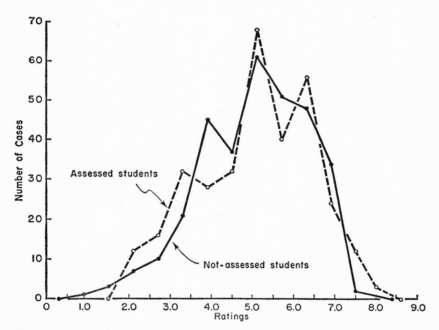

FIG. 5.1 Distributions of department ratings of Personal Soundness of all graduate students rated. The broken line shows the distribution for the 80 students who were subjects in the assessment study. The frequencies in each rating category for the assessment sample were pro-rated to make the curve directly comparable with that showing the distribution of ratings for students who were not assessed (solid line).

agreed to take part in the program of study. Of the 4 exceptions, 2 declined for reasons of physical disability, and the other 2 because of schedule incompatibilities; but none of those who attended the luncheon were unwilling to participate.

Exact figures are not available on the percentage of acceptance to subsequent invitations to the luncheon and to participation in the program. A conservative estimate, however, is that 65 to 70 per cent of those selected randomly as potential subjects were eventually subjects of study.

THE METHODS OF STUDY

These 80 subjects were studied in groups of 10 over a period of some six months. Each group of 10 subjects spent from Friday afternoon to Sunday afternoon at the assessment house, sleeping there and taking all meals there. The assessment day ran from 8 A.M. to 12 P.M. The assessors, like the subjects, made their home at the Institute during the three days of study. The distinctive feature of "living-in" assessment as a method of psychological research is that it provides a great variety of informal social interaction, in which the assessor is recognized to be in the role of participant observer. He, of course, observes the other assessors and himself as well as the subjects, for it is the total flux of events during the three days of assessment which is eventually to be interpreted and expressed in one or another of the kinds of summary statement in which observations during assessment are condensed.

This chapter deals chiefly with observations made and facts ascertained by the assessment staff during social interactions, including interviews, group discussions, improvisation, charades, a group competition in city planning, and several group problems, in addition to the sort of informal social interaction which took place at meals, during intermissions between procedures, and during the evenings after the conclusion of the day's work. Much of the data of assessment consists of test scores, and much of the total research enterprise is concerned with the development of measures that may be used outside the assessment setting; the aim of this chapter, however, is primarily to deal with impressions gained by staff members in personal interactions with the subjects, or from observing subjects in relation to one another.

Staff impressions based upon total observation of the subject in the assessment period were summarized chiefly in two ways: in the form of ratings on a set of 37 personality variables, and by use of an adjective check list containing some 280 common, personally descriptive adjectives. These two forms of statement of staff impressions were analyzed in relation to both Department Soundness and Staff Soundness.

ANALYSIS OF STAFF IMPRESSIONS: THE GOUGH ADJECTIVE CHECK LIST

Each staff member gave an adjectival description of each subject at the conclusion of the assessment period by checking the adjective that in his opinion best characterized the subject. Any adjective that had been used by two or more of the assessors to describe a given subject was included in the composite adjectival picture of that subject. (It was reasoned that any trait seen in a subject by more than one assessor was probably there.)

The coefficient of correlation between Department Soundness and Staff Soundness is .41, which is a statistically significant degree of agreement. The coefficient of alienation, however, is more than .9, which means that the disagreement is marked. In order to show both congruences and discrepancies in department and staff views of personal soundness, an analysis of the composite staff description of each subject was carried out for each of the two sets of ratings. Thus the adjectives that are significantly related to both department and staff ratings comprise the area of agreement; the adjectives that are significantly related to one or the other but not to both show the areas of disagreement, or at least of differences of view.

The method of analysis used was a group comparison of the top and bottom quartiles of each of the two sets of ratings. Adjectives which showed statistically significant differences are presented in Table 5.2.

A consideration of these adjectives suggests, first of all, that both department and staff raters in selecting examples of personal soundness choose persons who are efficient and well integrated in the pursuit of their goals; the emphasis is upon adaptability, organization, persistence, and resourcefulness. At the other end of the scale, subjects who receive relatively low ratings from both department and staff raters are

TABLE 5.2 *Adjective Descriptions by Assessment Staff of Subjects Rated Highest and Lowest on Department and Staff Soundness*

Highest 25 per cent			Lowest 25 per cent		
Dept. ratings only	Dept. and staff ratings (at .01 level)	Staff ratings only (at .01 level)	Dept. ratings only	Dept. and staff ratings (at .01 level)	Staff ratings only (at .01 level)
	adaptable organized persistent resourceful	appreciative friendly natural stable unaffected		immature unstable	anxious awkward effeminate emotional fearful high-strung moody self-centered
at .05 level:	at .05 level:	at .05 level:	at .05 level:	at .05 level:	
dominant	alert ambitious calm capable confident civilized dependable efficient foresighted helpful intelligent moderate realistic responsible serious	considerate fair-minded good-natured honest pleasant reasonable sincere sociable tactful tolerant trusting unassuming	dull inhibited interests narrow original peculiar queer self-punishing	confused dissatisfied distrustful defensive egotistical preoccupied tense undependable withdrawn	

primarily immature and unstable; confusion, undependability, dissatisfaction, and defensiveness go along with these characteristics. Effectiveness-ineffectiveness seems to be the dimension represented here.

The psychological assessors, however, place a premium upon certain less goal-oriented traits as well. Friendliness, lack of affectation, naturalness, fair-mindedness, tolerance, good-naturedness: these qualities temper somewhat the more exclusively efficient characteristics which are the preëminent manifestations of soundness in professional and scientific work relations. There is a slight touch of coldness about Department Soundness, combining, as it does, effectiveness with dominance, and omitting, as it does, pleasantness in human relations.

So far as Low Soundness is concerned, the psychological staff evidently takes a more relaxed view both of dullness and of personal peculiarities—including originality, it would seem. Originality, of course, sometimes appears a waste of time and motion, since it is in the nature of *umweg* solutions that they are the long way 'round. The staff may have here been discerning a kind of originality that is presently ineffective, but that is not to be discounted for lack of immediate results. In any event, whatever was here being seen by the psychological staff as original behavior was seen by department raters as unsound behavior. It is interesting in this connection that the correlation between department ratings on Soundness and department ratings on Originality is .62 for these subjects, so that in general the persons called original by the departments are also called sound by the departments; it is the psychological staff which calls some persons original whom the departments have called unsound.

STAFF RATINGS ON PERSONALITY VARIABLES

Staff ratings on personality variables were made separately for two subsamples of 40 cases each. After the first 40 subjects had been assessed, they were rated relative to one another; for this a 5-point scale with approximate normal curve frequencies was used. The variables and their definitions are given in Table 5.3, together with their correlations with Department Soundness. The first 40 cases are referred to as Group A, the second 40 as Group B.

Although the assessment staff rated the subjects on each of these 37 personality variables, an analysis of the interrelationships of the variables showed that only two clearly marked independent dimensions were involved. One of these may be called Stability-Instability; the other is General Responsiveness. (Actually, the cluster analysis revealed three other clusters as well: Intellectual Competence, Self-Assurance, and Masculinity. All three were significantly correlated with Stability, whereas the correlations between General Responsiveness and other clusters were as follows: Stability, .001; Self-Assurance, .001; Masculinity, —.02; Intellectual Competence, .40. The last-mentioned correlation may be mediated by Verbal Fluency, which emerged in the Responsiveness cluster but which is highly correlated with Intellectual Competence as well.)

TABLE 5.3 *Correlations between Department Soundness Ratings and Staff Rating Variables*

Personality variables and definitions	Correlations with department soundness	
	Group A	Group B
Personal tempo: rate of speech, quickness and intensity of expressive movement, general speed of response	.11	.13
Naturalness: freedom from pretense, being oneself	.06	.19
Vitality: general energy level, stamina	.30	.28
Intellect: general intellectual ability, "g," cortical power	.34	.30
Poise: ability to meet situations without becoming disconcerted or upset, unruffledness	.34	.34
Impulsiveness: inadequate control of impulse, acting without thinking, lack of deliberation and judiciousness	—.36	.09
Constriction: overcontrol of impulse, undue inhibition, lack of spontaneity	.29	—.17
Warmth: friendliness, responsiveness to others, approachableness	.02	.27
Effeminacy: effeminate style or manner of behavior, softness	.12	—.07
Positive affect: cheerful, animated, good-tempered, optimistic; *not* depressed, gloomy, irritable, sour, pessimistic, dispirited	.08	.21
Adjustment: general adequacy of adjustment	.45	.24
Drive: persistence, resolution, perseverance, directed energy	.30	.22
Sense of humor: capacity to appreciate and respond to wit and humor, and also a talent for amusing others	.08	.50
Good judgment: common sense, sense of reality, objectivity	.50	.24
Suggestibility: gullibility, the too-ready acceptance of things at their face value; lack of internal standards of judgment	—.11	—.21
Self-defensiveness: rationalizing, excusing, blaming, projectivity, anxiety about personal progress	—.14	.00
Self-insight: ability to verbalize the needs, desires, goals, etc. of which one's behavior is a function	.28	.20
Introspectiveness: tendency to concern oneself with one's own inner life	—.14	.04
Intraceptiveness: a subjective, tender-minded outlook on the world as opposed to an extraceptive, tough-minded one	—.05	—.15
Sensuality: acceptance of and capacity for sensual gratification	—.13	.25
Likability: personal reaction of the rater to the subject	.31	.50

TABLE 5.3 (*Continued*)

Personality variables and definitions	Correlations with department soundness	
	Group A	Group B
Positive character integration: sense of responsibility based on strong internally determined principles; conscientiousness; ethical sensitivity	.51	.14
Self-abasement: acceptance of guilt, humility, self-blame, intropunitiveness, feelings of unworthiness	−.21	−.24
Submissiveness: deference, willingness to be led, compliance, over-ready acceptance of authority	−.10	−.32
Deceitfulness: guile, subterfuge, duplicity, lack of frankness	.02	−.06
Verbal fluency: talkativeness, facility in conversation, use of varied vocabulary	−.01	.34
Rigidity: inflexibility of thought and manner, stubbornness, pedantry, firmness	.00	−.32
Potentiality: promisingness; probable future success	.53	.54
Originality: freshness of vision and creativity of thought; original approach to problems	.17	.39
Soundness: maturity; balance; integrity as a person	.52	.32
Self-confidence: confidence in one's own ability; easy self-assurance	.24	.33
Abundance values: sense of security and optimism regarding the future; absence of fears of deprivation, of being exploited, and of being cheated	.32	.18
Sentience: the seeking and enjoying of sensuous impressions, sensitivity, aesthetic enjoyment	.06	.15
Cathexis of intellectual activity: the degree to which intellectual and cognitive pursuits are valued, the emphasis placed on thinking, abstraction, and understanding. A person who cathects intellectual endeavor will seek out, enjoy, and sustain activity which involves cerebration and reflection. He will take pleasure in the thinking processes and will esteem their outcomes	.18	.21
Breadth of interest: wide-ranging knowledge; varied activities and interests; excellent fund of general information	.34	.36
Value for productive achievement as an end in itself: the extent to which a person values his own products quite apart from the social rewards they might bring him	.30	.06
Value for success as a means of acquiring status: the extent to which a person is productive because productivity is rewarded by superior status	−.10	−.10

The member variables of the Stability and General Responsiveness clusters, and their domain validities, are given in Table 5.4.

In view of the implications in the adjective analyses that department-recognized soundness was, at least in some cases, achieved at the cost of spontaneity and personal warmth, an analysis of the interrelationships of Department Soundness, Stability, and General Responsiveness seemed indicated. Such an analysis is shown in Figure 5.2, in which Department Soundness ratings are plotted in the space defined by two coördinate axes, Stability and Responsiveness.

TABLE 5.4 *Member Variables of the Stability and General Responsiveness Clusters in Staff Ratings*

Stability	Domain validities	General responsiveness	Domain validities
Staff soundness	.91	Lack of constriction	.86
Adjustment	.87	Verbal fluency	.74
Good judgment	.84	Lack of rigidity	.70
Positive character integration	.77	(Rapid) personal tempo	.70
Potential success	.77	Sense of humor	.69
Poise	.73	Impulsiveness	.68
Lack of self-defensiveness	.73	Warmth	.64
Abundance values	.71	Positive affect	.62
Naturalness	.65	Sensuality	.56
Drive	.62	Sentience	.53
Lack of deceitfulness	.59		

It is at once apparent from this figure that high stability combined with low responsiveness is the pattern endorsed by department raters (77 per cent of the cases in that quadrant being above the mean on Department Soundness). By contrast, if high stability is combined with high responsiveness, the probability that the person will be rated above average on Department Soundness is only .50.

This certainly supports the interpretation pointed to by the adjectives. Sensuality, Warmth, Sentience, and the like are not much called for in graduate school, and indeed they may be viewed with some disfavor. This is not entirely surprising, considering the nature of the cognitive enterprise and of scientific research, which calls above all else for reservation of judgment, distrust of immediate sense impressions, the rational reconstruction of experience, and deferment of gratification in the interests of distant goals. The scientific workers

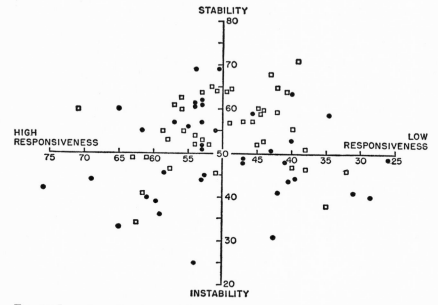

FIG. 5.2 Location of ratings on Department Soundness in relation to the staff rating dimensions of Stability and General Responsiveness. Ratings above the mean on Department Soundness are indicated by squares; ratings below the mean are indicated by circles.

among human beings are, in a sense, the most extreme extension of the whole trend of organic evolution, which is in the direction of detachment from totally unconscious participation in nature, toward intellection and conscious knowledge. Among the costs of such detachment for the person may be reckoned the loss of such joy as comes from immediate and spontaneous participation in what goes on around him.

CORRELATIONS WITH STANDARDIZED TESTS

Some of the test results are of interest in relation to these findings. Essentially what the foregoing analyses have pointed to is the existence of suppression and emotional detachment as fundamental elements in the character of sound scientists and scholars. The scores of these subjects on the Minnesota Multiphasic Personality Inventory bear out this interpretation. The highest individual scale correlation of

Department Soundness is with Hypochondriasis (.30); with Hysteria the correlation is .22, and with Paranoia it is .29. With Staff Soundness, on the other hand, Hypochondriasis correlates —.05; Hysteria, —.16; and Paranoia, —.03. To be considered along with these correlations, however, is the fact that subjects rated low on Department Soundness are much more likely than high-rated subjects to have at least one scale about 70 (that is, beyond the "normal" range). When the MMPI profiles were sorted into two groups—those which had clinical scale scores (*Mf* was expected) greater than 70 ("abnormals") and those which did not ("normals")—the coefficient of contingency was .42 against a dichotomization of Department Soundness ratings at the mean of the distribution, High Soundness being associated with all-normal profiles.

Thus it appears that suppressive mechanisms go along with less extremeness in psychopathology. One might speculate that perhaps Department Soundness is based rather too much upon the suppression not only of impulse, but also of behavior that might be construed as unsound. And these findings would suggest that such a suppression is achieved at the cost not of spontaneity alone, but of relaxation as well, since Hypochondriasis scale elevations reflect diffuse somatic complaints of the sort that arise from muscular tensions, cardiovascular imbalance, gastric upset, and so on. One would predict a relatively high incidence of psychosomatic illness in this group of highly rated subjects; not more psychosomatic illness, perhaps, than one would expect to find in the Low Soundness subjects, but more than one should expect in a group of persons who can properly be called healthy psychologically.

While noting these reservations, however, we should bear in mind that, for the most part, Department Soundness is correlated positively with traits that prove adaptive in almost any life situation. So much is indicated by the adjectives; test measures bear out the conclusion. Intelligence, as measured by the Miller Analogies Test and the Terman Concept Mastery Test, correlates .37 ($\pm.16$) and .26 ($\pm.16$), respectively, with Department Soundness. Several scales of the California Psychological Inventory are also related to the criterion variable: Responsibility, .34; Dominance, .32; Tolerance, .33; Psychological-mindedness, .37; Delinquency, —.27. The correlation of the Psychological-mindedness scale of the CPI is particularly interesting in view of a finding with the Strong Vocational Interest Blank. The only scales of the Strong inventory that are significantly related to Department Soundness are the original Psychologist key and the 1948 Kreidt revision of the Psychologist key. These correlations are .40 and .41, respectively.

Accuracy of self-description is also an important correlate of Department Soundness. An index of such accuracy was defined in terms of the percentage of agreement between the adjectives used by the assessment staff to describe a subject and the adjectives used by that subject to describe himself, when checking the same list. This adjective index, known as the Self-Insight Ratio, correlated .40 with Department Soundness.

Perceptual test measures are also associated positively with Department Soundness. Sixteen such measures were significantly related to the Department Soundness ratings. The tests or experiments included insight puzzles (nine puzzles constituting a test), Gottschaldt figures, the Street Gestalt Test, autokinetic movement, line movement, weight judgment, size constancy, memorial reproduction of a geometric figure (a Stanford-Binet subtest), retinal rivalry, judgment of the vertical by a subject lying in darkness on a tilted plane, and, finally, a masked figure—the word "summer" written twice, once in a normal fashion and again upside down and mirror-wise directly below the normal writing, at first glance creating, as we mentioned earlier in describing the case of Paul, the total impression of a corkscrew-like figure.

These significantly correlated measures seem to manifest three main factors in perception: (1) ease of insightful cognitive reorganization, both directed and spontaneous; (2) steadiness and resistance to stress upset in perceptual-cognitive functions; and (3) moderation between the extremes of several dimensions of perceptual-cognitive functioning, especially accuracy, variability, and reproduction of size. Tables 5.5, 5.6, and 5.7 show the variables grouped under these three factors, and their correlations with Department Soundness. It is worth noting that the relationships under factor 3 are expressed as correlation ratios, and all the subjects more highly rated on Soundness cluster near the middle of the distributions of scores on these variables.

Another source of evidence concerning soundness is the actual item pool of the MMPI. An analysis was carried out by correlating each

TABLE 5.5 *Correlations between Department Soundness and Perceptual Variables Related to Ease of Insightful Cognitive Reorganization*

Procedure	Measure	Correlation coefficient
Gottschaldt figures	Speed in completing trial 1	.25
Masked word	Speed in seeing word	.39
Street Gestalt	Number of pictures seen	.25
Line movement	Number of vertical-horizontal fluctuations in one minute	.26

TABLE 5.6 *Correlations between Department Soundness and Perceptual Variables Related to Steadiness and Resistance to Stress Upset*

Procedure	Measure	Correlation coefficient
Periscopic tracing	Quality of tracing of square	.26
Form memory	Quality of reproduction	.22
Form memory	High consistency of successive reproductions	.29
Tapping	Slow rate	.22

TABLE 5.7 *Correlation Ratios between Department Soundness and Perceptual Variables Related to Moderation between Extremes of Perceptual-Cognitive Functioning*

Procedure	Measure	Correlation ratio
Size		
Periscopic tracing	Size of square	.40
Form memory	Total size of reproduction	.23
Accuracy		
Perception of vertical	Total error, erect and leaning	.29
Size constancy	Error, object set	.45
Kinesthetic aftereffect	Directional error	.29
Weight judgment	Total shift in level	.24
Variability		
Autokinetic movement	Change in prevailing direction	.30
Kinesthetic aftereffect	Total deviation of judgments	.23

item with Department Soundness. The items showing differences significant at the .01 level are as follows:

A. Answered "True" more often by highly rated subjects:
    1) I loved my father.
    2) I am happy most of the time.

    3) I very seldom have spells of the blues.

    4) I have strong political opinions.

    5) I can stand as much pain as others can.

    6) I have no difficulty starting or holding my urine.

    7) I like to read about science.

    8) I am attracted by members of the opposite sex.

    9) Some people are so bossy that I feel like doing the opposite of what they tell me.

    10) My speech is the same as always.

    11) The only miracles I know of are simply tricks that people play on one another.

B. Answered "True" more often by less highly rated subjects:

    1) My hardest battles are with myself.

    2) I frequently ask people for advice.

    3) I have several times had a change of heart about my life work.

    4) There is very little love and companionship in my family as compared to other homes.

    5) It is not hard for me to ask help from my friends even though I cannot return the favor.

    6) I love to go to dances.

    7) I used to like hopscotch.

    8) I am very careful about my manner of dress.

    9) I shrink from facing a crisis or difficulty.

    10) I sometimes feel that I am about to go to pieces.

    11) Some of my family have habits that bother and annoy me very much.

    12) I have periods of such great restlessness that I cannot sit long in a chair.

The questions and answers tell their own story. It is evident that highly rated subjects claim to have greater equanimity, self-confidence, and objectivity and are somewhat more virile than subjects who receive low ratings. The latter picture themselves as unstable in mood, easily bothered or made restless, lacking internal resources, indecisive, and somewhat finicky and effeminate.

LIFE-HISTORY FACTORS ASSOCIATED WITH SOUNDNESS

Personal historical information concerning these subjects was gathered through two kinds of techniques: written responses to requests for certain of the more factual kinds of information (a biographical-data sheet and a life-data questionnaire), and a series of four interviews —the first two by psychoanalysts on the staff—focused on childhood and early adolescence, later adolescence and young adulthood, professional interests and activities, and philosophy of life. The aim of the interviews was to arrive at a formulation of psychodynamics in each case, as well as to get into the records the subject's own account of the events in his life.

The unreliability of such retrospective accounts must be admitted; a person's psychic defenses may be expected to be at their best on the occasion of a first interview with a psychoanalyst—especially if the person being interviewed has presumably been selected as an instance of psychological normality. It will not, therefore, be very strongly urged here that the interview data are accurate renderings of the actual life histories of the subject. At a minimum, however, one can claim to report what the subjects said to the interviewers when asked to tell about their lives. Actually, common sense would claim much more: these subjects seemed to respond with candor, seriousness, and coöperation with the interviewer in what was generally recognized as a piece of scientific work. Many of them were very much moved by the interviews and by their memories of their early life. Several said that they were discussing matters that they had discussed with no one else since their childhood. Three of the subjects wept in the course of the interview. There is no doubt that the life-history information was given with intense emotional involvement and at the cost of some pain to many of the persons interviewed.

Two kinds of use were made of the life-history material. First, it was used in case formulations in which the entire staff participated and in which the material was integrated with results from all the other techniques. Used in this fashion, it pointed to a number of significant determinants of personal soundness. From a methodological viewpoint, however, the information when used in that fashion was open to contamination and distortions in interpretation because of all the other information considered with it.

A second use of the material, however, frees it from such contaminating influences. All the life-history information for each subject was assembled in a folder, and all remarks that might identify him as one rated High or Low on Personal Soundness were deleted. A psychologist who had not participated in any of the assessments and who had no knowledge of the ratings and no personal acquaintance with the subjects, then used the interview material as the basis for filling out a life-history check list on each subject. This psychologist was instructed simply to indicate, for each check-list item, whether that factor was present or absent in the life history. Another psychologist who had not participated in the assessments was asked to assign a rating to each one of 22 life-history factors in terms of salience or importance in the interview material.

There were 25 items in the life-history check list. They are given in Table 5.8, together with their relative frequencies in groups of subjects rated High and Low on Department Soundness (N of 20 in each group).

The 22 items that were rated with reference to their salience or importance in the interview material were quite similar in content and coverage to the 25-item check list. Determining the salience or importance of a factor is, of course, somewhat different from simply noting its presence or absence. Some factors, if present, may be very important, and others are unlikely to be of striking importance whether present or absent. This may account for two notable differences in the results when salience ratings are averaged and the High and Low Soundness groups are compared on the items. The salient factors in the life histories of the High Soundness subjects were found to be as follows:

1. Reared in a stable family setting, marked by stability of home site, presence of both parents in the home, and economic security.
2. Father a respected and successful man.
3. Father valued and taken as a model by the son.
4. Early establishment of independence from the family.
5. Early establishment of enduring heterosexual relations.

The salient factors in the life histories of the Low Soundness subjects, as brought out in the analysis, were these:

1. Much overt parental conflict.
2. Target of some form of ethnocentrism.
3. Maternal emphasis on intellectual achievement.
4. Seductive mother.
5. Mother the dominant figure in the home.

The items in which the results from the check list differ from the salience ratings are chiefly those relating to dominating and driving qualities in the mother, and to the effects of group prejudice directed against the subject. A dominating and at the same time seductive mother may, under certain circumstances, set a pattern which is extremely difficult to alter, and which works against the development of mature masculinity. And it is only too plain that being born a Jew or

TABLE 5.8 *Relative Frequencies of Life-History Factors in Subjects Rated High and Low on Department Soundness*

Factor	Percentage of highs	Percentage of lows	Percentage difference
1. Early health record free of serious illness to subject or his parents or guardians	65	30	35*
2. Presence of both parents in home until adolescence	80	50	30*
3. Economic security of family unthreatened	85	50	35*
4. Stability of home site (including community stability)	80	40	40*
5. Absence of group prejudice directed at family	60	45	15
6. Presence of other siblings and positive relations with them	85	40	45*
7. Cultural coherence with the community (absence of conflicting group identities)	40	40	0
8. Absence of marked family friction, either overt or covert	60	25	35*
9. Warmth in home	70	55	15
10. Sophisticated, complex home environment	50	50	0
11. Strong and positively valued father	70	30	40*
12. Absence of fear of father	60	50	10
13. Paternal emphasis on intellectual achievement	70	40	30*
14. Positively valued mother	80	80	0
15. Absence of dominating and possessive qualities in mother	60	55	05
16. Absence of anxiety and anxiety-provoking qualities in mother	40	25	15
17. Absence of maternal ambitiousness for achievement in the child	55	45	10
18. Uniformly superior academic record	50	55	05
19. Development of professional interest in adolescence	75	70	05
20. Wide interests in adolescence	80	75	05
21. Early development of social facility	50	15	35*
22. Self-developed intellectual drives	95	85	10
23. Participation in organized athletics in high school or college	45	20	25*
24. Early positive heterosexual experience (intimacies in years from 14 to 18)	30	20	10
25. Current establishment of an enduring positive heterosexual relationship	90	45	45*

* Significantly (.05 level) more often characteristic of High Soundness subjects. Since the check list is essentially a statement of hypotheses, the one-tailed test of significance was considered appropriate.

a Negro may, under certain social conditions, be one of the most consequential facts of a person's life.

These chief differences in life history between the subjects rated High on Personal Soundness, and those rated Low, may be discussed under seven main headings:

1. *Health of the Subject and of Significant Persons during His Childhood.* One of the most striking differences between the subjects rated High and those rated Low on Personal Soundness is the uniformly excellent physical health of the High subjects and of their parents, and the frequent incidence of physical illness or hurt during the childhood of the Low subjects. In the case histories of the less sound individuals one finds, in addition to serious accidents and lengthy illnesses, such happenings as these: death of the mother in an automobile accident in the subject's childhood; alcoholism in both father and mother; psychosis in a guardian; death of the father from syphilis. Thus to a certain extent unsoundness in adulthood seems the consequence of tragic circumstance in childhood.

2. *Integrity and Stability of the Home.* This refers, first of all, to the continuing presence of father and mother with their children within the same four walls during most of the years of the subject's childhood. The Lows tended to be the products of homes broken by death, divorce, or illness, or by frequent long absences of the father. A part of the picture is the economic security of the family and the stability of the community itself. In addition to the tangible stability evidenced by the fact of continuing presence of both parents and the tendency of the family to live for long periods in one house, there were of course more subtle, and perhaps actually more determinative, emotional and qualitative evidences of family integrity. The check-list item "absence of marked family friction" showed one of the greatest percentage differences between the High and Low subjects. No doubt all these factors are generically related to one another. What they add up to, for the child, is an outer certainty which provides the psychological basis for the creation of the most important inner certainty: that both the world and oneself are stable and worthy of trust.

3. *Imagery of the Father as a Respected, Successful Person.* There was a marked difference between Highs and Lows in this respect. The Highs almost always spoke of their fathers as individuals whom they sought to emulate, and who were on the whole much respected in the community. A number of the Lows either did not know their father

or knew him as a pronounced failure: the father was abandoned by the mother in favor of another man, for instance, or the father died of syphilis, or was an alcoholic, or was managed by the mother.

What seems to be important here is that the High subjects had throughout their childhood the continuing presence of a model on which they could base their own conception of potent masculinity. This is not to say that they were without ambivalence, or that they were uniformly fortunate in their resolution of the Oedipus complex; what it means most of all is that they formed some image of successful manhood which they themselves could realize in their own persons in adulthood. The Low subjects, on the other hand, were unable, simply for lack of the significant experience of it, to adopt in imagination the role of the respected "man of the house." If it is true that adult personality is largely a realization and synthesis of the possibilities that were given in childhood, then we shall have to say that the Lows are unable to take over the adult masculine role largely because no image of it existed for them to emulate; in a sense, adult masculinity was never one of the potentialities which they expected themselves to realize.

4. *Affection and Close Attention from the Mother*. Many of the High subjects were closely controlled at home; but the general picture was of a mother who was loving without being seductive, and solicitous without being demanding or overprotective. Or perhaps it would be more correct to stress the fact that the mothers of Low subjects *were* generally reported as seductive and demanding. The mothers tended to emerge as dominant figures in the lives of the Lows, in contrast to the emphasis among the Highs on the strength of the father. In a number of the High records there is special attention devoted to the incidents that represented the individual's emergence from dependence on the mother; typically there was an open struggle with maternal discipline for a brief period in early adolescence. In a number of cases, athletic activity at this time seemed somehow related to the break with the mother; other common means for formalizing the new status of the adolescent boy were such things as joining clubs or "gangs" and being more participative in high school social activities. The general High pattern was for the boy to make a fairly clear break from the home circle soon after graduation from high school; but many of the Lows remained dependent, especially on the mother.

5. *Presence of Other Siblings and Positive Relations with Them*.

The Highs, as a rule, had more siblings, and more friendly relationships with them, than did the Lows. This factor seems psychologically important for somewhat the same reason as the presence of a successful father: what is involved here is the presence in childhood of models for later adult experience and adult roles. The family is a community in microcosm, and fullest participation in the larger community in later life should be facilitated by richness of interpersonal experience and flexibility in role-taking, determined in large part by the roles available in the family circle. If, as a boy, one has had both an older and a younger brother, one can be both an older and a younger brother to men; and if one has had both an older and a younger sister, one can be both an older and a younger brother to women. Thus complexity and flexibility of one's role repertoire should be increased by complexity of the role-opportunities present in the family. This assumes, of course, essentially positive and undistorted sibling relationships, so that the repetition of childhood patterns is spontaneous and free rather than compulsive.

6. *Athleticism and Competitive Play*. Highs included several young men who were widely known for their athletic prowess: several college swimmers, the captain of a fencing team, a Rose Bowl quarterback, and so on. Mountain climbing and skiing were also mentioned by the Highs. The Lows, as a rule, took little part in competitive sports. The Highs were more robust physically and more given to strenuous exercises; physical courage, stamina, general vigor and the virile expression of aggression seem to be indicated by their records.

7. *Sexual Expression*. Both Highs and Lows appeared to be somewhat slow in coming to sexual expression with other people. The records show a low incidence of sexual intimacies before age 20. Highs and Lows differed markedly from one another, however, in the capacity for forming enduring sexual ties with women. Of the Highs, 90 per cent were either married or were having sexual relations with a woman whom they had known intimately for at least a year; but only 45 per cent of the Lows had established such enduring relationships. Many of the Highs reported problems in sexual adjustment during the first year of marriage; however, the general pattern was to solve these problems successfully and to arrive at a stable relationship. Several of the Lows were either overtly homosexual or effeminate but sexually quiescent. A somewhat rarer pattern, but one found in a few of the Lows, was overcompensated masculinity with promiscuous heterosex-

uality. In general, the Highs were characterized either by mature, easily achieved masculinity or by a solution in which femininity was sublimated and masculine sex drives were satisfied in a stable marriage marked by close dependency on the wife. The Lows were characterized either by manneristic femininity—resulting either in homosexual relations or minimal sexual "outlet"—or by a "masculinity" that protested too much.

SOME CASE-HISTORY PARTICULARS IN HIGH SOUNDNESS SUBJECTS

This solid core of excellence and developmental ease characterizing the more highly rated subjects as a group deserves to be emphasized, but certainly should not be overemphasized. When one looks at cases individually, irregularities and complexities that the group averages had obscured immediately become apparent. Perhaps an overly bland picture of ease and integration among High Soundness subjects has been conveyed by these group comparisons. If so, it should be said at once that no especially blessed individual turned up in this assessment; the luckiest of the lives here studied had its full share of difficulty and private despair. This statement could be documented at considerable length. At the risk of having the reader conclude that the assessment staff psychologists do not know neurosis when they see it, we shall present briefly some facts about some of the subjects who were rated as above average by both Staff and Department raters.

The mother of one highly rated subject became psychotic during her son's adolescence and has been psychotic since then, though living at home much of the time. The father was alcoholic and inclined to wander; he abandoned the family on several occasions, and they were in extreme financial straits during the depression of the 1930's. These adversities are of the sort that often produce mental illness, but in this person they produced strength—not ease, certainly, but a complex kind of durability and integrity that showed itself in crucial moments in group and personal interactions. Still, there were many neurotic incapacities in his character, with disturbances in intimacy being most marked; he maintained his integrity partly by being separate and solitary. His Rorschach contained 87 per cent pure form responses, and the only color he saw in the ink blots was "blood dripping from the injured paws of a dog" on Card II. He, too, had been injured, but he had somehow emerged with the visible signs of personal soundness both in the assessment setting and in his professional relations.

Another highly rated subject, although Jewish, had taken pains to make himself unidentifiable as a Jew. Further, he admitted (painfully) to violent anti-Semitic feelings, which, however, did not find expression in action; he "leans over backward" in his dealings with other Jews. This uncomfortable posture marred the essential soundness of an individual otherwise distinguished by high intelligence, responsibility, and a very good sense of humor.

One of the most "promising" professionally of the scientists in the sample has already been honored by being chosen for a most-desired academic position in his field. In view of his early achievement and his promise of more to come, his response to Card 17BM of the Thematic Apperception Test is of interest:

> Here we have an acrobat, a member of a vaudeville troupe. He is gyrating high on a rope above an applauding audience. As he hangs there he reflects a bit grimly that his place could be taken with equal success by a monkey. As he strains his muscles and things (*sic*) of his low place in society, life seems for a moment unsavoury to him. Sliding now down the rope to the stage and bowing off in a storm of applause, he goes sourly to his dressing room and smashes the mirror which reflects his painted and powdered body. However, unable to change his position in life, he must continue as he is, and will do so until an aging body forces him into retirement and poverty.

The applause of the crowd, according to the subject's interpretation, is dust in the mouth to this muscular performer; his mood is sour and he finds life unsavoury; he is grim and strained in his triumph. This depressive note in the subject's response suggests a certain undercurrent of pessimism and self-dissatisfaction, if not actual disgust, beneath a surface that impressed the psychological staff, and his professional colleagues as well, as being outstandingly sound.

Still another highly rated subject was involved in an unusually severe Oedipal relationship, but one in which the opposition to the father was out in the open, if not always successfully carried through. He had mustered considerable adolescent rebellion, but generally failed of independent achievement at crucial moments. The Rorschach record contained numerous responses in which animals were seen as "mangled," "bleeding," "battered up," "shot full of holes," "horrible," and, on Card X, "black and angry." On Card IV, the so-called "father card," this subject saw "some terrible creature of the sea," and then he commented, "I wouldn't like to meet *him* at all." Finally, after a long pause, he added, "I give up." At the risk of being somewhat fanciful, one might say that the Oedipus situation is essentially unresolved, and that the subject sees his position as highly vulnerable. Nevertheless, unresolved Oedipus and all, this subject possessed to a notable degree the traits which both department and staff raters thought of as sound.

Another subject, a refugee, had endured extremely trying circumstances in Europe during the years of the Nazi terror, and they had clearly left their mark. Still, he communicated a high seriousness of purpose and an ethical purity which were truly impressive, and which earned him his above-average ratings on both Department and Staff Soundness. His personal difficulties, however, are reflected in his MMPI profile. His scores were as follows: Depression, 92; Masculinity-Femininity, 86; Hypochondriasis, 80; Hysteria, 75; Psychasthenia, 72; Paranoia, 62; Schizophrenia, 61; Hypomania, 50; Psychopathic Deviate, 48. This profile, seen in a clinic, would indicate a severely disturbed person. It seems probable that the subject had many neurotic disabilities, which, however, were somehow integrated into a personality that not only functioned, but functioned impressively well on its own terms.

There is little point in multiplying examples, although it would be possible to do so. The conclusion to which the assessment staff has come is that psychopathology is always with us, and that soundness is *a way of reacting to problems, not an absence of them.* The transformation of pathological trends into distinctive character assets and the minimization of their effects through compensatory overdevelopment of other traits are both marks of "sound" reaction to personal difficulties. At times, indeed, the handling of psychopathology may be so skillful and the masking of pathological motivations so subtle that the individual's soundness may be considerably overrated. There is no doubt that some of our apparently "balanced" subjects were balanced quite precariously, and that their stability was more semblance than fact. It is possible to mistake for soundness what is actually rigidity based on a sort of paralysis of affect engendered by a fear of instinctual drives. These cases of pseudo-soundness were probably few, however. The coherence and sensibleness of the correlates of both Department and Staff Soundness suggest a substantial validity in both the external criterion and the staff assessments. The existence of psychopathology in even the quite sound individuals has been emphasized here partly by way of counteracting the sort of trite determinism with which so many clinical studies seem to conclude: broken homes leading to delinquency; psychosis in the parents being passed on, through whatever mechanism, to the offspring; unloving mothers rearing hateful children; catastrophe breeding catastrophe. Undoubtedly such correlations exist in nature, and they were, indeed, found in our own investigation; but considerable variance remains unaccounted for. What we should like to suggest here is that within the population of subjects of ordinary physical and psychological integrity, soundness is by no means exclusively determined by circumstances but may be considered in the nature of an unintended—and perhaps largely unconscious—personal achievement. Our High Soundness subjects are beset, like all other persons, by fears, unrealizable desires, self-condemned hates, and tensions difficult to resolve. They are *sound* largely because they bear with their anxieties, hew to a stable course, and maintain some sense of the ultimate worthwhileness of their lives.

6

Psychotherapy and Creativity

I⊤ IS difficult to be objective about psychotherapy, so subjective in essence is the activity itself. In introducing some of my own
attempts to muster some degree of objectivity in such research, I must
beg the reader's indulgence for a time while I put forward certain of
my retrospections which I think are relevant. In later chapters the
objective research itself will be reported in detail.

What I propose to do here is first to take a look backward at my
own experience with psychotherapy and to say whatever I think I
can say with some confidence about it; this done, I shall offer some
further thoughts concerning recent experimentation with certain
psychoactive drugs in psychotherapy. These considerations arise as
much as a result of my own research in creativity as of my work in
therapy. Let me say at the outset that I consider psychotherapy to
have proved remarkably recalcitrant to scientific research, for reasons
that I think we should consider in some detail if we are to evolve new
approaches that offer promise of improvement in theory and technique.

But first, a look backward. Psychologists of my age (40 in 1962)
in the United States entered upon their profession at a time when the
march of events had produced extraordinary turbulence in the more
culturally advanced settlements of men and had at the same time prepared the way for radical unsettlings in cultures less developed.
Whether we were physically engaged in the war or not, we knew
the challenge to our own values posed by the actions of many men
just like us. The killing of one man by another has actually never
required much sanction, but when times are easy we like to think it

does, and we like to think that great communities are responsive to the rules against killing which are made effective easily enough when only a few individuals are involved. The second World War left no doubt that such morality as we had achieved was extremely feeble. And at war's end we saw an awesome triumph of intellect announced by the burning up of guilty and guiltless alike in atomic holocaust. Yet even that was a pale horror in comparison with what had engendered it: a genocide attempted in clerical coldness, a storm of violence and rapacity which had stopped just short of shaking down all that our culture had built.

These horrors, let me add immediately, had very little personal meaning to most of the people I know, in the sense in which a death in the family would have meaning, or going hungry for a few days in a row would have meaning. Human beings are nothing if not callous to suffering in the large. When I speak of these events as horrors, I do so by imagining their meaning to the people directly involved, and by considering them in the light of the advanced ethical sensibility that is part of the Judaic-Christian heritage. To most young Americans who were beginning their graduate training in psychology in 1946, these events were not personally horrible. Nonetheless, the events themselves and their ethical implications were there for all of us to live with, though they were more like an almost unnoticed though general contamination in the climate than like something so palpably real as a scheduled examination or a potential rise in pay; they were effective conditions of our existence, but ones to which we paid little conscious attention. I think, however, that they had a most important influence upon the development of interest in psychotherapy that occurred especially in the years between 1946 and 1955. Their subtle influence came in the framing of questions that were rarely stated articulately, they seemed so useless. "What does it all mean?" and "Why am I here?" were the questions, and unfashionable though they were in the worlds of pragmatism and logical positivism whose philosophies had become so dominant in science, they nevertheless lay behind much of the restlessness of sensitive minds in that decade. And though no one seemed really to know just what psychotherapy did have to offer, it seemed vaguely like a promise that meaning indeed was there, if only we understood our own individual existence a little better; that the restlessness would pass as meaning became clear.

Along with *this* disquiet, however inarticulate or only dimly apprehended, there went the perennial disquiet which youth experiences at the point of entrance into the responsibilities of maturity. William Butler Yeats puts it this way in a poem:

> Even the wisest man grows tense
> With some sort of violence
> When he sets out to accomplish fate
> Know his work or choose his mate.

Knowing one's work, in the case of clinical psychology in 1946, presented more than the usual difficulties so far as the matter of identity is concerned. Not only were we living the half-life of graduate students, we were trying to find out about a field of study which was trying to find out about itself. And the Socratic injunction "Know thyself" was being taken very seriously; as though one can, in any serious way, know oneself. Still, I think that basically the injunction was being taken properly, as an instruction to a machine to become a mechanic for itself. And this was a third major motive for our interest in psychotherapy, interest in ourselves as a machine somewhat in need of adjustment or tuning up—or even a major overhaul. In brief, besides the state of the great world and the vastly interesting personal circumstances attendant upon the beginning of adulthood, there was sometimes neurosis to be dealt with, and all its train of ills.

I shall not prolong this historical review by considering the way in which clinical psychology itself became an important force in the field of therapy, which of course at that time it was not. Essentially what happened was that we plunged into therapy for ourselves, and found out about it the hard way, as patients, as therapists, as researchers. In retrospect, some of the enthusiasm may seem to have been unwarranted, but retrospect would be graceless to say so. The atmosphere was one of excitement, uncertainty, and need, and psychotherapy was there with its tacit promise that things would all make sense if we but developed a sufficient degree of trust, autonomy, initiative, industry, and those various other good things that one had to have in just the right amounts in order to answer the question "Who am I?" William James concluded near the end of a questioning life that he was a "badly mixed critter," but those of us who knew of his conclusion either thought that he was joking or felt that he might have done a lot better if only he could have had some psychotherapy.

Whatever the tone of my remarking on this may be, it is no exaggeration to say that the majority of clinical psychologists in the United States by 1950 were recommending psychotherapy for everything from warts to worrisomeness, and of my personal acquaintances in the field I should say at least 80 per cent of them were actively engaged in psychotherapy either as patient or as practitioner, and usually as both. I must add myself to their number, if for no other reason than to tell you of a dream I had in mid-course.

The dream was one of almost total darkness. Gradually in the darkness I discerned shadowy figures, almost lost so shadowy they were; first one or two, then a few more, then by the tens and by the hundreds, all dimly bodied forth. Soon I realized that I could see them only from the waist up, and that from the waist down they were caught in a mire, an oozy swamp which was gradually sucking them downwards out of sight. Then I saw that each of the figures was holding on for dear life, left hand and right hand, to the hands of two other persons in the mire. Suddenly the dream became a nightmare, for in an instant of recognition and realization I knew that each one in the swamp thought that with his right hand he clasped the hand of someone on firm ground, and with his left hand he clasped the hand of someone deeper in the swamp, but that actually everyone was stuck to the same extent in the swamp and each had the same illusion. Then I recognized the dim figures in the dream, one after another; those lost figures were psychologists and psychiatrists all, and in the light of day they were connected with one another in some such wise as in my dream.

This dark dream no doubt had many meanings, but certainly its chief mood and meaning was disillusion. Disillusions pass just as illusions do, and often both illusion and disillusion are necessary steps in our understanding of reality. The state of affairs in psychotherapy (even in such a hotbed of self-examination with the help of someone else as Berkeley, California, was in those days) was never quite that bad. But neither was the picture very rosy, and the dream told something of what I was feeling and reflected one aspect of the then-current reality. A great many psychotherapists, myself included, were often at a loss to know what was going on in the cases they were treating. Out of this feeling came a recognition of the urgent need for research, with its own particular sort of siren song: "Let's get some facts to go on." Moreover, psychiatrists and psychoanalysts were obviously not much interested, in the main, in any sort of scientific inquiry into psychotherapy. Quite evidently, if anything of scientific value was to be discovered it would have to be discovered by psychologists. So, a lot of us set to work, again with considerable enthusiasm in the sowing, to which the yield perhaps does not measure up. Nevertheless, we set to work in earnest.

It was very much in the spirit of scientific inquiry that I myself approached the topic of personality change. I wrote in my doctoral thesis that my intention was "to check up on such matters as could be checked up on" in the psychotherapeutic enterprise, by which I meant that for the sake of making a beginning I was willing to limit myself to observations of an objective sort, and preferably those that were susceptible of crude quantification and enumeration as well. Thus I adopted a practical, functionally modest, and down-to-earth definition of *improvement* in the patient, and depended upon the opinions of persons other than the patient or the therapist for the evaluation of relative degrees of improvement in the patients I studied. By taking advantage of such further objectivization as psychological tests could achieve, I was able to develop measures that could predict which patients would be judged as "improved" and which would be judged as "unimproved." In the intervening years, these measures, and particularly my prognostic scale, which on the basis of much other evidence I finally named the Ego-strength scale, have proved useful in performing that sort of task. The conclusion was quite clear: patients who possessed greater ego-strength at the beginning of therapy, even though obscured by the usual clinical overlay of anxiety and depression, would be better off, i.e., would have shown more "improvement," by the end of therapy. I discovered, however, that the Ego-strength scale would also predict improvement over time in those patients who did not receive psychotherapy, but were only on a waiting list for it. Moreover, the scale predicts favorable reaction to stress and challenge in many different situations. My own conclusion is that many behaviors that appear to change as a result of psychotherapy are actually influenced little or not at all by the therapy, and that the observed changes are produced by endogenous processes of a counteractive sort which are set in motion within the reasonably strong ego after some trauma has produced a temporary regression.

To say this, however, is by no means to say, as some psychologists have said in interpreting these results and others like them, that "psychotherapy is no blessed good," or words to that effect. Hardly a general thing at all can be said about psychotherapy in the round, for the word is used by so many different people to refer to such various realities. But even if one does delimit its usage so that it denotes conventional psychiatric practice in which a patient is treated by a psychiatrist or psychologist who meets the usual qualifications of training and licensing, and the treatment methods used are not somatic but psychological, it remains difficult to generalize concerning the effectiveness of psychotherapy. My own impression is that from two-thirds to three-fourths of all patients who feel bad enough at some time to go to see a psychiatrist will say that they are feeling much better if asked about the matter some six months later. As I have indicated, however, perhaps two-thirds of these patients would say so just as strongly if they had had only one visit with the psychiatrist, so that the margin of difference made by such extended psychiatric treatment is slight if one takes crude enumeration of this sort as adequate to the task of appraisal. At the same time, most therapists know many cases in which improvement was striking and in which the coherence of events made the therapy plainly an important causative factor in the improvement. No one with extensive experience in the practice of psychotherapy can possibly accept any general statement impugning its value.

The source of this difficulty in appraising the effectiveness of psychotherapy is important to understand. It rests, as I see the matter, upon certain limitations of scientific method that as scientists we readily accept in order to make our observations, but then tend to forget as we formulate our interpretations. For psychologists more particularly, it rests upon that besetting difficulty which Fechner strove with so valiantly but which no one has eased: the mind-body problem, or, to consider it in its most relevant aspect in research on psychotherapy, the subject-object distinction. Science by its method limits itself to appearances of a public or potentially public sort, and in the interests of verification insists upon objectification. This works quite well so long as the objects do not have feelings; and it works—not quite so well, yet well enough for many purposes—even when the objects *do* have feelings. But if the question I am asking myself is "Why was I ever born?" or "Why live?" there are no objective answers that can be satisfying to me. The "question" is a feeling which cannot be "answered," but which can only give way to another feeling, "How good it is to be alive!" And the human transaction that enables the one feeling to give way to the other is a *transaction between subjects*, the objective indices of which are extremely subtle and highly variable at best. One can make tape-recordings, take motion pictures, count heart beats, measure muscle potentials, note the number of minutes spent together, ask questions (True-False questions, open-ended questions, questions in disguise), get interpretations of inkblots, or do any number of those tricks of the trade with which we are all familiar. They avail little, for the vitalizing transaction is a matter of feeling, having an existence and known only in the subject, or, as I prefer to say, in the realm of spirit. My own interest in the attempted empiristic solutions of the mind-body problem came to an abrupt end the first time I heard of Liebniz' wry rejoinder to Locke's dictum that there is nothing in mind that was not first in sense. Said Liebniz, "Nothing except mind," and that's all there is to that. This argument can proceed no further, nor can any of the great arguments of classical philosophy progress through analysis, for at heart they are matters of sentiment. One of the troubles of the sometime scientist who is also sometime psychotherapist is that his sentiments are mixed, and are especially mixed when he undertakes to do research on psychotherapy.

From the point of view of the subject, then, the essence of the beneficence that psychotherapy may bring is entirely of the spirit. The appearances that may accompany such spiritual beneficences are variable and elusive, and the superficies of "adjustment" to any given cultural norm may yield a rather bad fit to the behavior of the person who has benefited from psychotherapy. And to make matters even more difficult for the research psychologist, the moment of genuine encounter, the vitalizing transaction, may pass almost unnoticed at the time. It is ephemeral, as frail as love or blessedness, as passing as the moment of grace or the beginning of creation, the fecundating act; it has its being in the imagination and the spirit, while the dull machinery of routine thought chugs monotonously along and the inertia that makes us think the same thought in just the same way so many thousands of times over continues its hebetudinous reign. In almost all appearances we remain the same, even though we are different. To put the matter commonly, I have never known any case, no matter how successful, with treatment both thorough and inspired and with real movement felt by the patient and therapist, in which at the conclusion of the work the patient was not readily recognized by friends and neighbors, and in a million ways, some of them measured by the best psychological tests, *just about the same.*

And yet he had had a different sort of time and was likely to have a different sort of time in the future. So I feel that we must look to the ephemeral and the subjective in psychotherapy, perhaps more than to traits of personality that are consistent and objectifiable, if we are to appraise its value.

I realize that this view claims for psychotherapy a privacy which seems to put it beyond the kind of criticism that objective research can support. Nevertheless, I must say that I am increasingly reluctant to make the research process a part of the treatment process, and I would urge that we seek ways of doing research on basic problems in therapy without using cases in actual treatment. The subject-object distinction is most relevant here. Research must be objective, but to be objective may be simply the worst thing in the world from the point of view of psychotherapy, or of any creative activity. The artist has a perfect right to say to the critic, "Go away and leave me alone," for in fact whatever the artist does he must do alone. There is a Kentucky hill folk version of an old English song which puts it just right. The verses are:

> You've got to cross that lonesome valley
> Y'got to cross it by y'rself
> There h'ain't no one gwine to cross h'it for you
> Y'got to cross it by y'rself.

Needless to say, the research into creative process that my colleagues and I at the University of California have been doing has been dogged by exactly this difficulty: in attempting to be objective and scientific in relation to an activity so subjective and artistic, one can expect to be sorely tried by both the limitations of psychological measurement and the inherent epistemological impediment. Yet, as with psychotherapy, the phenomena seemed to cry aloud for objective investigation: one can hardly find an area of psychological study in which subjectivity has so cluttered the premises. One can only shoulder the burden, accept the limitations, and try to reconstruct with the aid of imagination the living process of which our correlation coefficients give us a murky picture. James Joyce in a famous passage in *Ulysses* likens Irish art to "a cracked looking glass"; my own eyes have been sorely strained these past few years in trying to find in some two hundred thousand Pearsonian correlation coefficients the dim outline of that mysterious process we call psychic creation.

One gets tired of such tedious peering at even the most indubitably valid numbers, of course, and I myself took the occasion a couple of years ago, when the Center for Advanced Study offered me a year's respite from my usual work, to explore a more subjective route to knowledge about the potentialities of mind for fantastic imaginings. Having heard of Gordon Wasson's successful expedition in search of the "divine mushroom" of Mexico, I decided to go there myself and eat the mushroom. I was prepared to make a journey to the Indian villages to obtain the mushroom, but I was spared the difficulties, and perhaps missed the fun, of doing so when I learned that the Institute of Biological Research at the National University was at work on a scientific study of the mushroom's effect and that the scientists there had a large store available. Through the courtesy of Drs. A. Nieto and D. Escobar, I was privileged both to read their extensive protocols based on experiments with students and to sample the substance myself. My own interest has been in the implications of the unusual inner experience for the psychology of imagination and for the mind-body problem; I did, however, see an analogue between the enlivening of imagination and the psychotherapeutic goal of broadening of consciousness. And so I commended the mushroom to the attention of a colleague of mine at Harvard University, Dr. Timothy Leary, who was an active practitioner of group therapy. He became interested in its possibilities as a vehicle for inducing change in behavior as a result of the altered state of consciousness that the drug produces. Since he has had the initiative in exploring the therapeutic possibility of the mushroom—or more exactly, of psilocybin, the chemical ingredient that produces the conscious-altering effect—I shall recommend that the reader search out the report of Leary and his co-investigators on psilocybin's application to group psychotherapy (with convicts in a Massachusetts prison). Let me point out, however, the grounds in theory for hoping that creative growth may be facilitated by the use of psilocybin or similar relatively harmless psychoactive drugs in conjunction with the more conventional psychotherapeutic agents of suggestion and analysis. What has emerged most clearly from my own research on creativity is the fact that the creative person is able to find in the developmentally more primitive and less reasonably structured aspects of his own mental functioning the possibility of new insight, even though at first this may be only intuitively and dimly grasped. He is willing to pay heed to vague feelings and intimations which on the grounds of good sense are put aside hastily by most of us. Characteristically, the creative individual refuses to be content with the most easily established perceptual schemata or perceptual constancies, even such obviously adaptive ones as the discrimination between what is inside the self versus what is outside the self, or the conviction that there are things in the world that are absolutely unmoving, or the notion that all effects have causes, or that time passes moment by moment in a succession of states rather than in an unstoppable flux. You will recognize these of course as the basis of what we usually call a sane mind, a clear sensorium, a sense of reality, and so on. But creative people sometimes do without these and without many other basic constancies, leading them at times, as you might imagine, to give an impression of psychological imbalance. There is reason to believe that many creative individuals deliberately induce in themselves an altered state of consciousness in which the ordinary structures of experience are broken down. The ordinary world may thus be transcended: in mystical states, in feelings of being possessed, in prolonged trances or deep reveries, and even at times in psychosis. The point is that these deviations from perceptual constancies may permit a more inclusive and more valid perception, once the stress involved in extending the boundaries is relieved. In brief, a kind of transcendence of apparently adaptive but in some sense crippling limits may thus be achieved. Something of this sort is necessary if neurosis is to be cured, for the constancies *there* are properly called compulsive and imprisoning.

At this point, let me introduce a note of caution to accompany this note of hope. Certainly not everyone can profit from letting neurotic defenses go on such short biochemical notice. Defenses, like other perceptual screens, usually exist for some good reason, however uneconomic they may seem when we look at the limits they set to breadth of experience. The psychic defenses themselves are part of the ego, and in terms of the availability of psychic energy it must be said that the immediate effect of such a drug as psilocybin is ego-enervating. As nearly as I can judge the matter in the hundred or so cases I have observed closely, the weakening of ego-functioning persists for several days after the most striking and immediate effects of the drug have worn off. The experience is often a pleasant one, let me add, but to speak technically in terms of ego structure and functioning we must say that the ego is weaker. The continuing therapeutic effects seem to be achieved during the new period of ego-synthesis that follows if more conventional psychotherapeutic measures are then employed. The drug by itself is primarily debilitating, a term which I hope can be used non-invidiously here. Whether the ego of modern man needs to be strengthened or weakened is quite another matter and involves complex questions of species survival and of evolution. In the practical case of the moment, however, we always give considerable thought to whether the individual ego we are dealing with can stand being weakened for a while, or whether the main need is not to be be-nerved. It is this decision which it behooves us to approach cautiously.

Whether or not these drugs do prove eventually to be of use in psychotherapy proper, they certainly open up to the psychological scientist the possibility of experimenting with methods for making contact with emotionally isolated individuals, of rendering unhealthy psychic defenses temporarily inoperative, of broadening consciousness and freeing imagination: in brief, of restoring to creative freedom that part of the self which uneconomic repression has severely limited. They may make it possible to initiate mechanically the process that occurs as one aspect of psychic creation. Such drugs confront us once again, and rather savagely in fact, with the mind-body problem: it seems quite apparent at this point in our exploration of the psycho-active drugs and of psychosurgery that minute alterations in the biochemical matrix of personality can produce dramatic changes in both outward behavior and inner experience, and that moral judgment itself can be radically affected. For good or ill, that is the direction in which all the recent research on the experimental production of altered states of consciousness is leading us, and the two areas of work, psychotherapy and creativity, are vitally involved in the outcome of these new developments.

7

Psychotherapy as Vitalizing Relationship

To say of the moment of genuine encounter—"the vitalizing transaction," as I have called it—that it may be "as frail as love or blessedness" is perhaps to put too much emphasis on the fragility of the live and growing thing that psychotherapy is designed to nourish. Certainly many psychotherapists take a hardier view. In fact, psychotherapeutic patience aims to overcome precisely the febrile quality of the state of "being in love" and the disillusion that time brings if there is no capacity for growth and change in the relationship. Recall Housman's poem in *A Shropshire Lad*:

> Oh, when I was in love with you
> Then I was clean and brave
> And miles around the wonder grew
> How well did I behave.
>
> But now the fancy passes
> And nothing shall remain
> And miles around they'll say that I
> Am quite myself again.

The fact of the matter is that psychotherapy properly practiced is a discipline of considerable technical complexity, and diagnosis is by no means either name-calling or even "labeling" or "pigeon-holing." Diagnosis itself is, if really well done, a form of relationship calling for a fineness of empathic understanding and, to return to my earlier phrase, "genuine encounter."

In what follows I shall try to place psychotherapy in the context of personal relationship in general. The material on which I shall draw formed the basis of my doctoral dissertation some years ago, and it reflects my interest then in finding the best terms in which to describe what I was at that time calling "personal interaction." My interest was in the general problem of describing people in their relationships with other people as much as it was in exploring the special case of two persons who talk to each other for the express purpose of inducing changes in the behavior of one of them.

Thus viewed, psychotherapy becomes a proper subject for investigation by one interested in the problems of personality in general. Although it remains a special case, it calls less for a special interest. It rather recommends itself as a conveniently delimited (in time and space) interaction between persons, with the roles fairly definitely but by no means rigidly defined, and with a well-demarcated beginning, course, and termination. In the teaching- and research-oriented institutions in which this study was conducted, it is also a situation that is rendered most available for intensive scientific investigation.

This coupling of the problems peculiar to psychotherapy with those relevant to the broader domain of all personal interaction derives from two converging lines of thought and research. The first of these, stimulated by practical needs in the psychiatric clinic, has to do with the prediction of response to brief psychotherapy. The second, with implications more broadly social but no less urgent and pragmatically important, is concerned with the conditions that make personal interactions mutually satisfying, constructive, and on-going, on the one hand, and antagonizing, destructive, and stultifying, on the other.

My research design attempted to represent the convergence of these two lines of thought. Placing psychotherapy in the broader context of personal interaction immediately brings about a shift in the balance of interest between therapist and patient. The patient has been too much the center of attention in psychiatry, and the importance of the personality of the therapist, both in theory-making and in clinical practice, has been too much ignored. The study of the therapeutic process is certainly incomplete without a thorough evaluation of the extent to which it is the therapist as well as the patient who determines the form of the interaction.

PERSONAL INTERACTION IN GENERAL

Two persons are interacting with one another when they are in perceptual contact and mutually influence each other's behavior.

Let us call such a situation a personal interaction. In what terms can it best be described?

Like all other events, it has, first of all, a space-time coordinate. That is, we might begin by stating where and when it occurs. These two facts alone give it a distinct character, and greatly delimit the set of other possible characteristics that personal interactions in general might have. Two persons meeting at a lively party on Saturday night are likely to have a personal interaction quite different from what they might if they were to meet in church the next morning, even though they were otherwise the same people. The personal interaction of two male ulcer patients meeting in a men's gymnasium where they had gone to get some exercise is likely to be quite different from that which might result had they found themselves serving on the same committee of the Junior Chamber of Commerce. For almost any two people, Monday morning at work in the office can be very different from Friday afternoon after work in a bar.

So much for space-time coordinates as determinant of the form of personal interaction. Having placed and dated it, we next need to know whom it involves. Even in the same place and at the same time, two men are likely to interact differently from two women, or from a man and a woman. People who bear a superior-subordinate relation to one another will interact differently from those whose relation to one another is coordinate. Such differences as older and younger, stronger and weaker, stupid and intelligent, rich and poor, psychotic and sane, will make a difference too in the form of personal interactions.

Related to such differences as these, but not entirely co-extensive with them, are the need-structures of the persons involved. There are some persons whose needs are so intense that they force almost all their personal interactions into the same form, thus limiting greatly the range of possible response on the part of the other person. Such a necessitous and undifferentiated character may be given to all interactions by, to employ a Freudian-type characterology, the orally deprived person, who strives desperately and incessantly to *get* from others, fearing starvation and abandonment if he is not immediately fed (love, or admiration, or applause in some form). So, also, to continue with the dramatis personae of the Freudian theatre, may the anal-compulsive, with his needs for order and balance, react frantically to interaction with a person who is seen as threatening to upset things, or who flaunts various derivative forms of anal indiscipline.

There are, of course, many less compelling and theoretically unclaimed needs for which satisfaction is sought, and generally found, in personal interaction. From other people one may get information, entertainment, helpful criticism, praise, blame, money for services rendered, inspiration, sexual satisfaction, food, transportation, votes, and even psychotherapy. Which brings us to the special case that is the focus of this investigation.

PERSONAL INTERACTION IN PSYCHOTHERAPY

Psychotherapy for private patients who have some disturbance in interpersonal relations but are not sick enough to require hospitalization generally takes place in the office of a psychiatrist or a psychologist, and is usually accompanied, more or less immediately, by the payment of a fee. It is begun at the behest of the patient, who has come to the opinion that his mind is not working properly, or who at least knows that his body is not working properly and that medical men have told him that the cause lies in his mind. The patient is usually very unhappy, and his personal interactions in the past have been unsuccessful in satisfying his needs (some of which, indeed, he may not be aware of).

In order to get psychotherapy, then, the patient must go to the therapist and must pay him money. The therapist, on the other hand, receives the patient in his office and takes money from him (though not in person, of course). He may have many reasons for accepting this patient in psychotherapy. One reason may be that he needs the money, or at least thinks that what he can buy with the money would be nice to have. Another reason may be that he likes to help people who are in trouble (behind this reason may lie a host of other reasons). Or, it may be an expression of his own creative selfhood to help others grow. Then again, he may be moved chiefly by curiosity, scientific or other: he may like to find things out, to discover the truth of matters. In addition, there is a certain amount of gratification to be had from being a person of power and wisdom, to whom others come for help.

It is certainly more bolstering to one's self-esteem to be a psycho-therapist than to be a patient.

Besides all these motives, it sometimes happens that the therapist is himself quite unsuccessful in other personal interactions, and doing psychotherapy is one of the few ways in which he can really get into contact with other people.

To these specific motives for doing psychotherapy must be added still other characteristics of the therapist which will influence the interaction: his physical appearance, his bearing and manner, his basic attitudes toward people in general as well as toward patients in particular, his views on religion, politics, and art, his group identity, his ability to obtain direct sexual satisfaction, the strength of his own impulses and his way of handling them, his tolerance of the impulses of others; what he desires, what he fears, what he has, what he wants but can never get; his loves and his hates; his basic family relationships; in short, his personality.

Not all these things will bear directly on the therapeutic interaction, of course. Some will simply not be relevant; other characteristics of the therapist may be so handled by him that they play a minimal role in the relationship. When we say that a therapist's skill has increased, we mean partly that he has learned how he affects the patient, and that he is able to produce desired effects deliberately, with fore-thought. Forethought requires some degree of imagination, so that it is imagination which determines scope in therapy. Because the thera-pist can imagine, he can understand; and, understanding, he can take action to affect. If the therapist has imagination, no personality is alien to him.

As we have suggested, the motives and needs of both patient and therapist may indeed be many. Withal, the therapist is usually com-mitted to a certain integrity in the practice of his high art, so that his chief duty to himself and his patient with regard to his own motiva-tions is simply *to realize their existence* and to deal with them as part of this particular personal interaction called psychotherapy. Psycho-therapy is, before it is anything else, an interaction or transaction be-tween two people.

This much we had fairly clearly in mind before starting the present study. As the research progressed, however, other facts that were only partly apprehended before suddenly emerged with new distinctness and greater importance. For these, there is no ready statistical evidence. They will, therefore, be presented simply as one observer's account of what he thought he saw emerging from a mass of first-order impressions.

There was, first of all, the importance of unconscious communication as a determinant of the forms of many of the interactions. These psychiatrists and these patients learned things about one another that they did not put into words and that they probably still cannot verbalize. They learned what the other person wanted, what he believed in, how he felt toward them, toward the clinic, toward the psychologist, toward psychotherapy, toward life in general, and probably the patients learned almost as much of these things about the psychiatrists as the psychiatrists learned about the patients.

A second important fact which seemed to emerge was a need for some theory of roles to rationalize the various interactions. Newcomb[1] has pointed out that "the most persistently self-maintaining systems within the organized human personality—including, in particular, the self-system—are those which have to do with role relationships." In view of this, it is not surprising that in personal interaction, which is largely interpersonal role relationships, the role-structures and role-perceptions of the individuals should give to the interaction its predominant form. Certainly, much of what happened in these psychotherapeutic relationships may best be explained in terms of such a theory. To this end, some effort has been made to clarify the notion of roles in personality, and these considerations will be presented in a later section, when we are ready to discuss specific interactions in detail.

Meanwhile, we shall proceed to a description of the sample, and the psychological procedures used in this investigation.

Description of the sample

The sample consists of six psychiatric residents and 33 outpatients. They participated in psychotherapy on the outpatient services of two mental hygiene clinics.

Four of the psychiatrists were men, two were women. The patients numbered 12 men and 21 women. The patients were among the first

[1] Newcomb, T. M., "Role Behaviors in the Study of Individual Personality and of Groups," *J. Personality*, 18, 3, 273–289.

36 new patients (three of these later dropped out) to begin therapy at the clinics in the year this study was started. The psychiatrists constituted the full complement of new psychiatric residents assigned to outpatient service for a six-month period beginning at the same time. The psychiatrists were all comparatively inexperienced in intensive psychotherapy, and none of them had been, or was being, analyzed. They had the benefit, however, of weekly individual consultations with experts in psychotherapy, of seminars devoted to case presentations and theoretical discussions, and of considerable psychoanalytic orientation in the clinics as a whole.

The original design of the research called for a total of 36 patients, six to each psychiatrist. This aim was not achieved, for in spite of whole-hearted cooperation on the part of the director of outpatient service, it became necessary, for administrative purposes, to assign seven patients to some therapists and only five to others. In addition, three patients, for reasons extrinsic to the therapy situation, were unable to return after one or two visits, resulting in one therapist's carrying only three patients, while another carried only four.

The total number of visits for those remaining in the sample ranged from 5 to 56. Patients who came only a few times and then dropped out were nevertheless retained in the sample, since this sort of action is representative of what generally occurs in outpatient clinics. To impose some arbitrary requirement as to length of therapy would introduce bias, since some selective factor is operating in causing a person to continue the relationship. So long as the therapy was not terminated for some reason extrinsic to the therapy situation itself, the case was retained in the sample. More will be said later about some of the reasons for early terminations.

Procedure

Both psychiatrists and patients were given a battery of five tests: the Rorschach, Minnesota Multiphasic Personality Inventory, Form 60 of the Levinson-Sanford Ethnocentrism scale, a sentence completion test, and an intelligence test. Because of many invalidations of the sentence completion test, it was later excluded from the data to be analyzed here. The intelligence test given to the patients was a short form of the Wechsler-Bellevue, consisting of Comprehension, Similarities, Digit Symbol, and Block Design. The psychiatrists were given the Michigan Vocabulary test. The experimenter interviewed most of the patients three times; each of them at the beginning of therapy and three weeks after therapy had begun, and many, although not all of them, at the close of therapy. He talked at some length with the therapists, anywhere from 10 to 20 times each, and held a formal two-hour interview with each therapist at the close of the six-month residence on outpatient service. At this interview, each case was discussed in detail.

In addition, the experimenter followed each case by reading the therapist's notes in the patient's chart, and thus was able to keep fairly well abreast of what was going on.

At the conclusion of the therapist's residence on outpatient service, each case was rated independently for degree of improvement by two judges, on the basis of a perusal of the charts and the therapist's report on the case in an interview with the judges. The judges were two heads of departments at one of the clinics; one of them was the director of outpatient service, and the other was the chief of the psychology section.

The rating form recognized three degrees of improvement or lack of it, defined as follows:

1) *Much Improved:* Considerable or complete relief of presenting symptoms; significant changes in ways of experiencing the world and relating to people; better capacity for love and work; modification of character defenses; decrease in hostility and anxiety.

2) *Improved:* Some decrease in symptoms; attainment of at least superficial insight; improved attitude toward trying to get along with others; somewhat more stable behavior in general.

3) *Unimproved:* Little or no relief of symptoms or change in behavior; no increase of insight, even of the superficial sort.

Results

The results of this study may be divided into three general areas. The first deals with the accuracy of prediction of outcome of psychotherapy from the test results of the patient. Here we shall use this sample as a cross-validation group for the testing of certain prognostic indices and prediction scales derived by other investigators on other samples, as well as to test certain hypotheses of our own.

The second general area deals with the possibility of improving prediction by considering the test results of therapists as well as those of patients. This is done by obtaining judgments from skilled clinical psychologists, based upon a consideration of test results.

The third area deals with particular therapist-patient relationships; it is treated by employing qualitative and largely anecdotal material. In view of the general disrepute into which the anecdote as scientific evidence has fallen, the account of things given on such a basis will not be strongly urged. The interview material there cited, however, does seem to illumine the test data and outcome ratings very greatly, and it is therefore well worth inclusion. While such observations in themselves cannot afford scientifically acceptable answers, they do pose some quite interesting questions which another research may be designed to answer.

ROLES IN INTERACTION

So much for the use of personality tests in predicting the outcome of psychotherapy. While sharing the interests of the clinician in that important practical problem, we spoke earlier of being a least as much interested in the more broadly social problem of identifying the conditions that make some personal interactions mutually satisfying, constructive, and on-going, while others are antagonizing, destructive, and stultifying.

The ramifications of this general question are, of course, considerable. Indeed, they suggest many fascinating problems for psychological investigation. What is the psychological basis for an enduring friendship, or an enduring enmity? Why do adult persons love one another, or hate one another? What makes for extremely successful marriage, or for divorce? Is it indeed true that nations cannot get along with one another, or is it diplomats who do not agree? (One is reminded of the Mauldin cartoon whose caption is a newspaper dispatch which describes glowingly the not-to-be-denied spearhead of a certain Allied attack. Above it Mauldin drew a picture of some very tired, dirty, hungry, and sick-of-it-all young men, who, as it happened, were the spearhead. Nations, like armies, are finally only some people, who may get along or not get along with one another.)

In the 33 instances of personal interaction that have been intensively studied in this investigation, many of these larger problems are presented in microcosm. In attempting to understand them, we have come gradually to accept a conceptual scheme whose basic unit of analysis we have called the "role-integrate." This scheme relies upon some common-sense notions of perception as it functions in personality.

We might begin by distinguishing between the sorts of roles that are "played" and the sorts of roles that are "lived." We will be talking always about the latter. One who *plays* a role is *acting as if* he were the sort of person who might live that role. On the stage, and all too often in real life, a role is acted. Psychologists in the Office of Strategic Services during World War II observed that some psychopathic candidates for O.S.S. irregular warfare assignments proved excellent at role-*playing* and were over-rated as to personal effectiveness on this account. While he is good at role-playing, the psychopath is curiously deficient in role-taking, or what we have here called role-living. Such living of a role involves the integration of certain consistent ways of behaving socially in relation to other people; for example, in a fatherly manner, or as a clown, or a rebel, or a big brother, or a helpful soul, or a gay blade, and so on. If we call such socially recognized consistency in behavior "role-integrates," then we may describe the total personality as a set of such role-integrates, themselves more or less synthesized into an organic whole in the mature person.

Certain role-integrates may be more appropriate than others for certain situations. One mark of the healthy personality is the flexibility of these role-integrates, and the ease with which the appropriate one becomes predominant over the others. A person's feeling of being himself all the time is largely dependent on the consistency of his role-integrates, and the extent to which he lives them rather than plays them.

Now the importance of such an analysis for the understanding of personal interaction is precisely this: the role-integrates that come to the fore in a given person in a given relationship may do so largely because of the other person in the interaction, or at least because of how he is perceived. One may speak not only of the differentiation of the structure of role-integrates within the perceiving person, but also of the differentiatedness or undifferentiatedness of his perception of the role structure of the perceived person. In general, a well-differentiated role structure goes along with differentiated perception of the roles of others.

Perhaps we can make clearer here what we mean by differentiation of perception of the roles of others. Let us take as examples two of the more important culturally and biologically defined roles: man and woman. Both men and women are also persons, with an immense variety of individual role-capacities more or less unrelated to their gender. To some men, however, woman are women, and to some women, men are men. That is to say, persons may be perceived by other persons as being, above all, members of a certain sex, and this single perception tends to blur other distinctions and subtle differences which actually exist in the perceived object. It is the unfortunate fate of Negroes, Jews, and other members of minority groups in our society to be perceived, above all, as Negroes, Jews, *et al.*, by an uncomfortably large percentage of the population (including other Negroes and Jews). They are almost forced to act the role assigned them, and to be, above all, Negroes and Jews. They have been perceived, by others and sometimes by themselves, in an undifferentiated fashion.

It is just this sort of undifferentiated perception of the roles of others that leads most often to destructiveness and stultification in personal interaction. This is not always the case, of course, for rather rigidly adhered-to roles occasionally tend to complement one another and, in the case of psychotherapy, to eventuate in a favorable therapeutic outcome. In general, however, rigidity of role-perception tends to retard therapeutic progress, or, if the roles indeed clash, to force the termination of the therapy.

By way of illustration, we may consider in some detail a few of the interactions in this sample, giving especially close scrutiny to some of the cases that did not progress as the test results would have predicted, or that eventuated successfully in spite of an apparently poor prognosis. In some of these examples the predominant role-integrates of therapist and patient proved complementary and conducive to success in therapy; in others they proved complementary, but conducive to failure; in others they were incompatible, and caused abandonment of the therapy; and in still others at least one of the interacting persons was sufficiently flexible so that an appropriate role-integrate was brought to the fore and ensured the successful outcome of the therapy.

Therapist A and four of his patients

We shall begin by a brief description of the therapist. He is a man in his late thirties, of authoritative bearing and demeanor. In conversation he tends to make pronouncements, to pontificate, to supply rare information. He is particularly well-read and authoritative on the subject of Roman history and law. He has a strong interest in the history of sex symbolism and sex practices through the ages and in different parts of the world.

Both from test data and interview material it is evident that this therapist cathects intellect very strongly. His Rorschach protocols are filled with erudite responses, and in taking down the record the experimenter several times had to ask him to stop and to spell some of the words. On the Michigan Vocabulary test he scored at the 98th percentile of college seniors in both Physical Sciences and Biological Sciences, and at the 93rd percentile in mathematics (in contrast to his three low scores on Fine Arts, Sports, and Human Relations).

In looking at the Rorschach inkblots, this therapist showed a very strong tendency to interpret variations in shading as indicating vista. This is a highly selective response to shading, involving as it does an actual distortion of the medium, in contrast to the reaction to shading as surface texture. A set of perceptual preferences or habits so markedly deviant in this direction leads one to look for an associated lack of spontaneity in responding to the environment, and a certain coldness and non-receptive attitude toward personal interaction. A rigid conscience, concern with status, and maintenance of psychological distance through intellectualization are some of the other character traits that go along with this way of perceiving the world.

One of this therapist's woman patients (not included in this sample) developed a strong "negative transference" to him after two visits, and in an outburst of rage at him informed him that he was "a conceited prig" and "always trying to play Swami." On the next visit, this patient brought a very large dog to the therapy hour with her; she complained during this hour about how different this therapist was from her previous therapist. By way of pointing out to the patient that different people have different ways of doing things, Therapist A said, "Now here we have a dog. You trained that dog, didn't you? Someone else might have trained the dog differently. Well, this situation is just like that. Some psychiatrists have one way of doing things, others do things differently." This illustrates fairly well the therapist's basically authoritarian attitude toward therapy, although it certainly would not be fair to infer that his technique is consistently auhoritarian. By intention he assumes a non-directive approach, though he is always liable to "tell the patient what's what." Furthermore, this authoritarianism pervades his whole attitude, his manner of speaking, his very posture as he sits in his office.

Two of this therapist's patients responded quite well to psychotherapy and were clearly improved at the end of several months. Two others, however, in spite of having very favorable scores on tests that predict response to therapy, terminated therapy after about one month, with no improvement. It is of some interest to examine the nature of these four interactions.

This therapist's most successful case was a 38-year-old woman, of German birth and rearing, who entered therapy to "try to understand" what caused her stomach upsets and her pre-menstruation irritability and hostility toward her husband. In contrast to her therapist, this patient responded to shading primarily as surface texture, a perceptual preference generally related to passivity, compliance, contact-craving, and a generalized hunger for food, security, and love.

The patient smiled frequently throughout her interview with the psychologist and gave a definite impression of sensitivity, desire to be liked, honesty, and high intelligence. Asked how the therapy was going (this was after the third therapeutic session), she offered hesitantly, "The doctor seems to me to be very aggressive. He keeps asking me many questions about sex practices, and seems to want to stay always on that subject. Of course, I suppose he knows what he is about." When next seen by the psychologist, a couple of months later, this patient was carrying a copy of Freud's *General Introduction to Psychoanalysis*, and she spoke of the need for a better translation of Freud. Asked about her relations with her therapist, she replied that they were "very, very good." She said that she had a great deal of confidence in him. "At first I didn't think I would like him, and was afraid to tell him things, but now all is different. I am beginning to understand the real reasons why I do a lot of things. Often I wish to telephone him during the week and tell him things I have thought of. I feel better all the time, and I think much of it I owe to the Doctor. He has a very positive approach to problems. He is sure of himself, and I think that is good. Also, I have gotten much out of reading the books."

When several weeks later one of the staff psychologists interviewed the therapist about this patient, he reported that she was getting along very well. She was enjoying sexual relations with her husband more than she ever had before, and she was also becoming more able to tell her husband if she really did not want relations at a certain time (though previously she had felt it necessary to submit silently). In talking about the patient, the therapist referred to her as "one smart woman" and spoke admiringly of the way in which she was able to "pick things up." He said also that "the transference there is really getting hot." It seemed evident that there was a certain amount of counter-transference as well, and that the patient was improving in this situation in which she was a little girl being taken care of by a superior, authoritative, and approving person—to her, a benevolent father. She was undoubtedly participating in a process of intellectualization, but there was real emotional gain as well. Even though the personal interaction was marked by a large element of innocent eroticization, which might militate against lasting improvement in the long run, it remains true that the short-term gain was definite and worthwhile. And perhaps one is not really entitled to skepticism about its enduring character or its inferiority to a more skillfully managed psychoanalysis, since it is rather difficult to assess the lasting effects of either.

The other patient with whom this therapist had marked success was a 39-year-old, neat-appearing, soft-voiced woman who at first gave an impression of sedateness, which later seemed closer to flatness of affect. Both the Minnesota Multiphasic Personality Inventory and Rorschach indicated some psychotic tendencies, although there was a healthy amount of anxiety shown on the Multiphasic, and good recovery of interpretative capacity on the colored cards of the Rorschach after an initial poverty of response. Her history indicated brief previous lapses into a sort of schizoid withdrawal, with the possibility that she had been actively psychotic, although not hospitalized, several months earlier.

This difficult case showed distinct improvement during six months of therapy. In recording his impressions of this patient after her third visit, the therapist wrote, "This is a 39-year-old infant, who still craves Mama in what she says and does. She is weak and functions in an ineffectual way. She retreats from situations she is powerless to control." The urgency of the patient's infantile needs aroused the therapist's defenses, and he rejected her needs as strongly as he rejected the infantile part of himself. He showed a rather open contempt for her weakness, and doubted that she was capable of being "improved" by anything he could do. She was more or less beyond the pale. As he remarked in the outcome-rating session, "She just views me as some-one to talk to—she's never talked to anyone about herself before. If she found someone down the street from her to talk to, it would have the same effect." Of significance, however, is the fact that what this therapist was continually doing with the patient was insisting on the realities of her life-situation, relentlessly refusing to cater to her regressive tendencies, and continually buttressing the integrative and reality-oriented forces within her. At a crucial time in her life, he stood for hard facts and being sensible, playing a role that was natural for him and happily conjunctive with the needs of the patient.

This same therapist produced quite a contrary effect on two women patients who seemed, on the basis of test results, to be good bets for improvement in psychotherapy. Both these women termi-nated therapy in the second month, and, by a curious coincidence, im-mediately following the session in which the therapist had suggested doing the usual physical examination at the next hour. They were rather similar in personality structure, as indicated by the tests; both were diagnosed as mild cases of hysteria. Afraid of their own aggres-sive and sexual impulses, they dealt with them generally by over-control and by achieving distance from them through strong repres-sion and conversion mechanisms. The measure of safety they had thus achieved (though at the price of severe headaches) was suddenly threatened by our therapist's frank approach to sex in psychotherapy. When in addition he proposed to undress them in the interests of medical knowledge, they found physical distance safer than psycho-logical distance in guarding them from their own impulses; and so they terminated therapy and were rated unimproved. A slower thera-peutic approach to central conflicts might have resulted in more successful outcomes for these two patients, but the needs of the therapist and the role he assumed were simply incompatible with *their* needs and *their* roles. They had to be modest while he had to be frank.

Conflicts of sex role

One of the male therapists in this sample suffered acute anxiety which seemed to stem from his basic doubt as to his own sex role, and a fear of the passive desires that he experienced. This not uncommon conflict, while its effect was pervasive and influenced many of his personal relations, became especially intense in interactions involving other men with similar problems. We shall describe here one such interaction involving a male patient who was similar to the therapist.

This therapist, a quite intelligent and sensitive individual, experienced specifically genital homosexual desires, and was in an acute state of conflict because of them. His very complex system of defenses was organized around his fear of such impulses, which he was firmly resolved not to indulge. His Minnesota Multiphasic Personality Inventory profile, while within the normal range except for the Masculinity-Femininity score (T-score of 76), showed a patterning of scores, especially in the interrelations of Hysteria, Paranoia, and Schizophrenia, which indicated that he was experiencing considerable stress. The Rorschach record, a long, complex, and highly original one, showed a great deal of inanimate movement and many vista responses. There was much less human movement than one would have expected from a person of such intelligence and originality, suggesting perhaps an inhibition of fantasy life because of the danger of confronting, even in fantasy, the intense impulses which found expression in the inanimate movement responses. The impulses are intellectualized rather than transformed in fantasy.

If we accept response to color as an indicator of ability to handle emotional stimuli, it would seem that frequently this therapist must either dissociate or be overwhelmed. He gave two pure color responses, and one response where color is the primary determinant and the form is poor (CF-). Three other responses employed color in an arbitrary fashion (that is, it is not an essential part of the percept), but with good form. He recovers quite well on Card X, however, and at the very end gives three good color responses where form is primary. In brief, the therapist was an exceptionally intelligent and capable person with a disturbing problem of his own.

The patient can perhaps best be introduced simply by including here the psychological report that the research psychologist wrote in reporting his test results.

At his first appointment for testing, this 38-year-old architect seemed quite self-possessed, gracious, and almost condescending. Deliberate in speech and movements, he had a very distinctive bearing and mien, and in conversation showed himself quite intelligent and well-informed.

On the Rorschach the patient gave many highly original, imaginative responses, which in spite of their unusual nature showed excellent correspondence to actual forms present in the blots. His responses were generally complexly determined, with a good deal of attention to such surface characteristics as texture and color. For the most part, however, he saw movements or vistas in the blots, and in such abundance that one suspects that the psychological equivalent of such easy distortion of the medium is a facile use of projection as a defense. Undoubtedly in this patient there is a good deal of residual magical thinking, which ordinarily tends to be discounted somewhat by his high intelligence and his excellent correspondence with reality in its formal aspects. Perhaps another way of saying this is that for most purposes he sees the world as it is and is able to take cognizance of it in gaining his own ends, but in certain highly significant personal relations and in dynamically important sorts of relations he continues to act on erroneous premises whose beginnings lie in the animistic period of his childhood.

Some clue as to the nature of these erroneous premises may be gained from some of the specific responses. There is considerable passive, feminine imagery, generally followed immediately by strong, masculine, centrifugal action. On Card VII, which frequently elicits unconscious material about the subject's mother, he sees a bay and "a huge harbor . . . gives the harbor impression . . . sort of the feeling of a shelter. I seem to associate it with safety, for some reason. Some place you could go and lock yourself in." At this point the patient made a long and almost compulsive digression to tell of his recent travels about the world, and how when he began to feel the uneasiness which led to his present condition he decided to go from one port to another, seeking a place where he could find rest. As he named each port and described his entry into it, he would say, "But no . . . I could tell that that wasn't it . . . it just wasn't it."

Along with the archaic oral longing expressed in this imagery there goes a considerable amount of castration anxiety, with frequent symbols of it occurring in the content of the responses. Fears of the passive, feminine position resulting from identification with the mother have led to counterphobic aggressive action, especially toward men. There seems also to be some guilt about the death of the father, an unconscious belief that it was his hostility which caused his father to die. The result of this constellation is a sadistic superego and a great need to defend against homosexuality by repression and projection.

On the occasion of his second visit for testing, three weeks after the first, the patient had lost his self-possessed air, and was dressed sloppily in contrast to his earlier almost dapper appearance. He was also unshaven. He seemed somewhat confused and uncertain of himself. In general, he looked as though he had had a bad three weeks.

On this occasion he was given the Minnesota Multiphasic Personality Inventory. The Multiphasic, which generally gives an accurate picture of present clinical state as well as a description of the dynamic inter-action of control and defense mechanisms, shows severe overt pathology in a personality which ordinarily is rather well-controlled but which is currently being pushed almost to the borders of a psychosis by unac-ceptable id-impulses. The defenses seem over-extended, but the picture is of a personality actively engaged in a struggle for a new equilibrium. The danger of a psychosis should not be minimized, but the patient does have certain health-tending strengths which make the psycho-therapeutic outlook fairly hopeful.

Within the therapy itself, the whole area of passivity toward the father, fear of seduction and castration, and repressed hostility which may burst out suddenly, provides the crucial problems which the therapist must handle.

Following the first two interviews with the patient, the therapist wrote:

> From a distance, I find this patient attractive, both physically and intellectually. He uses words very effectively and is bright. His con-fusion with relation to his own social role—i.e., ambivalence toward the working class and attempted, but unsuccessful, identification with the upper class is very apparent and lends a note of insincerity to him which shines through. This is apparent in the tendency—just percepti-ble—to obsequiousness with higher status people.

Several trends previously suggested by the test results are evident in these remarks. The opening phrase, "from a distance," expresses the sort of perception which the patient's vista responses on the Rorschach had suggested as typical. The reference to "obsequiousness with higher status people" may very well be an expression also of passivity toward the father, interpreted here by the therapist as having to do primarily with class identification.

The therapist's verbalizations in talking about this case are also re-vealing of some of the dynamic under-currents. In remarking on the irregularity with which the patient kept appointments, he said, "Whenever I felt we were really getting close, then he would miss his appointment." Again, "He was very obsequious to me at times . . . sort of putting me up there." Other remarks of this sort were, "He just wants me to be a wedge for him," and "He'd like for me to be over him."

The interaction finally took on an extremely anxious and hostile character, and after a session in which for the first time there was considerable overt homosexual content, the therapist became openly angry and the patient did not return for several weeks. When he finally did call to make another appointment, the therapist demanded to know why he hadn't called to break previous appointments if he did not intend to keep them. The therapist reported that he then asked, "Well, now, have you decided whether you really want to come in?" The patient replied in an "enraged" tone, "Of course I do." The therapist remarked to one of the staff psychologists later that this was the first expression of hostility toward him in the course of the therapy. He then added, "But the things that guy would say about me if he would only talk ought to be in print. I mean, wouldn't be fit to print."

The uncertainty of both therapist and patient about the sex role of both himself and the other person finally generated so much anxiety that the situation became intolerable. The interaction simply could not go on. Eventually the patient was transferred to another therapist who reports that there has been considerable improvement and continuing progress.

It should not be thought that the therapist was himself entirely unaware of these disturbing under-currents in the interaction. He sought consultation on the case with a number of skilled people, and during this period of time he also tried to make arrangements for a personal analysis. It was evident that the relationship was a significant as well as a disturbing one for him too, and perhaps ultimately it will prove to have been quite a beneficial one. He displayed a high degree of conscientiousness and personal integrity, and it is not to his discredit that his own needs and problems were at that particular moment in his life too pressing for him to carry out successfully his very difficult task.

A therapist in spite of himself

Another male therapist who had a few problems of his own was nevertheless quite successful in several difficult cases. In his Rorschach record there was a definite preference for the use of shading as perspective, and an inhibition of human movement percepts. There was also considerable castration symbolism in the record; his fears seemed centered on failure of potency and competence, perhaps related to the fact that he was now beginning psychiatric training after many years in general practice and was much older than the other residents. He saw the animal on Card VIII as "trying to move along, looks like he's stuck a little bit, his foot dragging." Later he returned to this response and added, "One can see a sort of strain in this animal—a sort of concern about not being able to move along." He saw a rooster on Card III, and remarked of the percept, ". . . though that tail doesn't go along with the rooster." On Card IV he saw a foot and a leg, remarking that "the leg is heavy compared to the rest of the drawing." The middle section of Card V was seen as "a rabbit that doesn't have much speed or action left in it—the way it's extended out—just stretched out."

All of this therapist's Minnesota Multiphasic Personality Inventory scores were within the normal range except Masculinity-Femininity (71). The one curious feature of an otherwise rather innocuous record is a score of 56 on the Lie Scale. An elevation on this scale, if earned in good faith, betokens an uncommon and slightly pretentious sort of moral goodness, appropriate perhaps to a cleric but rather unusual in a psychiatrist. A compulsive and unrealistic tendency in this direction was shown also on the Levinson-Sanford scale; the therapist wrote on the test booklet, "Let's leave Jews, Catholics, Protestants, Mohammedans and all, out of these questions." The evident intent of this remark was to express a sort of super-non-ethno-centrism, but it showed a rather astonishing failure to grasp the actual purpose of the questionnaire. The therapist in general is reluctant to commit himself to any opinions or to express any hostility.

The patient was a short, dark, pleasant-faced fellow who appeared rather sad, lackadaisical, and passive. His peak score on the Minnesota Multiphasic Personality Inventory was on Depression, with a secondary peak on Psychasthenia. This is the profile of a depressive character, chronically pessimistic about things, a bit worrisome, generally seeing the world through blue-colored glasses. He reminds one of the Thurber character who was introduced with the comment, "This is my brother Ed. He's given up." (*The New Yorker*, Sept. 1, 1934).

At the time of the first testing session, this patient was quite obviously depressed, speaking slowly and in a low tone. When he was seen again a couple of weeks later, he still did not seem very energetic, but he was not nearly so depressed. One of the staff psychologists asked him what had caused him to feel better, and he replied, "Oh, I don't know—guess it just sort of wore off."

The brief notes on the Rorschach written by the research psychologist at the time of testing were as follows:

> The impression given by the Rorschach is of a very passive, rather castrate individual who is afraid of expressing hostility, or, for that matter, of feeling it. He is otherwise in excellent contact with reality, and he responds well emotionally. He should be able to relate easily to people and to form normal emotional bonds with others. He has adequate inner resources. His chief problems seem to be in the area of dependency, and great sensitivity to rejection, especially by father figures.
>
> The patient's symptomatology seems to be expressed chiefly as a way of life, although some of his anxiety is probably somatized gastro-intestinally. It is to be expected that successful psychotherapy with him would have to be a long process, and that it would continue only with a very accepting and tolerant therapist who would not arouse the patient's strong castration anxiety. Ultimately it might be possible for the patient to assume a more phallic role, but the change could be expected to be very slow and gradual.

In commenting on this patient early in the therapy, the therapist characterized him as, "Congenial—pleasant—not digging or probing. Accepts life—wants general happiness and security." A few weeks later he remarked, "I can take it easy with him compared with most of the people around here." This comment referred to his professional colleagues at the clinic, with whom he was having some difficulties at the time.

Essentially what happened in the therapy was that the therapist made it clear that the patient had nothing to fear from *him*. One of the patient's chief symptoms was a "frightened feeling in my stomach when I'm around the boss" at work. This seemed to be a repetition of his childhood fear of his very stern step-father, who in his drunken rages often threatened to kill his wife's children. The patient recalled that the step-father had a gun to do it with, too.

The therapist, however, apparently did not have a gun and was anything but threatening. He was more encouraging than anything else. The patient accepted the encouragement, and decided that maybe he would be better off if he weren't working for any boss at all, but working for himself instead (a view in which the therapist heartily concurred). He finally decided to try to start his own doughnut business, and shortly thereafter brought in a dozen doughnuts for the therapist, who found them delicious.

TWO CONSCIOUSLY PSYCHOTHERAPEUTIC THERAPISTS

Probably the most important thing to be said about the two therapists who remain to be discussed is that they were able to make almost all their personal interactions with patients into genuinely psychotherapeutic interactions. Both of them had high intelligence, honesty of purpose, and a conceptual scheme of sufficient scope and subtlety to enable them to cognize their roles clearly as well as to feel them and be emotionally committed to them.

These two therapists, a man and a woman, were, in addition, reasonably burdened by their own private neuroses. However, they were remarkably self-aware, and they dealt with their own feelings and motivations as important parts of the phenomena of the therapeutic situation, to be used in helping them to understand the patient, and in helping the patient to understand himself.

We will begin by describing two of the patients of the male therapist, and indicate briefly what happened in the two interactions.

The first patient, age 31, was a tall, athletically-built man of rather prepossessing appearance. He spoke in an intelligent, competent manner. He was obviously very tense, however, and seemed to be controlling himself only with some effort. He displayed a certain amount of hostility toward the testing procedure, but was overtly cooperative and uncomplaining.

The patient's Minnesota Multiphasic Personality Inventory is typical of the most clear-cut cases of psychopathy or impulse neurosis. Basic to the personality structure is a very deep and primitive oral fixation, with subsequent reaction formation against it. Direct satisfaction of libidinal impulses is sought, rather than repression or substitution. Conflicts tend to be acted out, and there is a constant flight from anxiety rather than an attempt to endure it. Associated with the underlying orality and passivity is considerable hostility which is also expressed orally (by such means as sarcasm, invective, and biting). What is most feared is the passivity, and dominance-submission is the characteristic conflict.

There is a considerable tendency toward self-dramatization. The primitive oral longing may lead to alcoholism or drug addiction, and sexuality in such cases is usually polymorphous perverse. Such anxiety as is not handled by character defenses may be expressed gastrointestinally.

The Rorschach showed poverty of inner resources, an inability to sublimate or obtain substitutive gratification. Impulses are responded to in an uncontrolled fashion. Depression and anxiety are evident, the depression being the more prominent of the two. There is a good deal of sexual preoccupation, and judgment defect manifests itself chiefly in that area. Otherwise, contact with reality is good.

The patient had been divorced once, and he was not married to the woman with whom he was presently living, although they had been living together for several years. He came into the clinic purely on an impulse, although he had occasionally entertained the idea in the past because of a vague feeling of dissatisfaction with certain aspects of his own behavior, such as his promiscuity, his predilection for prostitutes as sexual partners, and his tendency to look for unusual forms of excitement and entertainment when drunk. His common-law wife was fairly tolerant of these failings, but he was worried that sooner or later he would get in trouble with the police, which would interfere with his profession as a teacher. He appeared to have no particular anxiety or neurotic symptoms.

The therapist reported that the therapeutic interviews were generally "very man to man . . . the patient manipulated the situation so that we seemed to be sort of jolly buddies rather than patient and doctor. He refused to admit of any professional distance between us." The interviews were more like casual chats than therapeutic sessions. There was, nevertheless, a very strong transference. As the transference increased in intensity, and the patient's passive desires got closer to the surface, his acting out of this conflict began to take a very hostile form. It manifested itself both generally, toward all the people in his environment, and more particularly, toward Jewish girls. (The therapist, as it happened, was Jewish; the patient was not.) It finally became evident that it was more than coincidence that every Saturday afternoon or evening, following the therapeutic hour, the patient succeeded in seducing some Jewish girl or other, generally taking a different one each week. He seemed to have an especial preference for girls who were interested in psychology or psychiatry, either as an amateur preoccupation or because they were themselves psychiatric patients.

In addition, this patient found the occasion to hurl the epithet "dirty Jew" at a Jewish person of his acquaintance, although actually he had always liked this person and had never before had any particular aversion to Jews. It seems reasonable to entertain the notion that his partial identification with the therapist, and his own passive homosexual desires toward the therapist, caused a violent resurgence of his counter-phobic defenses and a rejection and abasement of all that was Jewish, feminine, and weak.

The therapist dealt with this situation by a gradual summing up of the material in such a way that it became quite evident that hostility was being displaced from the therapist to other Jews, and that Jewishness was especially repugnant partly for the reason that it represented part of the patient himself. When his hostility towards the therapist was thus recognized and out in the open, the patient became rather quiet, hesitant, and soft in manner. The therapist reported observing an actual "flattening" of the patient's facies at this time, together with a general settling down of a depressive mood.

On one occasion, the patient came in drunk, having been out drinking all night. At this time he gave vent to considerable hostility, its first object being the psychological tests and the psychologist. When the therapist pointed out that this too might be displaced, the patient turned violently upon the therapist himself, and began to compare psychologists very favorably with psychiatrists.

The patient's hostility was evinced plainly in his expressive movement during this hour, as he began many aggressive gestures which he quickly inhibited. Finally he broke down and cried. Afterward he said he felt better, "like after sleeping with a woman." Following this, a good deal of passive homosexual material emerged in his associations, and this was dealt with very effectively and in an anxiety-relieving manner by the therapist.

All the gain that the therapist would claim for this patient after six months of psychotherapy was that the patient had been rendered more available for treatment. In view of the extreme difficulty of working with such psychopathic character disorders, this modest gain is indeed rather praiseworthy. The therapist had acted like a therapist, putting behind him a number of other, unpsychotherapeutic responses he might have made: as, for example, a Jew to an anti-Semite, or a fairly moral and rather inhibited character to a thoroughly amoral and impulse-ridden one.

The second case was that of a woman of 27, who had recently been divorced. Upon seeing her for the first time, one recalled only in retrospect that she was rather pretty and quietly well-dressed; the first impression she gave was of tremendous agitation, simply a huge volume of anxiety erupting through her defenses. She came in looking frightened to death, an expression almost of terror on her face. She twisted her hands constantly. She refused at first to take any of the tests. When the first Rorschach card was presented to her, she quickly looked away, and stared steadfastly into a corner of the office, refusing to look at the card. After a few minutes of silence, the research psychologist remarked, "Well, as you know, of course, everything you say will be held against you." The ironic tone of this, combined with the obvious element of truth in the statement (do any psychologists *really* think that the patient believes "there are no right or wrong answers"?), caused her to laugh, and she forthwith turned around and glanced at the card, giving a quick response to it. She finally took the entire test, although it took a very long time to administer, and throughout it she voiced exclamations of dismay in a despairing tone of voice.

In spite of all this, the examiner did not get the impression that the patient found the testing quite so trying an experience as her surface behavior would indicate. There was a distinct feeling of emotional contact with her, and in fact there was something subtly seductive about much of her behavior.

The brief clinical report on the Rorschach and Minnesota Multiphasic Personality Inventory was as follows:

> The patient displayed a rich, imaginative fantasy life on the Rorschach. This capacity for vicarious experience is used far more often than techniques for obtaining direct attainment of goals; the patient seeks to sublimate and substitute rather than gratify her impulses. There is some emotional response of a direct sort, but it is greatly overbalanced by the tendency to experience in fantasy rather than in fact. Contact with reality is excellent throughout, and there is evidence of considerable sensitivity. The patient's appeal is for oral sustenance; contact-craving is expressed in the use of shading as texture in rather striking fashion.
>
> The Minnesota Multiphasic profile was highly elevated on many scales, its configuration suggesting a severe hysterical neurosis, with

displacement almost as prominent a mechanism as repression. Phobias and obsessive thinking were the chief forms of displacement. A central problem is control of impulsivity. The Multiphasic picture verges on that of a ruminative-obsessive personality, but the hysterical elements are somewhat more prominent.

Psychotherapy may be effective in relieving some of the grosser symptomatology in this patient. Her subtle manipulative techniques in interpersonal relations will certainly yield much more slowly to analysis, however.

The therapy concentrated to an unusual degree upon a working out of the interpersonal relationship of the therapist and the patient. This relationship was entered into quite intensely by the patient, and every hour was a concentrated emotional experience. Here are the written comments of the therapist about the patient after a couple of months of therapy:

A markedly labile person emotionally, with considerable range and spontaneity of feeling which maintains one's interest and provokes considerable reactive and empathic feeling. This patient's feelings are often exaggerated and displaced, but their liveliness and forcefulness are appealing to me. Her range of interests and sensitivity to certain of these interests coincides with much that is also significant for me. With this patient I have a strong feeling of interaction which is at once pleasant and unpleasant. The stimulation and interest it provokes is pleasant; the degree of anxiety frequently present in the patient and consequently in me to a lesser degree is sometimes unpleasant. This patient gives me the constant impression of a clinging, demanding, beseeching need for affection and involvement.

In this situation, again, the temptation was great to carry on something less than psychotherapy. The personal relationship might very easily have become, unrecognized, an infantile sexual one, with the primary emphasis being on what each could get from the other. No doubt most of the patient's relationships in the past had been on just that level. The therapist succeeded in breaking that pattern, however, by constantly analyzing the patient's behavior and being consistently honest in recognizing the feeling between them. The resulting interaction was, as the therapist described it at the rating session, "hectic," but it resulted in very considerable improvement in the patient. There was marked abatement of anxiety and guilt, and several of the patient's phobias disappeared (fears of open places and of riding on buses, and a fear that when she looked at a man she would be forced to stare at his genitals). She was also much less depressed, and she was able to consider with some hope the possibility of making a happy life for herself.

The other "consciously psychotherapeutic" therapist, a woman of 33, had a very rich and complex personality; she was highly sophisticated culturally and active intellectually. She gave an unusually large number (13) of human movement responses on the Rorschach, as well as 5 inanimate movement responses and 4 responses involving animal movement. These were counter-balanced by a total of 21 responses to formal or surface characteristics of the blot, including 6 responses to color, 10 to form, and 5 to texture. The richness of the symbolic imagery in the movement responses, as well as a tendency to use color symbolically, suggests a highly sublimated personality, a capacity to elevate the merely personal to the artistic and to see the trivial and the commonplace in a context more cosmic and tragic.

The patient, on the other hand, was a statistician. Twenty-two of his 31 Rorschach responses were pure form, and he gave only one human movement response. The content was chiefly geographical (coast-lines, islands, maps), anatomical, and animal. Twenty-five of his responses were to large details; only three involved the whole blot.

This patient entered therapy because he had been suffering from a great deal of stomach upset, and because he had finally been told by his physician that it was probably due to emotional problems. Asked about what he expected from therapy, he replied, "I just want to get rid of my stomach disturbance. If that means that I have problems that I have to solve in order to get rid of the stomach trouble, then I guess I'll have to work on them. But what I'm really concerned about is the stomach discomfort."

This problem-solving approach to the emotional life was thoroughly characteristic of the patient, and was certainly understandable in the light of his unfortunate childhood history. His mother died shortly after his birth (in Germany), and his father left him with the maternal grandmother and departed, never to be seen by the patient again. He was taken care of by the grandmother and his aunt, being led first to believe that the grandmother was his mother, and then later being told that the aunt was his mother. He finally discovered that neither was his mother, and that his real mother had reportedly died needlessly as a result of some physician's laxity.

All this the patient related in a casual, unemotional tone, as though he were reciting a history lesson.

At age five, the patient was placed in an orphanage. Orphanages in Germany were no freer of anti-Semitism than was the rest of the country, and the patient, who was not only Jewish but also "looked Jewish," soon learned that even among orphans he was an especial outcast. It is not surprising that in this emotional atmosphere he came quickly to deny all personal feelings, to reject his own needs for love, and to interest himself solely in external reality, lest the sadness of his own life overwhelm him.

In the early stages of the pogrom in Germany the patient was sent to the United States by his uncle, to live with a distant relative in Minnesota. The patient, age 12, made the trip alone. There he went to high school, and by working after school and during vacations he saved $200 to help pay the passage of his uncle to this country. He lost contact with the uncle at the last moment, however, and never saw him or heard from him again. During the war the patient became an officer in the U.S. Army and returned to Germany, where he spent much time and energy in trying to find his uncle, but without success.

Quite alone in the world, the patient could hardly admit his dependent needs; only the independent survive. The therapist commented on the fact that when the patient talked about personal relationships, he seemed almost to be speaking a foreign language, so stilted and devoid of connotative meaning were his words.

When the therapist was asked to indicate the degree of personal congeniality she felt with each of her patients, and the possibility of personal friendship with them, she wrote of this patient:

> I would not feel congenial with Mr. R because he has such poverty of social interaction and because we have so little in common. I like his quietly confident air when he talks about international affairs, and as an acquaintance I might learn a good deal from him—I admire his intelligence, too. I would like him better as a patient than as a friend, because in the therapy situation I feel I can give him something that he needs—an interpersonal relationship, for an hour at a time. That is enough, because of the obstacle of his being unable to trust me. I also like his determination (to get well).

In the rating session, in reviewing the case, the therapist said:

> My first reaction was one of faint—I wouldn't say "dislike" . . . I'd perhaps say "distaste." Sort of intangible . . . his faint . . . well, you couldn't call it arrogance . . . but it was sort of reaching for that. At first I often felt as though he were interviewing me for Officer Candidate School.

This attitude and my reaction to it very soon dissolved. He began to soften up . . . acquired a sort of wistful, sad, cocker-spaniel look . . . as though he was just finding something . . . and in retrospect it seemed I was perhaps that mother he was looking for.

He found it difficult to talk spontaneously. So I fed him somewhat. Gradually he came to trust me more, though he still said there were important things he couldn't tell me about. At one point his talking seemed to come to almost a complete standstill, and the silence would sometimes last as long as forty minutes. When I'd look at him I'd see a very disconsolate expression on his face, as though he were waiting for something.

We finally broke through this silence, and then he began to talk his head off. He was living in a boarding house with two psychology students, who also were getting psychotherapy. He finally told them his secret, and was amazed to find himself accepted warmly by them. He got lots of support from them, and they encouraged him to talk.

In the next-to-the-last interview he reported an incident which seemed to have great personal significance. He told about finally getting up courage to talk to a seemingly well-adjusted girl sitting next to him in class. Upon talking with her a while, he concluded that actually she was a psychologically sick person and needed help. As he told me of this, he came spontaneously to recognize that he was partly talking of himself and of his own changing attitudes towards psychiatry. It was more or less on this note that the last interview ended, and he was transferred to another therapist, as I was leaving the clinic.

Again, the therapeutic gain in this case was fairly small so far as relief of the somatic symptoms was concerned, but the emotional gain may have been very great indeed. The patient was becoming willing to accept help, to become a bit dependent, to talk about his feelings, and even to sympathize with himself (indirectly, through sympathizing with the "well-adjusted girl" who really needed psychological help). If the psychological forces set in motion in this interaction continued beyond it, and got further impetus from his relationship with the next therapist, perhaps this patient may finally be able to live instead of merely to survive.

CREATIVE PSYCHOTHERAPY

There is something creative in psychotherapy thus carried on. To the old patterns of perception and action is added a force for change, so that they gradually become something quite different, though retaining many of their former elements.

We would suggest that there are two main principles to be seen in such truly creative personal interactions: first, a certain acceptance of things at face value, and, second, a willingness to let the other person be as he wishes, combined with an insistence on yourself being as you wish.

The first of these principles involves, in psychotherapy, a recognition that surface motivations are as legitimate in their own way as more deep-lying motivations. That is, one should not hold the consciously recognized and perhaps superficial motivations to be false or any less valid simply because unconscious and "deeper-level" motivations may partially determine them. There is an insidious tendency among some psychologists and psychiatrists to disparage, for example, stamp collecting (because of the alleged symbolic equivalence of stamps and feces) or to look askance at social protest (because authorities are fathers and protest is analogous to adolescent rebellion). What we propose as a first principle is: "Take things first for what they most plainly are."

The non-directive technique, properly applied, is an excellent instance of the use of this principle in psychotherapy. It has the advantage of keeping the therapist's remarks at the same level as the patient's, at least in terms of manifest content. Where the non-directive technique fails, when it does fail, is in its reluctance *ever* to proceed to deeper levels of meaning, resulting sometimes in a failure to interpret resistances at crucial points in the therapy. Often a patient is forced to terminate therapy "successfully" because of mounting rage against a therapist who is just too nice to have nasty thoughts about; better to give him a final bouquet (a list of improvements he brought about) than to proceed into all the unpleasantness that is brewing.

The second principle, to be what you wish and to let the other person be as he wishes, may, as it applies to psychotherapy, seem absurd on the face of it. After all, have we not said that the aim of psychotherapy is to induce changes in the behavior of the patient? Do we not want him to have fewer symptoms, better relations with people, a constructive set of social values, a happier outlook on life?

I would reply that while we may have all of these desires as secondary goals for the patient, we must wish for him, above all else, and if necessary even at the expense of those secondary goals, simply that he be free to choose what he wants. He may in the end choose to be much as he was in the beginning; the difference should be that he chooses freely and is not compelled by his own blind needs. It is, indeed, our faith that there are many things, to us undesirable, that a free man would not choose for himself; but we must be willing, in the final analysis and to state the case in its most extreme form, to grant the other's right to choose destruction and evil, if he does so freely.

If we accept this principle, we will not pity the patient, nor hold ourselves wise or good as compared to him, nor wish to impart to him our own virtues or visions. Rather, we will wish only to help him to understand himself, that he may be made more free to choose, and less the slave of his own history.

8

Signs from Psychological Tests That Promise Improvement in Psychotherapy

IN THIS chapter we shall consider in some detail and in an appropriately technical manner the *signs* that personality testing affords us of probable improvement in patients under psychiatric treatment, where the chosen method of treatment is psychotherapy. In other words, the correlates of change, as determined from psychological test results, will be presented. The subjects of study were the 33 adult psychoneurotics who participated in the research on the therapeutic relationships described in the preceding chapter.

This report is restricted to the test results only of patients, and it will adopt by choice the somewhat narrow conception of response to psychotherapy described earlier. To repeat that description: the criterion variable can be best characterized as an answer to the question, "Did the patient improve or not?" where the word "improve" means some fairly general changes in state from bad to good. Examples of such changes are these: (a) the patient feels better, is more comfortable, takes more interest in life, and the like; (b) important interpersonal relations are straightened out a bit; (c) physical symptoms have been relieved or cured; (d) important health-tending decisions have been made; (e) there has been an increase in insightful remarks and behavior.

The judgment as to whether or not improvement had occurred was made, as we have said, by two expert observers (heads of departments at the clinics) who had not had any part in the conduct of therapy. Each therapist made a formal presentation before these two judges of every case he had handled; prior to the presentation the judges had read all of the material concerning the patient that had been recorded in the clinical chart.

In the instruction to the judges it was emphasized that the crucial variable was *not* general level of functioning of the patient at the conclusion of therapy, but rather the *change in state* that had occurred between beginning and end of therapy. Further, it was made clear to the judges that part of their function was to evaluate the therapist's involvement in his own account of the therapeutic process, and to weigh that factor in coming to a best estimate as to the degree of change that had actually occurred.

On the basis, then, of two main sources of information (formal presentation of the case by the therapist, and an evaluation from the clinical chart), the expert raters assigned cases, first of all, into two main categories, those who had shown definite improvement and those who had failed to improve or who had improved only slightly. They were in close agreement on this crude categorization, differing on only 2 of the 33 cases. In addition, they assigned ratings on a 100-point scale to each case, so that the total sample was ranked in terms of the variable "Improvement." The correlation between the two independent sets of ratings was .91. The two disagreements were resolved by averaging the scale ratings. The final classification included 17 patients in the Improved group, 16 in the Unimproved.

SOME ILLUSTRATIONS OF CRITERION BEHAVIOR

It is of some interest to examine the kinds of incidents and outcomes that the judges considered indicative of improvement or lack of it. Here is a partial list of such incidents and outcomes, abstracted from the clinical charts of these patients. Some of these have been described in more detail in the previous chapter, in the context of the therapist-patient relationship.

Improvement:

1. A woman patient who had been frigid through four years of marriage which terminated in divorce now established an intimate

relationship with another man in which for the first time she experienced orgasm in sexual intercourse.

2. A man who entered therapy in a very depressed, anxious, and physically upset state, and whose troubles centered on his relations with his foreman on a construction job (a relationship in which he was outwardly submissive and cooperative but inwardly enraged), finally learned to "stand up to" the foreman and express his feelings. There was a clear advance in his feelings of independence and self-esteem, and toward the conclusion of the therapy the patient left his former job and started a business of his own.

3. A woman with menstrual difficulties related to unconscious hostility toward her husband because of his disregard of her own wishes in sexual intercourse became conscious both of her anger and her retaliative tactics, with consequent disappearance of the menstrual difficulties and a more candid and unmartyred relationship to her husband.

4. A woman who had been recently divorced after an extremely traumatizing marriage and who entered therapy in a state of tremendous agitation and anxiety, so incapacitating that she could not sit in the lobby of the clinic or cross a street or look anyone in the face, gradually lost her phobias, experienced a great reduction in anxiety, and became able to associate comfortably with other people.

5. A man suffering from severe gastric disturbances which he considered unrelated to any emotional problems entered therapy upon the strongly worded advice of the internist. His dissociation of affect from the death of his mother and subsequent disturbing childhood years in an orphanage was gradually broken down and he reexperienced his own sense of forsakenness and finally came to terms with it, crucially aided by the support and understanding of the woman therapist.

Lack of improvement:

1. A very dogmatic and dominating man who entered therapy at the insistence of his wife (who complained of his overbearingness with her and their three children) proved too overbearing for the young woman therapist as well. The therapist was unable to handle the negative counter-transference that developed, and the therapeutic

interaction became simply a battle, with consequent lack of improvement in the patient.

2. A woman of forty, who had never been married and who suffered from continual headaches and disturbing sexual impulses which she attempted to suppress, found herself obliged to terminate therapy for some good reason precisely after the hour at which the therapist had told her he would give her a physical examination on the occasion of their next appointment.

3. A man with a history of homosexuality attempted to seduce his male therapist, who responded with anger as well as some anxiety. The patient had to be transferred to another therapist.

4. A psychopathic young man who had a long history of rebelliousness, brushes with the law, and employment instability entered therapy because, he said, he happened to be passing by the clinic and wondered what it would be like to be a patient. He liked it for a while, especially as he happened to be assigned to an attractive woman therapist, but after a few months he hitchhiked off in a southerly direction, leaving a chatty farewell note for the psychiatrist in which he addressed her by her first name.

5. An engineer of extremely masculine appearance and manners complained of a "psychic malfunction" and wanted "a few treatments to get at the nuclear material and get things cleared up." His therapist insisted on taking a nondianoetic, unhurried approach to the matter, which annoyed the patient, who nevertheless remained in therapy in the expectation that something would eventually happen.

One might summarize the kinds of outcomes in the Improved group as follows: (a) the patient generally reported a feeling of well-being at the conclusion of therapy, in contrast to depression and anxiety at its start; (b) specific symptoms, such as headaches, frigidity, or impotence, gastric disturbances, menstrual difficulties, skin disorders, etc., tended to be relieved or totally cleared up; (c) in some cases there were significant changes in the direction of more mature interpersonal relations, especially with parents, parent-substitutes, or spouses.

The failures in psychotherapy could often be traced to the inability of the therapist to handle some particularly difficult problem. Perhaps with more experienced psychotherapists some of the patients who did not improve would have made some progress; however, there seemed little doubt that the cases that were marked down as therapeutic failures were basically more difficult problems. As we shall see later from the test results, it was generally the more disturbed individuals who did not improve.

TEST CORRELATES OF IMPROVEMENT

The test battery given these patients before psychotherapy began consisted of a shortened form of the Wechsler-Bellevue Intelligence Scale, the Minnesota Multiphasic Personality Inventory, the Rorschach Psychodiagnostic and the Ethnocentrism Scale (in Form 60 of the University of California Public Opinion Study scales). The patients themselves were all receiving psychotherapy for the first time, and they began the course of treatment just at the time that their therapists were starting a six-month period of service in the outpatient clinic. The therapists were psychiatric residents who had had little experience in intensive psychotherapy.

Most of the patients had one hour of treatment a week for six months. Of the 33 patients, 12 were men and 21 were women. They ranged in age from 20 to 45. All but 3 of them were high school graduates, but only 2 were college graduates. As a group they could probably be characterized as lower-middle-class socioeconomically. Two-thirds of them were gainfully employed.

All of the testing was done by the experimenter. Conventional controls were exercised to prevent contamination in the prediction of outcome from the tests. The controls were as follows:

(a) Only the experimenter knew the test results. The psychotherapists were informed of this condition before the experiment began, and were told that they would be given information concerning the testing only if in their judgment it was essential to the diagnostic formulation and the handling of the case. In three cases such information was requested by the therapist during the course of the therapy. The information given was not comprehensive, but was in response to some specific point. These cases were retained in the sample in spite of their being exceptions to the general rule, for their exclusion would be as likely a source of contamination as their retention.

(b) The judges of outcome had no knowledge of the test results.

(c) The test protocols were identified by a code number rather than by name, so that clinicians who attempted to predict outcome had no knowledge of the patient beyond that afforded by the test results themselves.

The design of the present study, so far as prediction of outcome is concerned, is a replication of some earlier work by Harris and Christiansen,[1] who used in an almost identical clinical setting a similar criterion of outcome of therapy and the same clinical tests, except that they did not employ the Ethnocentrism scale. It is, therefore, in some respects a cross-validation of their findings, or at least it offers further evidence on some of the questions they discussed. Their results will therefore be compared with the present findings whenever such comparisons seem relevant.

The Wechsler-Bellevue Intelligence Test

As we have said, an abbreviated form of the Wechsler scale, consisting of the Comprehension, Similarities, Block Design, and Digit Symbol subtests, was used. Harris and Christiansen, using the same subtests, had found no significant relationship between Improvement and Intelligence. In this sample, however, the two variables were associated positively, the Pearsonian correlation coefficient being .46, which is significant at the .01 level of confidence. The mean of the Improved group was 122; that of the Unimproved group was 112.

The mean IQ of the total sample was 117, as compared with a mean of 108 in the Harris-Christiansen study. An important difference between the two samples so far as method of selection is concerned should be noted: the Harris-Christiansen sample consisted of already hospitalized persons who were given psychotherapy because of delayed recovery from physical disease, surgery, or accident, whereas almost all the patients in the present study had elected on their own initiative to seek psychotherapy at the clinic, and in their waking hours went about the business of life in an upright position. This difference might well account for the IQ difference between the samples, as well as for the fact that these self-referred patients were a good standard deviation above the general population mean in intelligence. Simply being aware of the fact that psychotherapy is to be had

[1] Harris, R. E., & Christiansen, C., "Prediction of Response to Brief Psychotherapy," *Journal of Psychology*, 1946, 21, 269–284.

and that it makes sense to seek it when you are in personal difficulties is probably related positively to general intelligence and cultural sophistication.

It is also to be expected on theoretical grounds that greater effectiveness of cortical functioning (which presumably reveals itself on the Wechsler-Bellevue) should be associated with a factor of modifiability in personality structure. Intelligence certainly involves the ability to cognize relationships adequately, including emotional relationships, and to correct one's cognitions on the basis of new evidence. It would seem that in this sample, at any rate, the more intelligent patients were better able to use the psychotherapeutic relationship to induce desired personality changes.

The Minnesota Multiphasic Personality Inventory

The MMPI analysis may be divided into three main sections: (1) group differences between the Improved and Unimproved cases on MMPI scales; (2) prediction of outcome from MMPI profiles by clinical psychologists skilled in the use of the test, as well as by certain rational indices or rules for mechanical sorting of the profiles; (3) development and cross-validation of a prediction scale. The first two enterprises will be reported in this chapter; the development and cross-validation of a prediction scale will be reported separately, however, as it involved work with a number of other samples and raised some other test-specific questions.

Group comparisons on the usual diagnostic and validity scales are shown in Figure 8.1. Only on the Paranoia scale was there a significant difference between the means of the Improved and Unimproved groups (t of 2.6, $p < .02$). The Unimproved group profile is consistently higher on almost all scales, however, and the peak is at Schizophrenia, with the average T scores for Psychasthenia and Depression also being greater than 70. The sorts of individuals who earn profiles like this are usually schizoid; in *An Atlas for the Clinical Use of the MMPI*,[2] most of the 8,724 profiles carry a diagnosis of reactive depression with underlying schizoid trends. This diagnosis fits well with the observation by Harris and Christiansen that poor prognosis is generally associated with what they call "subclinical psychotic

[2] Hathaway, S. R., & Meehl, P. E., *An Atlas for the Clinical Use of the MMPI* (Minneapolis, Minn.: University of Minnesota Press, 1951), 668–669.

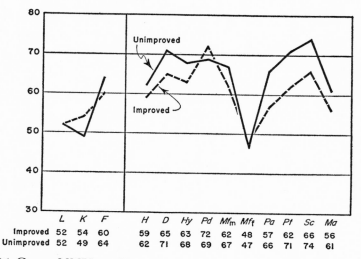

	L	K	F		H	D	Hy	Pd	Mf$_m$	Mf$_f$	Pa	Pt	Sc	Ma
Improved	52	54	60		59	65	63	72	62	48	57	62	66	56
Unimproved	52	49	64		62	71	68	69	67	47	66	71	74	61

Fɪɢ. 8.1 Group MMPI profiles of the Improved and Unimproved groups.

trends," referring to a more severe ego dysfunction than first clinical impression seems to indicate. Depression and anxiety are salient features of the clinical picture in almost all patients who seek psychotherapy in the outpatient clinic; but the patients who fail to improve are those in whom paranoid and schizoid features underlie the psychoneurotic symptoms. A reasonable guess would be that their personal difficulties are more chronic and characterologically based, in contrast to the more acute and situation-linked problems of the patients who improve.

The 33 individual MMPI profiles were also given to clinical psychologists for prognostic evaluations. Eight clinicians independently attempted to predict outcome from the profiles, having no other information concerning the patient beyond age and sex. Each clinician sorted the 33 records into two groups, predicting either that the case would be improved or that it would be unimproved. Of 264 (8 × 33) such classifications, 164 (62.12 per cent) were correct. The sum of the eight values of chi square was 20.46, which for 8 df yields a p less than .01. The three best sorters had a pooled accuracy percentage of 69.7 per cent. All of the sorters were more often correct than in error, but it should be pointed out that an average accuracy of 62 per cent when 50 per cent would be expected by chance is a fairly modest achievement in clinical prediction. Even the best of the MMPI analysts would be well advised to be tentative in their prognostic formulations.

Rational indices and rules for mechanical sorting produce substantially the same accuracy of prediction as do sortings by clinicians; actually, such indices are slightly more effective. Two fairly simple and obvious mechanical predictors were put to the test. The first of these employed the rule that for any profile with all scores within the normal range (i.e., greater than 30, less than 70) improvement should be predicted. Ten profiles met this requirement, and 9 of these cases had in fact improved. Twenty-four of 33 profiles (73 per cent) were thus classified correctly (chi square of 8.1, $p < .01$). Exceptions were then allowed in the general rule: e.g., profiles with only D, or with only D and Pt, greater than 70 would be called Improved. Both exceptions led to an accuracy of prediction between 75 and 80 per cent.

In addition to these sorting rules, a simple index of subclinical psychotic trends was defined by summing the scores of four scales (F, Pa, Sc, and Ma) usually found elevated in psychosis. This index correlated — .40 with outcome as it had been rated on a 100-point scale.

It is of some interest that the same indices that predicted response to psychotherapy worked equally well in another setting, with a sample apparently quite different from the patient sample at this clinic. In the previously reported study of personal effectiveness in male graduate students in their final year of work for the doctorate, in which ratings were obtained from faculty members on certain dimensions, such as originality and personal soundness, the averaged faculty ratings on personal soundness for 40 such students correlated —.40 with the index defined by the sum of F, Pa, Sc, and Ma, and had a contingency of .52 with a mechanical sorting of the MMPI profiles using the rule that all profiles having no clinical scale elevation (except D) of 70 or above should be called Sound, while all others should be called Unsound.

The "personally sound" graduate students were different from the "personally unsound" students in the same way that patients who profited considerably from psychotherapy differed from patients who profited little or not at all. As one would expect, however, there was a difference in absolute level of adjustment; the distribution of scores on a Prognosis for Psychotherapy scale showed a clear progression in group means from the Unimproved patients through the Improved patients and the Unsound graduate students to the Sound graduate students.

What these relationships indicate, it would seem, is that the patients who are most likely to get well are those who are not very sick in the first place. Another way of putting this is to say that patients who are more integrated to begin with are better able to use the psychotherapeutic relationship to solve whatever problems brought them into therapy. A corollary is that the potential gains from therapy should increase as therapy progresses, at least up to the point where the critical problem for the patient is to become genuinely independent of the therapist. By that time, of course, the therapeutic process has become internalized, and personality problems have been brought "into the ego," to be dealt with rationally and objectively.

The Rorschach Psychodiagnostic

The Rorschach analysis was carried out according to the same general design as the MMPI analysis, with the exception that no prognostic scale was developed. Average profiles were determined for the Improved and Unimproved groups, using the Klopfer-Kelly conventions for the scoring and nomenclature of determinants. Individual scores on the Harris-Christiansen Rorschach Prognostic Index were computed, and the relationship of Outcome to that index was calculated. Finally, the test protocols, including both content of responses and profiles of determinants, were given to clinicians for sorting.

All the Rorschachs were administered by the experimenter, with all the verbalizations and relevant behavior of the patient being recorded. The tests were scored independently by the experimenter and by one other clinical psychologist who had had several years of experience both in the scoring and in the interpretation of the Rorschach. The experimenter himself had had approximately three years of clinical experience with the test, in addition to a graduate course in its scoring and interpretation. The two independent scorings showed a high degree of agreement; discrepancies were reconciled in a conference on review of the scoring. The Improved and Unimproved groups did not differ significantly on any Rorschach determinant, nor on any of the important ratios, such as W, D, Dd, plus S, M: sum C, and so on. This finding is consistent with Rorschach results in the graduate student sample previously referred to; in that study no significant relationship was found between any Rorschach determinant or combination of determinants and the criterion variable, Personal Soundness.

The Harris-Christiansen Prognostic Index correlated .00 with Improvement. Most empirical Rorschach indices fail to hold up under cross-validation, so that this is not a surprising finding.

Somewhat contrary to the expectation of most persons who have worked with the test, however, is the finding that experienced Rorschach interpreters were not able to predict outcome of therapy on the basis of the Rorschach evaluation. Four clinicians, all of whom were highly trained and experienced, both in the use of the test and in general clinical practice, attempted the sorting task. They had at hand all of the responses of the patients, as well as a summary of the scoring in terms of the usual ratios and profile of determinants. Only one of the four sortings approached significance, and that was in the negative direction; that is, the sorter was more often wrong than right in predicting outcome.

The Ethnocentrism Scale

Certain theoretical considerations had led to the inclusion of the Ethnocentrism scale in the test battery. Levinson[3] had found, in a study at this same clinic, that ethnocentric patients showed a personality syndrome of a sort that would be resistant to change through psychotherapy. High-scoring patients were described by her as having the following characteristics: "rigid, constricted personalities . . . stereotyped, conventionalized thinking . . . undifferentiated egos . . . narrow range of experience, emotionally and intellectually . . . weak interpersonal relationships, expressed in terms of dominance-submission." The low-scoring patients, on the other hand, were marked by their "desire to be loved and fear of being rejected . . . expressed directly in interpersonal relations and in a very personalized way . . . the frequency with which low scorers discuss their relationships to others is striking."

These considerations suggested the hypothesis that patients who scored high on the Ethnocentrism scale would be less likely to enter

---

[3] Levinson, Maria H., "Psychological Ill-health in Relation to Potential Fascism: A Study of Psychiatric Clinic Patients," in T. W. Adorno, *et al.* (Eds.) *The Authoritarian Personality* (New York: Harper, 1950), 891–970.

deeply into the sort of personal interaction that occurs in psycho-therapy. From the very beginning of therapy they would find it necessary to narrate the comings and goings of their somatic com-plaints, and to minimize the importance of their psychological prob-lems as the cause of their somatic disturbances. According to this notion, ethnocentric patients would tend characteristically to isolate affect and to avoid psychological self-examination; they would be strangers to their own inner life.

While the psychological formulation itself was not checked on in any detail in the present study, the hypothesis that it led to (i.e., that Ethnocentrism would be negatively related to Improvement) was confirmed. The correlation of the E scale with Improvement ratings was —.64, making it the best single predictor employed in this study.

Several reservations, however, should be noted. In the first place, scores on the E scale are negatively related to intelligence, which can be presumed to be a somewhat more basic psychological variable than ethnocentrism. As Gough[4] has pointed out, many of the items in the E scale are written in such an extreme fashion that a person of some intelligence and education could not agree with them, even though the sentiment expressed might win his approval if the form of its statement were less clearly irrational. Since Improvement is correlated positively with Intelligence in this sample (.46), one would expect a negative relationship between Improvement and Ethnocentrism on the basis simply of their common relationship to Intelligence.

When Intelligence is partialled out, however, some relationship re-mains. The coefficient of partial correlation between Ethnocentrism and Improvement, with Intelligence held constant, is —.34. Partialling intelligence out in this manner is not strictly correct, of course, except in a mechanical way. Actually, some underlying emotional-cognitive variable such as rigidity, which is complexly related both to intelli-gence and to ethnocentrism, may be accounting for a large part of the correlation of both of those measures with the capacity for psycho-logical change as shown by improvement in therapy.

There is one other reservation to be noted. Four of the psycho-therapists in this study were Jewish, a fact which might have affected both the ethnocentric patient's attitude toward them and their attitude toward the ethnocentric patient. In several of the therapeutic inter-

[4] Gough, H. G., "Studies of Social Intolerance: I. Some Psychological and Socio-logical Correlates of Anti-Semitism," *Journal of Social Psychology*, 1951, 33, 237–246.

actions, such patient attitudes came into the open and were dealt with therapeutically; and in at least one case the therapist admitted candidly to the psychologist that his own response to the patient's anti-Semitism was disruptive of the relationship.

In spite of these reservations, however, the relationship between ethnocentrism and capacity for psychological change through psychotherapy is a striking one. If confirmed, it would be of some theoretical importance. It may, indeed, have implications for social communities as well as individuals, inasmuch as it suggests that the social organization that fosters prejudice might well be forfeiting the kind of emotional flexibility that is necessary if in time of crisis it is to cure its own ills.

9

Ego-strength and the Power to Rally from Setback

EVERYONE alive has troubles and problems, and as we learned from our studies of especially "sound" individuals, the most important consideration in determining personal effectiveness is not the amount of trouble or misfortune (within limits) a person encounters, but *how he responds* to the vicissitudes and challenges of life. This capacity to meet problems without being dismayed or overwhelmed, to endure suffering and face great loss without foundering, is an aspect of psychological strength and vitality that deserves special study.

In what follows, we shall first describe the development and cross-validation of a scale originally designed to predict the response of psychoneurotic patients to psychotherapy. Consideration of the scale content and its correlates, however, has suggested that a somewhat broader psychological interpretation be placed upon it, making it useful as an assessment device in any situation where some estimate of adaptability and personal resourcefulness is wanted. It appears to measure the various aspects of effective personal functioning that are usually subsumed under the term "ego-strength."

The scale consists of 68 items from the Minnesota Multiphasic Personality Inventory, selected from a total MMPI pool of 550 items on the basis of significant correlation with rated improvement in our 33 psychoneurotic patients who had been treated for six months in a clinic. The test responses of the patients were obtained before psychotherapy began, so that the scale, so far as logic of construction is concerned, is designed to predict whether or not after about six months of therapy the patient will have improved.

The sample of 33 patients, as we have seen, was divided into two groups: 17 patients who were judged to have clearly improved, and 16 patients who were judged to be unimproved. And although the sample was small, the cases were intensively studied, and the two skilled judges who had thoroughly acquainted themselves with the course of the therapy (although not themselves involved in it otherwise) were in considerable agreement (r of .91) in their independent ratings of degree of improvement. While one would not ordinarily base scale development on a sample of this size, it was reasoned here that a small number of well-studied cases who were classified with high reliability, and, as collateral evidence indicated, with high accuracy as well, would serve better than the practical alternative, which was to get a large sample in which the therapist's rating of outcome was accepted uncritically.

When the Improved and Unimproved groups were scored on this 68–item scale, the mean of the Improved group proved to be 52.7, that of the Unimproved group 29.1, a difference which is significant well beyond the .01 level (t of 10.3). The odd-even reliability of the scale in a clinic population of 126 patients is .76. Test-retest reliability after three months in a sample of 30 cases is .72.

The 68 items of the scale are presented below, arranged in groups according to the kinds of psychological homogeneities that, in the judgment of the writer, are involved in the item content.

Physical functioning and physiological stability. 153. During the past few years I have been well most of the time (T). 51. I am in just as good physical health as most of my friends (T). 174. I have never had a fainting spell (T). 189. I feel weak all over much of the time (F). 187. My hands have not become clumsy or awkward (T). 34. I have a cough most of the time (F). 2. I have a good appetite (T). 14. I have diarrhea once a month or more (F). 341. At times I hear so well it bothers me (F). 36. I seldom worry about my health (T). 43. My sleep is fitful and disturbed (F).

Psychasthenia and seclusiveness. 384. I feel unable to tell anyone all about myself (F). 489. I feel sympathetic towards people who tend to hang on to their griefs and troubles (F). 236. I brood a great deal (F). 217. I frequently find myself worrying about something. (F). 100. I have met problems so full of possibilities that I have been unable to make up my mind about them (F). 234. I get mad easily and then get over it soon (T). 270. When I leave home, I do not worry about whether the door is locked and the windows closed (T). 359. Sometimes some unimportant thought will run through my mind and bother me for days (F). 344. Often I cross the street in order not to meet someone I see (F). 241. I dream frequently about things that are best kept to myself (F).

Attitudes towards religion. 95. I go to church almost every week (T). 488. I pray several times every week (F). 483. Christ performed miracles such as changing water into wine (F). 58. Everything is turning out just like the prophets of the Bible said it would (F). 420. I have had some very unusual religious experiences (F). 209. I believe my sins are unpardonable (F).

Moral posture. 410. I would certainly enjoy beating a crook at his own game (T). 181. When I get bored, I like to stir up some excitement (T). 94. I do many things which I regret afterwards (I regret things more or more often than others seem to) (F). 253. I can be friendly with people who do things which I consider wrong (T). 109. Some people are so bossy that I feel like doing the opposite of what they request, even though I know they are right (T). 208. I like to flirt (T). 430. I am attracted by members of the opposite sex (T). 548. I never attend a sexy show if I can avoid it (F). 231. I like to talk about sex (T). 378. I do not like to see women smoke (F). 355. Sometimes I enjoy hurting persons I love (T).

Sense of reality. 33. I have had very peculiar and strange experiences (F). 349. I have strange and peculiar thoughts (F). 251. I have had blank spells in which my activities were interrupted and I did not know what was going on around me (F). 48. When I am with people, I am bothered by hearing very queer things (F). 22. At times I have fits of laughing and crying that I cannot control (F). 192. I have had no difficulty in keeping my balance in walking (T). 62. Parts of my body often have feelings like burning, tingling, crawling, or like "going to sleep" (F). 541. My skin seems to be unusually sensitive to touch (F).

Personal adequacy, ability to cope. 389. My plans have frequently seemed so full of difficulties that I have had to give them up (F). 82. I am easily downed in an argument (F). 32. I find it hard to keep my mind on a task or job (F). 244. My way of doing things is apt to be misunderstood by others (F). 555. I sometimes feel that I am about to go to pieces (F). 544. I feel tired a good deal of the time (F). 261. If I were an artist, I would like to draw flowers (F). 554. If I were an artist, I would like to draw children (F). 132. I like collecting flowers or growing house plants (F). 140. I like to cook (F). 380. When someone says silly or ignorant things about something I know, I try to set him right (T).

Phobias, infantile anxieties. 367. I am not afraid of fire (T). 525. I am made nervous by certain animals (F). 510. Dirt frightens or disgusts me (F). 494. I am afraid of finding myself in a closet or small closed place (F). 559. I have often been frightened in the middle of the night (F).

Miscellaneous. 221. I like science (T). 513. I think Lincoln was greater than Washington (T). 561. I very much like horseback riding (F). 458. The man who had most to do with me when I was a child (such as my father, stepfather, etc.) was very strict with me (T). 421. One or more members of my family is very nervous (T). 515. In my home we have always had the ordinary necessities (such as enough food, clothing, etc.) (T).

The pretherapy characteristics of patients who improve in therapy, as compared with those who do not improve, might be summarized as follows:

Improved: (a) good physical functioning; (b) spontaneity, ability to share emotional experiences; (c) conventional church membership, but nonfundamentalist and undogmatic in religious beliefs; (d) permissive morality; (e) good contact with reality; (f) feelings of personal adequacy and vitality; (g) physical courage and lack of fear.

Unimproved: (a) many and chronic physical ailments; (b) broodiness, inhibition, a strong need for emotional seclusion, worrisomeness; (c) intense religious experiences, belief in prayer, miracles, the Bible; (d) repressive and punitive morality; (e) dissociation and ego-alienation; (f) confusion, submissiveness, chronic fatigue; (g) phobias and infantile anxieties.

From an inspection of these differences, one might easily be led to envy the mental salubrity of psychoneurotic patients who are about to improve. Their actual mental distress, however, has been detailed in the case material presented earlier and will not be repeated here. What the group comparison really reveals, of course, is the *dimension* on which the improved and unimproved groups differed. Had the improved patients been compared with an exceptionally healthy nonclinic group of subjects, the same items might well have emerged as descriptive of the difference between the groups, but with the characteristic responses of the improved patients being exactly opposite to those listed above. In other words, the nature of the criterion behavior determines the *nature* of the dimension that the item analysis will reveal, but the question of the *strength* of that variable in the criterion groups must be answered separately.

In this case, it is suggested that what is being measured is a general factor of capacity for personality integration, or ego-strength. The greater vividness of psychopathology often tends to obscure the ego-synthetic or constructive forces in the behavior of a psychologically disturbed individual, so that a prognostic evaluation is generally more difficult to make than a diagnostic evaluation. Nevertheless, in spite of the saliency of psychopathology in the clinical picture, it may be presumed that the patient has certain latent strengths which will gradually show themselves, particularly as the psychological crisis that brings him to therapy subsides. What the item content of the prediction scale seems to indicate is that these strengths are of the sort that are generally ascribed to a well-functioning ego, and that latent ego-strength is the most important determinant (within the patient) of response to brief psychotherapy.

Such an interpretation would, of course, have relatively little warrant without supporting evidence from other samples. The obvious next step is to inquire into the relation of the scale to other measures in new populations.

CORRELATES OF THE PREDICTION SCALE

In this further inquiry, one clinic sample and two nonclinic samples were studied. The clinic sample consisted of 77 female and 50 male patients; the nonclinic samples consisted of 160 male Air Force officers and 40 male graduate students.

The first step was to obtain adjective descriptions, by objective and skilled observers, of high and low scorers on the prediction scale. This was made possible by administering the MMPI to graduate students who were participating in intensive three-day psychological assessments being conducted at the Institute of Personality Assessment and Research. Following the assessment periods, the staff members of the Institute filled out an adjective checklist with the purpose of describing each one of the subjects in the assessment, on the basis of the subject's socially observable behavior in situational procedures, interviews, and informal social interaction. A composite staff impression was thus assembled. The 10 highest and 10 lowest scorers on the psychotherapy prediction scale were then compared by item-analyzing the composite adjective list for the two groups. The adjectives that showed a statistically significant difference (.05 level) between high and low scorers are listed below. (The staff observers were, of course, in ignorance of the test scores of the subjects.)

> *Adjectives checked more frequently about high-scoring subjects:* alert, adventurous, determined, independent, initiative, outspoken, persistent, reliable, resourceful, responsible.
> *Adjectives checked more frequently about low-scoring subjects:* affected, dependent, effeminate, mannerly, mild.

The general impression conveyed is of greater resourcefulness, vitality, and self-direction in the high scorers, and effeminacy, inhibition, and affectation in the low scorers. This picture is supported by staff ratings of these same subjects on a number of psychological variables which it was thought could be inferred from social behavior in the assessment setting. The psychotherapy prediction scale correlated significantly with Vitality (.38), which was defined simply as "general energy level," and with Drive (.41), defined as "persistence, resolution, perseverance, *directed* energy." In addition, the scale showed low but positive correlation with several other variables descriptive of effective functioning. These are: Self-confidence (.24), Poise (.24), and Breadth of Interest (.25). Significant negative correlations are with Submissiveness (—.40), Effeminacy (—.34), and Intraceptiveness (—.34). As in the adjective descriptions, the high scorers on the scale emerge as more adequate physically, more at ease socially, and somewhat broader culturally. Low-scoring men are effeminate, submissive, and inclined to turn inward rather than to be emotionally outgoing.

The relationship of the prediction scale to intelligence was next investigated. Among the functions of the ego, as described by psychoanalytic writers, are these: perceiving, planning, synthesizing, and, in general, bringing the subject into an adaptive relationship to reality. Ego-determined behavior is what we are accustomed to calling *intelligent* behavior. Any scale that purports to measure ego-strength should be positively correlated with standardized measures of intelligence.

In the sample on which the scale was developed, its correlation with Wechsler-Bellevue IQ is .44. In the Air Force officer sample, the scale correlates .36 with total score on the Primary Mental Abilities test and .47 with the Intellectual Efficiency scale of the California Psychological Inventory. In that same sample it correlates .48 with the Potential Success scale developed at the Institute of Personality

Assessment and Research against a criterion consisting of faculty ratings of the probable professional success of the doctoral candidates studied. In the graduate student sample itself, the psychotherapy prediction scale correlates .39 with intelligence as measured by the Miller Analogies Test. Further, in the latter sample it correlates .52 with the Intellectual Efficiency scale. Thus it relates to general intelligence, as measured by a variety of tests, even in highly restricted ranges of intelligence. Certainly the ego-strength interpretation of the scale is supported.

The scale also is related to tolerance and lack of ethnic prejudice. In the standardization sample it correlates —.47 with the Ethnocentrism (E) scale of Form 60 of the University of California Public Opinion Study Questionnaire. In the graduate student sample it correlates —.35 with the Prejudice scale of the MMPI, and —.46 with the E scale. Its correlation with the E scale in the Air Force officer sample is —.23, and its correlation with the Tolerance scale of the CPI in that sample is .42.

Again, these findings lend some weight to the notion that what is being measured is general excellence of ego-functioning. The authors of *The Authoritarian Personality*, in their unquestionably successful search for the character defects that accompany ethnocentrism, found that high scorers on the E scale show "lack of differentiation of the ego." This is manifested among clinic patients in "a narrow range of experience, emotionally and intellectually," together with "rigidity and constriction," "stereotyped thinking," and so on. All of these things are thus, by inference, negatively related to scores on the psychotherapy prediction scale.

The relationship of the scale to the diagnostic and validity scales of the MMPI was determined in both the graduate student sample and the diagnostic study cases. The results are shown in Table 9.1. Surprisingly high negative correlations are found with most of the measures of psychopathology, averaging in the neighborhood of —.60 with Hypochondriasis, Depression, Hysteria, Psychasthenia, and Schizophrenia, and around —.50 with Paranoia in the clinical samples. What this suggests is that the prediction scale is picking up a general factor of psychopathology in the MMPI, reflecting degree of maladjustment or ego-dysfunction irrespective of differential diagnosis. In other words, it is related to general elevation of the profile, regardless of the pattern.

TABLE 9.1   *Relationship of Ego-strength Scale to Diagnostic and Validity Scales of the MMPI in Clinic and Student Populations*

Scale	Male Clinic Patients ($N = 50$)	Male Graduate Students ($N = 36$)	Female Clinic Patients ($N = 77$)
F	−.49	−.36	−.47
K	.31	.31	.31
Hs	−.62	−.67	−.63
D	−.60	−.53	−.67
Hy	−.39	−.61	−.63
Pd	−.48	−.07	−.34
Mf	−.04	−.43	.07
Pa	−.62	−.07	−.49
Pt	−.71	−.54	−.71
Sc	−.55	−.44	−.64
Ma	−.04	−.33	−.21

The correlations are, of course, partly a function of overlap of items (generally scored in the reverse direction) between the prediction scale and the diagnostic scales. The amount of net overlap for each scale is shown in Table 9.2. The very fact of overlap itself testifies to

TABLE 9.2   *Item Overlap of Ego-strength Scale and MMPI Diagnostic Scales*

Scale	Items Scored in Same Direction	Items Scored in Opposite Direction	Net Overlap
Hs	None	2, 43, 51, 62, 153, 189, 192	Seven items, scored opposite
D	58, 241	2, 32, 36, 43, 51, 153, 189, 208, 236, 270	Eight items, scored opposite
Hy	253	2, 32, 43, 51, 109, 153, 174, 189, 192, 234	Nine items, scored opposite
Pd	82	32, 33, 94, 231, 244	Four items, scored opposite
Pa	None	109, 341	Two items, scored opposite
Pt	None	22, 32, 36, 94, 189, 217, 344, 349, 359	Nine items, scored opposite
Sc	None	22, 187, 192, 241, 251, 349	Six items, scored opposite
Ma	109, 181	22, 100, 251	One item, scored opposite

the character of the scale as a measure of general excellence of ego-functioning, manifested in this instance by absence of chronic psychopathology.

The raw score means and standard deviations of the samples studied are presented in Table 9.3. The values are fairly consistent in the

TABLE 9.3   *Ego-strength Scale Statistics*

Sample	N	Range	Mean	SD
1. Standardization sample	33	15–62	41.94	13.30
2. 1st cross-validation sample*	53	26–58	40.10	7.62
3. 2nd cross-validation sample	52	23–60	41.04	8.18
4. 3rd cross-validation sample	46	22–61	42.06	9.32
5. Clinic diagnostic cases	127	23–60	41.97	7.36
6. VA mental hygiene clinic patients	52	22–59	41.79	7.38
7. I.P.A.R. graduate students	40	37–60	50.92	5.62
8. Air Force officers	160	38–60	52.73	4.05

* Scores on abbreviated scale prorated for length of scale.

TABLE 9.4   *Conversion Table for Use of Ego-strength Scale in Clinic Samples*

Raw Score	T Score	Raw Score	T Score
22	25	46	57
23	27	47	58
24	29	48	59
25	30	49	60
26	32	50	62
27	33	51	63
28	34	52	64
29	36	53	65
30	37	54	67
31	38	55	68
32	39	56	69
33	40	57	70
34	42	58	72
35	43	59	73
36	44	60	74
37	45	61	75
38	47	62	76
39	48	63	78
40	49	64	79
41	50	65	80
42	52	66	82
43	53	67	83
44	54	68	85
45	56		

clinical samples, with somewhat higher means for the graduate students and Air Force officers. In Table 9.4, a chart is given for conversion of raw scores into T scores comparable to other MMPI scales.

CROSS-VALIDATION OF THE SCALE AS A PREDICTION INSTRUMENT

The prediction scale was tested on three new samples of psychotherapy patients, in order to see whether it was doing the job for which it was designed. The patients were psychoneurotic, the psychotherapy was brief (very close to six months in all cases), and the clinical setting was similar to that in which the scale was developed. All the patients took the MMPI at the beginning of therapy, and all were rated as to degree of improvement at some date following termination of therapy. The cross-validating samples are described below.

1. Fifty-three patients who were given psychotherapy because of delayed recovery from injury or physical disease. Ratings of improvement were made by expert judges (who had not taken part in the therapy) on the basis of terminal interviews. At a final rating conference, these 53 patients were ranked in terms of degree of improvement. This sample of patients had been studied some six years earlier by Harris and Christiansen, who showed that patterns of test scores on both the Rorschach and the MMPI were predictive of improvement. The same pretherapy MMPI's were now scored on the prognosis scale. Only 39 items of the 68 could be used, however, as these patients had been given a shortened form of the MMPI, containing only the items that make up the clinical and validity scales of the test. The correlation with terminal rating is .42.

2. Fifty-two patients who had received brief psychotherapy during the preceding five years at a clinic. The sample was obtained by asking therapists who had worked at the clinic during that period of time to nominate patients whom they remembered as clear examples of exceptional improvement, complete lack of improvement, and moderate improvement. The latter group consisted of 27 patients, while the two extreme groups numbered 9 and 16 respectively. The degree of relationship between pretherapy prognosis scale scores and this trichotomy, as determined by computation of *eta*, is .54. The means were as follows: Unimproved, 32.75; Improved, 43.07; Exceptional Improvement, 49.66.

3. Forty-six patients who were part of the current patient load on the psychiatric service of a general hospital. All of these patients had had approximately six months of psychotherapy at the time the rating was obtained. Ratings were made by the therapists themselves, on a 9-point

scale of improvement. The correlation with pretherapy prognosis scale scores is .38.

These correlation coefficients are of about the magnitude that one would expect for a scale that is giving a valid measure of patient variables related to outcome of psychotherapy. It is reasonable that there should remain considerable unaccounted-for variance, quite apart from whatever error variance is contributed by the fallible criterion and predictor measure; for there are many important determinants of outcome of therapy besides the personality of the patient. The personality of the therapist, e.g., is also important. In addition, there is a subtle interactional factor that results from the combination of a particular patient with a particular therapist, which is not infrequently the crucial determinant of outcome in a given case. Then there are, of course, life-situational variables outside of the therapy, affecting both patient and therapist, individually or jointly. It seems safe to say that no standardized test is likely to achieve any very high order of correlation with therapeutic outcomes. At the same time, the effort to construct measures of the different sources of variance tends to advance the research problem somewhat, and to make new questions answerable.

To recapitulate: this MMPI scale was developed for the purpose of predicting response to psychotherapy, and upon inspection of its item content and its personality and intelligence test correlates it was interpreted as being essentially a measure of ego-strength. The scale is now known as the Ego-strength scale of the MMPI, and its conventional abbreviation is *Es*.

The relationship of the scale scores to therapeutic outcomes in several cross-validating samples leads to the conclusion that a significant determinant of personality change in psychotherapy is strength of the ego before therapy begins. Among the characteristics that are collectively referred to as ego-strength are physiological stability and good health, a strong sense of reality, feelings of personal adequacy and vitality, permissive morality, lack of ethnic prejudice, emotional outgoingness and spontaneity, and intelligence.

Since the patients who seek psychotherapy are almost invariably in some sort of psychological difficulty, it must be evident that these characteristics are usually not salient features of the clinical picture at first contact. The evidence suggests, however, that such strengths are latent in the personality, and they emerge as therapy progresses. By implication, it seems probable that the kind of personal crisis that brings the person of good ego-strength to the clinic is more situation-linked and less characterologically based (i.e., less chronic) than the personal difficulties of the person with poor ego-strength.

The scale should be useful both as a research instrument and as an additional clinical indicator on the MMPI. Considerable caution should be exercised in the clinical use of the scale, however. Certainly it should not serve as the basis for categorical recommendations to treat or not to treat certain patients; the grounds for such action in a clinic should properly involve values as well as facts, and in any event the kind of crude measuring device presented here represents a fairly low order of "fact." Any prognostic assertions made on the basis of this scale should be quite tentative, and probably should be accompanied by a visual image of the kinds of scatterplots that may give rise to correlations in the general neighborhood of .45.

As a research instrument, the scale should prove useful in giving some assessment of the role of "patient variables" in determining the complex outcome that is involved in response to psychotherapy. It may also be of some value in assessing the kind of change that occurs in therapy. One may ask, for example, whether there is actually an enhancement of ego-strength as a consequence of therapy, and get an answer by comparing pre-therapy with post-therapy scores on the scale. Or one might inquire whether the therapy itself is causing the change for the better in patients who improve; evidence on the issue might be obtained by setting up a research design that would use as a control group a sample of patients who are matched with the therapy sample in terms both of *Es* scores and of present need for psychotherapy, but who differ in that they do not receive psychotherapy.

In addition, the scale may be useful as an assessment device quite apart from the clinical situation. Its correlates with personality variables in normal samples are similar to the pattern of relationships seen in clinic samples, and in general it seems to be measuring constructive forces in the personality. Thus it may serve as a predictor in any situation in which an estimate of personal adaptability and resourcefulness is called for.

The workings of the especially strong ego both in countering setbacks and in *permitting* regressions will be the subject of some of the studies to be reported a bit later in this volume. At this point, however, it may be useful to give a very brief resumé of the determinants and marks of ego-strength as the term is here being used, drawing both upon these statistical findings and upon general observation of normal psychological functioning.

Ego-strength is, first of all, a function simply of intelligence. Since comprehension of experience depends mostly on the degree of organization in the central nervous system, the scope of the ego will vary with the quality of the brain.

Scope does not depend solely upon cognition, however. Psychodynamics enter chiefly in relation to the mechanism of repression. Repression operates in the service of homeostasis, and so serves an economic function that is indispensable in maintaining the organism in an integral form in its environment. However, repression may be so extensive as to become a false economy; when broad areas of experience are lost to consciousness through repression, the ego may be said to be less strong (i.e., less able to adapt) as a consequence. To state the matter positively, ego-strength requires a flexible repression-mechanism, so that the person may be said to be optimally open to experience, though capable of excluding phenomena that cannot be assimilated to the structure of the self.

Physiological stability and regularity of physical functioning is the biological matrix in which the ego thrives, or attains maximum strength. Generally speaking, the ego is at its strongest in the years of physical maturity, granting good bodily health. Ego-strength is increasing as the organism grows towards maturity, levels off in the "prime of life," and declines thereafter with increasing age.

The crucial years in determining ego-strength are the first five years of life. Severe ego-dysfunction in those years is virtually irreversible. In the normal course of development, a regular sequence of ego-crises and ego-achievements may be discerned. The first achievement of the ego in relation to experience is the attainment of a stable and facile distinction between inner and outer sources of stimulation. This is the indispensable basis of the "sense of reality"; an inability to make this distinction is the primary mark of functional psychosis, in which introjection and projection no longer operate under the control of the ego. Paranoias and psychotic depressions and excitements are the diagnostic syndromes consequent upon such ego failure. A strong ego, on the other hand, consistently recognizes the independent and autonomous existence of objects other than itself, and also is able to take a reflective attitude toward its own existence and the laws of its being.

Building upon this basic distinction of inner and outer sources of experience, the ego gradually attains mastery of bodily functions involving intake and output, which includes experiencing the erotic component in such functions. Such later character traits as the ability to get and to give good things, to hold on to what one wants and to let go when necessary, to be able to rise to the occasion, to make things go, to build and to conserve, to understand and to predict, all have their beginnings in the early years when the most important of ego-crises occur. The later achievements of the normal ego involve primarily the synthesis of these earlier acquisitions of mastery; the most important outcomes have to do with personal identity in work and in love, and finally with the individual's participation in community experience, which would include some understanding of man in relation to nature, and of nature itself.

10

Ego-strength and the
Management of Aggression

In this chapter we shall consider some observations incidental to the validation of the MMPI Ego-strength scale just described. Most of the correlates of the scale seem to fit in well with the concept of ego-strength as one generally finds it used in the psychoanalytic literature. In the present study, however, in which the subjects are healthy, well-functioning men of generally superior abilities, there appeared as significant correlates of the Ego-strength scale a cluster of traits seemingly more related to egocentrism: competitiveness, marked power-orientation, and disregard of the rights of others. The aim of this chapter is to report these findings and to seek to give some theoretical account of them.

By way of background, recall the information just presented concerning the validity of the *Es* scale. The scale was constructed originally for the purpose of predicting response to psychotherapy, and for this it appears to have substantial predictive efficiency, producing correlations of .38, .42, and .52 against rated outcome in three cross-validating samples. It has also been shown to increase significantly following psychotherapy.[1] It consistently has high negative correlations with the MMPI clinical symptom scales, as indeed a measure of ego-strength should have. Thus it is related positively to the ability to recover from psychological distress, and negatively to the tendency to develop psychiatric symptoms.

[1] Barron, F., & Leary, T., "Changes in Psychoneurotic Patients with and Without Psychotherapy," *Journal of Consulting Psychology,* 1955, 19, 239–245.

The scale also, as we have seen, correlates positively with measured intelligence. In some half-dozen samples in which the measures of intelligence included the Wechsler-Bellevue, the Miller Analogies, the Primary Mental Abilities Test, the Wesman Personnel Classification Test, the Terman Concept Mastery Test, and the Idea Classification Test, the *Es* scale correlated from .35 to .45 with those measures.

Other aspects of ego-strength find representation among the observed correlates of the scale. Consistently in studies using the living-in assessment method, the *Es* scale has correlated significantly with ratings of such dimensions as Vitality, Drive, Self-confidence, Poise, and Breadth of Interest. In a study of courage and fighting ability under enemy fire (in infantry combat in Korea), the scale achieved excellent discrimination between fighters and non-fighters, the fighters (those who fired back and fought back) scoring higher on *Es*.[2] In group psychotherapy,[3] the scale has been found to have positive relationship to active participation in the group process. In still another study,[4] it has been reported to be the only MMPI scale correlating positively with favorable aspects of functioning, such as *W* and *M*, on the Rorschach test.

In the present investigation, the *Es* scale correlated with other measures as follows:

a. With independence of judgment in a group situational test based on the Asch[5] experiment. The Pearsonian *r* was .33.

b. With ability to orient oneself correctly to the vertical plane in darkness, in spite of the distorting influence of a tilted visual frame.[6] The correlation between this ability and *Es* was .28.

c. With absence of implicit anti-democratic trends. The correlation of *Es* with the Fascism scale was −.34.

d. With ratings of overall effectiveness in a variant of Charades known as The Game. Here the correlation was .34.

e. With intelligence. *Es* correlated .41 with the Terman Concept Mastery Test and .42 with the Wesman Personnel Classification Test.

All in all, these correlations and those observed in other samples indicate consistency and validity in the *Es* scale; the unexpected find-

2 Cline, V. *et al., Task: Fighter,* A research report of the Human Research Unit No. 2, OCAFF, Ford Ord, California, April, 1954.

3 Leary, T. & Coffey, H., "The Prediction of Interpersonal Behavior in Group Psychotherapy," *Group Psychotherapy,* 1954, 7, 7–51.

4 Williams, H. L. & Lawrence, J. F., "Comparison of the Rorschach and MMPI by Means of Factor Analysis," *Journal of Consulting Psychology,* 1954, 18, 3, 193–197.

5 Asch, S., *Effects of Group Pressure upon the Modification and Distortion of Judgments.* Swarthmore College: Progress report on Office of Naval Research Project, Task Order N7Onr-38003, 1950.

6 Witkin, H. A., *Personality through Perception* (New York: Harpers, 1953).

ings described below should therefore require explanation in terms of ego theory.

SAMPLE AND METHOD OF STUDY

The men who constituted the sample for study in this investigation were 100 U.S. Air Force officers of the rank of captain. They were observed for three days in a program of living-in assessment, precisely of the sort described earlier, at the Institute of Personality Assessment and Research.

The majority of these men were combat veterans, and many of them had been decorated for valor during World War II. Of the 100, 96 were married, and most of these were fathers as well. In general, the sample was well above average in personal stability, intelligence, and physical health. This fact, of course, showed itself on the *Es* scale: the average *T*-score for the sample was 63, with a standard deviation of 5.7.

In an effort to achieve a personality description of each subject that would allow room for the expression of clinical inference and at the same time be readily amenable to statistical analysis, a set of 76 Q-sort statements descriptive of personal functioning was assembled. These 76 statements were used by each staff member at the conclusion of the three days of living-in assessment to sum up his impressions of each person studied. The statements were sorted on a nine-point scale, the frequencies at each point being such as to make the final distribution conform closely to the normal curve. The objective was to obtain an ordering of the traits according to *saliency within the person*, rather than to order the persons in relation to one another on a given dimension. These staff oberver Q-sorts were then composited for all staff raters (10 in all). It is thus the averaged staff judgments with which the individual subject is finally characterized.

These Q-sort descriptions were, of course, given without knowledge of the objective test performances of the subjects. No rater knew the *Es* scores of any of the subjects at the time he did the Q-sort.

RESULTS WITH THE Q-SORT

The relationship between *Es* scores and each one of the 76 Q-sort statements was determined. A total of 40 of the 76 statements proved to be correlated to a statistically significant (.05 level) degree with

Es. (This was an unusually large number of *Q*-sort correlates for an MMPI scale in the present study; most of the standard clinical indicators on the MMPI were significantly correlated with only two or three *Q*-sort items, the average for the entire test being fewer than five per scale.)

A Tryon-type cluster analysis of the entire *Q*-sort item-pool was carried out to discover what communities of variance existed among the items. In listing the 40 *Q*-sort items correlated with the *Es* scale, we have grouped variables according to their own intercorrelations; that is, clusters of interrelated items are presented together.

Cluster I. Items descriptive of general effectiveness
1. Efficient, capable, able to mobilize resources easily and effectively; not bothered with work inhibitions.
2. Derives personal reward and pleasure from his work; values productive achievement for its own sake.
3. Is self-reliant; independent in judgment; able to think for himself.
4. Is an effective leader.
5. Is counteractive in the face of frustration.
6. Takes the initiative in social relations.
7. Communicates ideas clearly and effectively.
8. Is persuasive; tends to win other people to his point of view.
9. Is verbally fluent; conversationally facile.

Cluster II. Items descriptive of aggressiveness; power-orientation, and disregard of the rights of others
1. Takes an ascendant role in his relations with others.
2. Is competitive with his peers; likes to go ahead and to win.
3. Emphasizes success and productive achievement as a means for achieving status, power, and recognition.
4. Is aggressive and hostile in his personal relations.
5. Manipulates people as a means to achieving personal ends; opportunistic; sloughs over the meaning and value of the individual.
6. Is rebellious toward authority figures, rules, and other constraints.
7. Is sarcastic and cynical.

Items in clusters not substantially represented among Es *scale correlates*
1. Is masculine in his style and manner of behavior.
2. Is active and vigorous.
3. Prefers action to contemplation.
4. Undercontrols his impulses; acts with insufficient thinking and deliberation.

The *Q*-sort items that have a significant (.05 level) negative association with *Es* are the following:

Cluster III. Items descriptive of personal inferiority, lack of inner resources
   1. Lacks social poise and presence; becomes rattled and upset in social situations.
   2. Lacks confidence in his own ability.
   3. Is unable to make decisions without vacillation, hesitation, or delay.
   4. Would become confused, disorganized, and unadaptive under stress.
   5. Is suggestible; overly responsive to other people's evaluations rather than his own.
   6. Is rigid; inflexible in thought and action.
   7. Has a narrow range of interests.
   8. Has slow personal tempo; responds, speaks, and moves slowly.
   9. Tends not to become involved in things; passively resistant.
   10. Is pedantic and fussy about minor things.

Cluster IV. Items descriptive of excessive conformity and personal constriction
   1. Overcontrols his impulses; is inhibited; needlessly delays or denies himself gratification.
   2. With respect to authority, is submissive, compliant, and overly accepting.
   3. Conforming; tends to do the things that are prescribed.
   4. Tends to side-step troublesome situations; makes concessions to avoid unpleasantness.
   5. Is stereotyped and unoriginal in his approach to problems.
   6. Is self-abasing; feels unworthy, guilty, humble; given to self-blame.
   7. Is pessimistic about his professional future and advancement.

Items in clusters not substantially represented among Es *scale correlates*
   1. Sympathetic; feels for and with other people.
   2. Respects others; is permissive and accepting; not judgmental.
   3. Is effeminate in his style and manner of behavior.

DISCUSSION OF Q-SORT RESULTS

Most of the results from the use of the *Q*-sort technique are quite consistent with findings from other procedures and from other studies. High scorers on *Es*, it would seem, are effective and independent people, with easy command over their own resources. They are intelligent, stable, and somewhat original, and they make their presence felt socially. Men who score high are appropriately masculine in their style of behavior. Low scorers, on the other hand, are confused, unadaptive, rigid, submissive, and rather stereotyped and unoriginal; low scorers among men tend to be somewhat effeminate as well.

This much is readily assimilable to the concept of ego-strength as it is generally used by psychologists. The observations that are the central concern of this chapter, however, point either to inadequacies in the scale or to some theoretical difficulties in relation to the concept itself. The Q-sort items in Cluster II appear to describe certain features, in the characters of at least some high scorers, that are not usually thought of as associated with strength of the ego. There is a good deal of aggression, and perhaps even unethicality and destructiveness, implied in these items. There are at least some persons among the high scorers who are hostile and competitive, rebellious toward authority, opportunistic and manipulative, and sarcastic and cynical. If one thinks of a strong ego as one that is well integrated with a rational superego, then these persons might be considered to be improperly classified by the scale. To be brief about it, they appear to be manifesting more egoism than ego-strength.

The essential question here has to do with the existence and the management of aggression and hostility. Broadly speaking, hostility may be turned either inward, against the self, or outward, against objects. In an effective person, theory would hold, it is turned inward, in the service of the superego, to just the extent necessary for easy socialization; and outward, in the service of the ego, to just the extent necessary for the vigorous prosecution of one's own interests in gaining goods and prospering in life. Excesses in either direction would presumably characterize the weak ego. Extreme self-punishment, or, on the other hand, rampant hostility that draws retaliation, are both of them inefficient solutions in the management of aggression.

However, there is an economic consideration which must be borne in mind, and which may be crucial in explaining the present finding. Individuals differ in the amount of hostility and aggression that they carry about with them, and that it is the business of the ego to handle effectively. In persons with an excess of hostility, originating perhaps in more than the usual amount of frustration and disharmony in childhood, it might be expected that the question essentially resolves itself into this: will hostility be turned characteristically against the self, with the ego adopting a masochistic position in relation to the superego, or will the hostility be turned characteristically against objects other than the self?

The externally-directed aggressiveness which we have observed in some high scorers on *Es* might then be explained as an economic solution, and a mark of greater rather than lesser ego-strength, if indeed it can be shown that these persons were subjected in childhood to experiences of frustration and disharmony, more so than what one finds in other high scorers on the scale. Fortunately, there are some data that bear on this hypothesis and permit at least a partial check on it. Each person studied had been interviewed for two hours by a psychiatrist concerning his background, with particular attention to childhood history. The interviewer, at the conclusion of the study, then rated all subjects relative to one another, using a nine-point scale, on various psychiatric variables, including one called "Pathogenicity of Childhood." This was defined as "the presence in childhood of circumstances which commonly produce mental illness or psychological upset." (The interviewers, it should be mentioned, did not see the subjects at any time except during the interview, and knew nothing of objective test performances or of the assessment staff's reactions to the subjects.)

To check the hypothesis that "hostile" high scorers on *Es* had more pathogenic childhoods, average scores of each subject on the *Q*-sort items in Cluster II were determined. Then all subjects who had earned *T*-scores of 60 or more on the *Es* scale were ranked in terms of their Cluster II scores. This group consisted of 61 subjects. The top and bottom third of these (20 in each group, high Cluster II scorers being *more* aggressive and low scorers *less* aggressive) were now selected for comparison on life-history background factors, particularly the rating on Pathogenicity of Childhood. The latter comparison is presented in Table 10.1.

TABLE 10.1 *Comparison of High Ego-strength, High Aggressiveness Ss with High Ego-strength, Low Aggressiveness Ss on Ratings of Pathogenicity of Childhood*

	Subjects High on *Es*, Low on Aggressiveness (Cluster II)	Subjects High on *Es*, High on Aggressiveness (Cluster II)
Mean	4.4	5.8
S.D.	2.11	1.99
	$F = 4.45$	
	$p < .05$	

Considered in relation to the total sample, high scorers on both *Es* and Cluster II have had more pathogenic childhoods than the average subject, while persons who score high on *Es* but low on Cluster II have had less than the average amount of difficulty in childhood. The difference is statistically significant when the two groups are compared with one another. The interpretation seems justified that persons high on ego-strength, who nevertheless manifest considerable hostility toward others, are those who actually have more aggression in themselves to manage as a result of disturbing events in childhood.

Results supporting this interpretation are obtained when specific background information from the life-history interviews is considered. The interviewers, immediately upon the conclusion of each interview, used an "interview checklist" to record what they had learned of the subject and his background. The 267 checklist items were analyzed for differences between high *Es* scorers who were *high* and those who were *low* on Q-sort Cluster II. Thirty-three items showed differences significant at the .05 level. An overall description based on this analysis is given below, with the actual phrase from the significant checklist item given in italics.

Lows on Cluster II (Hostility and Aggression) were *warmer* in relating to the interviewer, were dressed both more *comfortably* and *inconspicuously*, and appeared to be both more *masculine* and more *reserved*. Highs were described as more *assertive*, more *self-assured*, and more *verbose*. Highs also appeared more *military* and held themselves *straighter*. As children, the Lows were *quieter* and tended more to *play with other boys*. The Highs were more *aggressive*, and their play was described as more *rough-and-tumble*. The Highs expressed *negative affect* toward their parents, while Lows had more *positive affect* and were more *dutiful* as children. The Lows were more often described as having had *stable* homes. The Highs, on the other hand, reported much more *family friction*. Highs describe their mothers more often as *practical*, while Lows describe their mothers as *warm* and *home-making*. No difference emerged in description of the father. In general, however, the Lows *idealized* their parents more. To the Lows, religion was *personally meaningful and important*, and they *spoke favorably of it* more often than did the Highs. Highs had more often been *separated* or *divorced* from their wives. Highs also had more frequently had *pre-marital intercourse* with their wives.

The overall picture from the life-history interview would seem to support the generalization that aggressiveness in persons of excellent ego-strength stems from life circumstances marked by relatively greater discord in the home during childhood and by friction in significant personal relations.

11

Rebelliousness, Morality, and Psychological Health

THE FIRST and most obvious consideration in the relationship of rebelliousness to morality and psychological health is one which by now has passed from iconoclastic protest to virtual stereotype. Nonetheless, it should not be disregarded. It is simply this: rebellion—resistance to acculturation, refusal to "adjust," adamant insistence on the importance of the self and of individuality—is very often the mark of a healthy character. If the rules deprive you of some part of yourself, then it is better to be unruly. The socially disapproved expression of this is delinquency, and most delinquency certainly is just plain confusion or blind and harmful striking out at the wrong enemy; but some delinquency has affirmation behind it, and we should not be too hasty in giving a bad name to what gives us a bad time. The great givers to humanity often have proud refusal in their souls, and they are aroused to wrath at the shoddy, the meretricious, and the unjust, which society seems to produce in appalling volume. Society is tough in its way, and it's no wonder that those who fight it tooth and nail are "tough guys." I think that much of the research and of the social action in relation to delinquency would be wiser if it recognized the potential value of the wayward characters who make its business for it. A person who is neither shy nor rebellious in his youth is not likely to be worth a farthing to himself nor to anyone else in the years of his physical maturity.

A second consideration which is certainly no news to most people, but which tends to get lost to psychologists who use phrases like guilt feelings, hostility, and anxiety, is that the healthy person psychologically is usually virtuous in the simple moral sense of the term. Psychologically healthy people do what they think is right, and what they think is right is that people should not lie to one another or to themselves, that they should not steal, slander, persecute, intrude, do damage willfully, go back on their word, fail a friend, or do any of the things that put them on the side of death as against life. This probably sounds like old-time religion, and in fact I am willing to be straightforwardly theological about this. I think there is an objective character to guilt, and when a person is false to his nature or offends against the nature of others then he is *in sin* and the place in which he has his existence is well described by the word "hell." I take "sin" here to be descriptive of the state of separation from the most basic sense of selfhood, or what some existentialist philosophers have called "the grounds of being." In whatever terms it is put, the fact is that a person is most alive and is functioning in such a way that *he knows who he is* and *you know who he is* and *he knows who you are* when his thoughts and actions are in accord with his moral judgment. The corollary is that when you do what you think is wrong you get a feeling of being dead, and if you are steeped in such wrongful ways you feel very dead all the time, and other people know that you are dead. There is such a thing as the death of the spirit. Many of the people whom we know as patients in our mental hospitals or as prisoners in our jails are in a condition of spiritual death, and their only hope is that someone can reach out to them, break through the walls of their isolation, *recognize* them. I think that too much has been made of the word love in this connection, for usually it connotes a feeling on the part of the person who is to give the love. The essence of the act of love as I understand it is the act of attention, and the affect that accompanies it in the person who is paying attention may be love, hate, sadness, or what have you. A real fight is an act of attention, a genuine condemnation is an act of attention, an understanding of final defeat is an act of attention. These as well as their positive counterparts are on the side of life, and the person who experiences them is in communication with other living beings and offers to them the possibility of community. The sort of philosophy of psychotherapy that prescribes blandness, nonjudgmentalness, and essential indifference on the part of the psychotherapist is simply a form of human debasement. Paying attention, caring, and being there yourself is all that counts.

Recall the research I described earlier on "psychotherapy as relationship." One of the therapists there was clearly an incompetent by all standards—AMA, APA, and probably the Bureau of Internal Revenue as well. Everything he did was wrong. After about six months of his residency, however, it became apparent that many of his patients were unaccountably getting better. Among his aberrant behaviors were such gross actions as telephoning a patient's foreman at work and telling him to stop bullying the patient, suggesting an unusual sexual technique to another patient whose wife was apparently frigid, and bluntly suggesting to a third patient that he should give up his job as an automobile repairman and get into the dispensing of food. The climax of the latter case was especially gruesome to the clinic, for the patient opened a doughnut shop of his own and on his final appointment appeared with a dozen doughnuts of his own making which he presented as a gift to the therapist, who without any insight at all offered them around to various other therapists and his supervisor, all of whom had difficulty swallowing them. Goodness knows I am not suggesting, in recalling the case of this incompetent fellow, that all psychotherapists go forth and do likewise, for he was he and we are we. But I will say that he was alive, even though so obviously misguided; to his patients, the only thing that was of consequence was that he cared about them and that he thought there was something different they could do which would be right.

12

The Crisis in Belief

THE WORD "crisis" is Greek in origin, and in that language its primary meaning is "decision." In medical pathology, a crisis is that point in the course of a disease at which a decisive change occurs, leading either to recovery or to death. In general, a crisis is a turning point, the end of one epoch and the beginning of another.

In speaking of "the crisis in belief," I refer to a point in the course of individual development at which the person must decide for himself whether the picture he has been given of the nature of the world is a true one. It is the point at which one is called upon to think for oneself about the important matters of cosmology and ethics. It is the time of decision about the meaning of life, the existence of God, the coerciveness of moral law, the place of man in nature, the freedom of the individual will, and all the other great issues with which philosophy deals.

Not all of us are philosophers, of course, but if we are human we must have a philosophy. Our intellect demands that experience should be accounted for; the need for things to be intelligible is a basic human need. Thus we are all, willy-nilly, philosophers of a sort, in the sense that we tell ourselves one story or another about most of the enduring issues with which systematic philosophy deals, and without which we cannot face life with any sense that it has meaning and worth.

The crisis in belief need not occur at any special age, and in fact it need not occur very conspicuously at all. For most people, however, it comes with adolescence, and it is ushered in partly by the challenge that the newly awakened and intense sexual and aggressive urges of puberty offers to morality and the civilized sexual code. It is a function as well, I think, of the growth of intelligence, which is beginning to reach full power concurrently with sexual maturation. It comes at that period when the mind, like the body, is getting ready to leave home in search of a new home of its own. Less dualistically, we may say that the maturing human form, freeing itself, under the push of natural development, of the habitat of its childhood, emerges into a new world in which it is no longer provided for and ministered to, but in which it must seek its own sustenance and meaning, and must choose anew for itself. With choice comes responsibility, self-valuation, and self-affirmation or self-rejection. The crisis in belief is often a time of categorical repudiation or total acceptance, of radical change or of rigid stasis. It is no exaggeration to say that it is a time of the greatest psychological danger, in which the integrity of the self is challenged, and in which old selves die and new selves are born.

As psychologists interested in the way in which psychological forms develop, and therefore, I shall add, intensely interested in the individual life, we "assessors" necessarily pay a great deal of attention to that part of the individual's history in which he was faced with a serious crisis of development. The work of assessment requires us to understand how a person came to his beliefs about the nature of the world and his own place in it, and how solidly founded and ready for action his philosophy of life really is. I need hardly say that in order to arrive at such an understanding we must not only inquire deeply into his beliefs on great issues, but must synthesize what we know of the nature and genesis of those beliefs with what we have been able to understand about his entire character and life history. Moral posture and beliefs about the cosmos are themselves frequently determined at least in part by psychodynamic forces, and a complete personality formulation gives an account not only of what actions our philosophy determines, but what forces our philosophy is determined by.

The study I shall describe in this chapter is focused primarily upon religious belief, and especially upon the adoption of atheism as one form of attempted resolution of the crisis in belief. My work on the psychology of philosophical beliefs has, however, been as a rule much more general in its scope and has attempted to deal with philosophical problems that have no necessary connection with a belief in supernatural beings. This research has concerned itself primarily with the psychological determinants of opinions on such philosophical questions as freedom-determinism, the problem of induction, and the rational justification of ethical prescriptions. I have sought to relate attitudes on these matters to such psychological events as the resolution of the Oedipus complex, the development of oral optimism or pessimism in the first two years of life, and prototypic images of good and evil consequent upon early experience and persisting as highly cathected complexes in the unconscious. The question of the existence of God is of course of central importance, in terms both of its implications for the nature of the objective world and of the psychological meaning of belief or disbelief in Providence, in heavenly justice and mercy, in life after death, and in the efficacy of prayer, and hence in the dependability of a benevolent supernatural power.

This research has been carried on by a combination of techniques, but with chief reliance being placed upon the intensive interview and upon the objective inventory method. An abbreviated example of the interview is given in Chapter 4, the case study of Paul. It was designed to elicit opinions and feelings about the philosophical problems mentioned above: freedom and determinism, theism, good and evil, and the like. The interviewer proceeded by posing certain questions or problem situations and asking for an analysis of them. One problem, for example, described the events leading up to a criminal action, in which the external and internal determinants of the person's behavior were made manifest. This problem served as the point of departure for a discussion of individual responsibility in affairs in which the individual appears compelled by forces within and without to act in an apparently irresponsible way. Another problem concerned a man shipwrecked alone on a desert island, with certain knowledge that he could never get off it. The question then was, could such a man, being part of no human community, do an evil action? This immediately led into the difficult problem of the locus of ethical sanctions, whether in society or in the individual, which in turn, of course, is central to the psychological problem of the internalization or externalization of the superego, with all its implications for the management of aggression and sexuality, and anarchic impulse in general.

Many other such problems were presented in the course of the interview, all of them with some hypothetical relevance to enduring philosophical issues. The general idea of assessing philosophical beliefs through the presentation of critical problem situations was later incorporated into a projective-type test, known, innocuously (as professional convention requires), as the Story Completion Test, in which the beginning of a story that clearly involves an ethical conflict is presented to the subject, and he is asked to complete the story as he thinks it would turn out. This test is scored both for sensitivity to the ethical issues involved and for relative internalization or externalization of the superego.

The chief inventory device used in these studies to supplement the interview is a test called the Inventory of Personal Philosophy. Developed in 1952, it has since been administered to more than 2,000 subjects, whose place of origin has included every state in the union and whose religious beliefs have included virtually every Christian denomination in America as well as Hinduism, Mohammedanism, Judaism, and varieties of atheism ranging from nihilism to the ambiguous denials and affirmations of emergent evolution. The Inventory includes a section on basic religious beliefs, another on social attitudes, a third on personal values and aspirations for oneself, and a fourth on preferences among well-known persons.

The section on religious beliefs contains four scales of a high degree of internal consistency. The scales are as follows: 1) Fundamentalist Belief; 2) Enlightened Belief; 3) Enlightened Disbelief; 4) Fundamentalist Disbelief.

The Fundamentalist Belief scale includes such affirmations as these: a) There is a God, and He is a person who is interested in each of us and hears our prayers; b) Human beings have a soul which survives the death of the body; c) Heaven and Hell are real places.

The Enlightened Belief scale contains these affirmations: a) I believe in God as a principle of order in the universe; b) Heaven and Hell are ideas or symbols rather than real places; c) Prayer brings spiritual comfort to individuals, whether or not each prayer is heard by God.

The Enlightened Disbelief scale contains such affirmations as the following: a) We cannot know for sure whether there is a God or not; b) Personal consciousness cannot continue after death, though there is a sort of immortality to men; c) The sum total of the reward and punishment we merit by our good or evil acts is paid over to us at the end of every moment of our existence.

The Fundamentalist Disbelief scale contains these assertions: a) There is no God; b) Heaven and Hell are lies invented by the clergy to control people; c) When the body dies, the person dies, and will never live again in any form; d) Organized religion is a racket; e) Prayer is a form of superstition and is degrading to the individual; f) There are no such things as good and evil.

Some information concerning the correlates of scores on these scales is available. One of the groups of subjects who took the inventory in the course of living-in assessment consisted of the previously mentioned 100 military officers, ranging in age from 27 to 49. They were seen in groups of 10 for three days of assessment at the Institute house, and they also took part in three days of group testing at the military installations in which they were based. Hence a variety of measures and ratings are available for correlation with the four belief scales I have described. It is not my intention to report the results of that study in detail here, but at least let me summarize briefly the correlation pattern for each scale. In doing so, I shall cite only those relationships that are significant at better than the .001 level of confidence (i.e., that would occur by chance on only one of 1,000 occasions).

FUNDAMENTALIST BELIEF

To begin with, fundamentalist belief was atypical of the officer sample as a whole. A measure of the consensus of opinion was obtained simply by constituting interest preference items that were selected by a majority of the officers into a single scale. This correlated —.38 with Fundamentalist Belief. Fundamentalist Belief is negatively associated with assessment staff ratings of Adaptive Flexibility and of Ability to Communicate. It is also negatively related to ratings of Integrity and Responsibility as a Commanding Officer. On the MMPI, the officers who scored lower on *Mf*, i.e., in the more masculine direction, tended also to get higher scores on Fundamentalist Belief. Such officers also scored lower on the Chapin Social Insight Test, on the Social Status scale of the California Psychological Inventory, and on an inventory measure of complexity of personality. To summarize: officers who expressed opinions of the fundamentalist sort were seen as less flexible, less able to communicate with others, and less able in command functions, and made scores indicating greater simplicity of personality structure and more pronounced masculinity. The sample as a whole, incidentally, was more masculine than the general population, so that extreme scores on masculinity in this group may have indicated a constricting amount of suppression of attitudes that are considered in this culture to be more permissible in women than in men.

ENLIGHTENED BELIEF

Enlightened Belief and Fundamentalist Belief are themselves highly correlated negatively, and so produce almost opposite correlational patterns. Enlightened Belief is associated most strongly with Integrity and Responsibility as a Commanding Officer, and it also correlates positively with the Self-assertiveness scale of the California Psychological Inventory and with the Self-maintenance scale of the same test. The Self-maintenance scale, incidentally, was developed against a criterion of duration of life among persons afflicted with tuberculosis; persons who express religious beliefs but of a relatively enlightened and nonfundamentalist sort are thus like those who are best chanced for life when stricken with an incapacitating disease. Enlightened Belief is also correlated positively with the *F* scale of the MMPI, and with a test measure of creativity based primarily on the Guilford creativity factor tests. The general picture is one of a strong personality, with internalized standards of right and wrong, ease of self-assertion and self-maintenance, and some degree of originality and ability to express minority opinions.

ENLIGHTENED DISBELIEF

Enlightened Disbelief correlates most highly with complexity of personality as measured by the inventory scale referred to above, and with the *F* scale of the MMPI. It also correlates positively with relative femininity of attitude as expressed in the MMPI *Mf* scale and with various measures of originality. Interestingly enough, it is also associated positively with *level of anxiety* as rated from the subject's handwriting by an expert in graphology. It goes along as well with the measures of Self-maintenance, Social Status, and Social Insight referred to earlier. In brief, the adult male who has arrived at opinions which can be described as enlightened disbelief in religion is one who is complex, original, relatively feminine, socially insightful and sophisticated, and withal rather anxious as well.

FUNDAMENTALIST DISBELIEF

Fundamentalist Disbelief, oddly enough—or perhaps not so oddly —has something in common with Fundamentalist Belief. Both scales are related negatively to staff ratings of Adaptive Flexibility. Fundamentalism in either direction thus appears to be associated with rigidity and lack of ability to adapt. Fundamentalist Disbelief also correlates negatively with the staff rating of Evaluation of Ideas and with intelligence as rated from handwriting by a graphologist. It is also negatively associated with the staff rating of fairmindedness. Thus the person who expresses extreme and angry disbelief in the claims of religion appears essentially rigid, prejudiced, and poor at evaluating ideas.

Neither the existence nor the nature of a crisis is readily inferred from inventory scores, of course, though in certain cases a certain pattern of scores will point clearly to internal arrangements of a turbulent sort. But in general what one has to do in this sort of assessment study in order to understand a person is to find out by interview just what happened when and with whom.

We have conducted this sort of inquiry retrospectively by interviewing alumnae of a college for women 25 years after their graduation from college, which does not give very exact data so far as the measurement of change is concerned, but which has the tremendous advantage of perspective over the years of maturity. Not all crises are over, of course, when one graduates from college, or even, I fear, when one has been out quite a long time. We certainly expect to find many of the graduating seniors still very much in a period of transition concerning basic beliefs and ideals, and indeed we were not surprised to find more than one of the distinguished long-gone alumnae in similarly unsettled states.

The alumnae, 50 in all, who presented themselves for study may be described as highly intelligent and highly educated women in the fifth decade of life, unusually stable and personally effective as a group, and generally of considerable importance in community affairs. I think it is fair to say that they tended to be unusually thoughtful persons who characteristically faced up to intellectual issues and required of themselves that they make sense out of life's puzzles. I describe them as highly educated not only because their undergraduate education took place in an institution whose tone in such matters is resolutely high, but because more than half of them went on to graduate work and almost all of them continued to educate themselves either by occasional courses of study, by travel, or by reading.

Of these 50 women, 7 said they were atheists. They were distinguished from the rest of the sample in a number of ways. To begin with, more of them were living alone and claiming to like it, four of them in totally unmarried bliss, and two others in a durable state of divorce. Several were strong supporters of feminism in the happy days when that "ism" was a suitable candidate for student support in girls' colleges. They were without exception notably devoted to *thinking* as a way of getting on in life; scholarship, science, logical analysis, intelligence as the touchstone of judgment—these were the values by which they lived. Whether because of native ability or because of special motivation, they scored much higher as a group on the intelligence test used in the study than did the rest of the sample. The test used was the Concept Mastery Test developed in the Terman study of gifted children, and the mean score of the confirmed atheists was 165, as compared with a mean of 135 for the rest of the alumnae sample and approximately 95 for the general population.

In one of the assessment procedures a curious correlation developed which perhaps should be attributed more to feminism than to atheism, but which has certain implications for ethics that warrant comment. The procedure was psychodrama, and the plot required the subject, who was cast as the worried wife of a husband whose consumption of alcohol had recently increased sharply, to respond to a house call from a close office friend, male, of the husband. The office friend was played by a "standard role player" who was a member of the assessment staff. He attempted, under the banner of solicitous friendship, to induce the wife to discuss her husband's private affairs with him, and he succeeded, whether husbands like the idea or not, in almost all cases. And the exceptions, who perceived the situation as one in which they were being asked to violate a confidential relationship, were not by any means the happily married women in the sample, but were instead numbered among the unmarried disbelievers.

There is one other noteworthy fact to report about the group of confirmed atheists. One might think that skepticism and rejection of religion would come about as a result of exposure to science and philosophy, or at any rate as a concomitant of higher education and the development of independent judgment. And as I have indicated, scientific thinking was one of the strongest values in the group of atheists. However, the general retrospective report of these women was that the crisis in their belief in God occurred between the ages of 14 and 16, and that it was in the nature of a sharp disillusionment and was accompanied by a terrible sense of loss. Several subjects reported remembering the moment when they suddenly thought to themselves that there was really no God after all. Two subjects spoke of tremendous emotional upset accompanying this; as one said, "I wept bitterly when I realized that it was all a lie." Another said, "Suddenly the hypocrisy of it all overwhelmed me." Although the data are too scanty to warrant any conclusion that could claim statistical support, I must say that I formed a strong impression from a scrutiny of the accompanying life history information, with the recurring circumstances of death or desertion by the father, that the crisis was an emotional (and perhaps sexual) as well as cognitive one, and that disappointment in the father and anger against him was the psychodynamic force that led to an affirmation of atheism. The atheistic claim that there is no God is essentially a denial of benevolent supernal power, as well as a repudiation of infantile wishes for love and for a staff of strength external to oneself. Whether or not the atheistic assertion is a true description of the objective world, it often reflects in the individual case a set of emotions that have arisen in relation to one's parents, and it can serve as a symbolic statement of one sort of attempted resolution of the Oedipus complex. In this sample, at any rate, atheism seemed to represent disappointment in the father, anger against him, repudiation of a need for his love, and affirmation of the self alone as sufficiently potent to carry on in life. Let me add that five of the seven women in this group who repudiated their need for a father at adolescence were later to pay for their independence at some length, for they entered psychoanalysis. Although it is obviously not a religion, psychoanalysis nevertheless furnishes its devotees with a dimly lit room, a periodic examination of conscience, a soothing acceptance of sin if not outright absolution, and a figure that sits comfortably at a somewhat higher level and can be construed as offering a chaste form of love and a dependable source of support.

I should perhaps mention that the atheism of these women was not phrased in the extreme manner of the items in the Fundamentalist Disbelief scale, for even those alumnae who were exceptional in this particular manner were much too urbane to be angrily cynical. They were more cool than hot in their disbelief. The assessment interviewers who wrote personality formulations of these subjects continually stressed their strong intellectual control, their emotional detachment, their lack of sexual expressiveness, and their marked need for autonomy, which to them meant solitariness. In terms of C. G. Jung's typology, these confirmed atheists tend to be introverted thinkers, with feeling being the inferior or undeveloped function and with energy characteristically invested in the subject rather than in the object. A nice question arises here as to whether the loss of a most important object at adolescence, as indicated in the repetition of the theme of abandonment by the father, gave rise to the introverted attitude, or whether an established introversion is more ready to perceive the object as unreliable and to interpret any absence as abandonment.

In addition to these confirmed atheists, there were five other subjects who described themselves as having once been convinced of the falsity of religious claims, but as having returned to religion after some years of disbelief. In these cases there is much more emphasis upon educational influences as leading to the initial disbelief. The first subject in this group is described by the interviewer as "no abstract thinker or worrier. She would follow popular feeling *in her set.*" She described herself as having become "agnostic" as a result of taking courses in comparative religion. After leaving college, however, she felt herself to be less agnostic than she had thought, and she eventually resumed church membership. Another of the subjects was described as having "no interest in abstract philosophy" by one interviewer, and by another interviewer as "not intellectual—a person with high social rather than theoretical values." She too began doubting "the basic tenets of the Christian religions" while studying comparative religion, but she finally decided to "resolve my feelings of doubt by choosing the most congenial religion of those available to me in practice." There is considerable emphasis in all five of these subjects upon adaptability, adjustment, reality-orientation, and integration.

Still another one of these five subjects is worth considering in some detail, for she was rated by the assessment staff as being exceptionally well adjusted, and indeed her life seemed agreeably proportioned, with secure community position, healthy and happy children, a professionally successful husband, and constructive social service activities through which she expressed something of her individuality and in which she felt worthwhile. This woman said that she decided to "drop" religion early in college, having reached the conclusion that it was "all a little too incredible." Chapel services were compulsory at the college at that time, and she always went to services, taking along "an interesting non-religious book" to read during the sermon. Shortly after graduation she married a man of exceptional eligibility in terms of the status symbols of that time and place, but with whom, she confessed, she was "not altogether in love." She had two children, and while they were "still very young" she began to feel quite unhappy, "always worn-out and cross." She began, she says, "looking around for a philosophy which would bring contentment." She found it in LeComte Nouey's book, *Human Destiny*, which she says enabled her to feel justified in returning to church membership and to religious belief. She now believes in a personal God, to whom she prays and in whom she finds support. Of her belief, she says, "It's satisfactory enough, and it fills a definite need. Sometimes I wonder, though, whether I just thought it all up to fill a gap in my life." She does not believe in the after-life. However, she says that her "unbelief" in this respect is "not complete or final; I may some day, in the future, come to believe in an after-life as well." The implication was that if she needed to believe it, she would believe it.

That she suspects that she has perhaps made rather too much of a good thing out of flexibility is indicated, however, in her T.A.T. stories, several of which communicate a sense of shallowness (as she sees it) and lack of profound meaning in her life. On Card 19, for example, she tells this story, which purports to deal with a single day in a girl's life, but which suggests the emotional tone of the subject's own life in its totality, as she perceives it.

> Virginia has had a thrilling day. She has had a good start on learning to ski. She emerged with no broken bones or even sprains, though she had a glorious day of climbing, sliding, leaping, staggering, and falling with her legs, skis, and ski poles all mixed up.
> The air was so clear, so wonderful—not as cold as all her friends had told her the horrid north would be. And how nice Johnny Evans was. So friendly, no more and no less. Everyone laughed a lot, and they the most of all.
> Better get ready, now! The day is by no means over. Square dancing tonight, with Johnny and all the others, then the long ride home, and serious business—job hunting again in a day or two.

"How silly I was," thought Virginia, "to be so childishly frightened about my luck up north. It's just like anywhere!"

But will Virginia find her grandfather's watch with the lost ruby of the Whitehall family? Or trace her friend Johnny's surprising ancestry? Read the December issue of *Bang* to find out!!!

This story, like all complex symbolic productions, may be interpreted at many levels of meaning. I find it most touching and poignant, and to interpret it is in some sense a shame. Yet: she tells us that she has emerged happily from the first years of a feared adulthood (the horrid north) with no damage done (no broken bones, or even sprains; in fact, it has been a glorious and exciting and lucky day up north). But, the day is not yet over; indeed, it is "by no means over." There are things not yet found out; Johnny, for instance, though he is so nice and so friendly (no more and no less) has a surprising ancestry (where did the beasts begin?). And then there is the lost ruby which should pass on from generation to generation, encased in a patriarchal time-piece (this jewel of sexuality, agent of transmission of the matter of life through the generations). And fear with it, that true generation has not passed through her, or seized her for its fulfillment. And the final sentence: "Read the December issue of *Bang* to find out": the sum of the tale. A "bang" is, of course, what one gets out of life, and December is the last issue of the year. The final crisis of selfhood is still before her, and the very facility of her adjustment seems to represent the greatest danger to her integrity. So far as religion is concerned, I feel that this woman would have evolved a very different interpretation of experience out her transitory atheism if she had had the courage to sound her own depths instead of accepting pragmatically what seemed to satisfy her immediate needs. As things stand, I believe that she perceives herself unconsciously as having forfeited profound experiences in the interest simply of facile adjustment. (Which is not to say that she is "right" in this self-perception; the story is a deeply experienced one.)

I should perhaps pause at this point to make it plain, if it is not already so, that we are not here concerned with the validity of religious beliefs in their cognitive aspect. Rather, we are concerned with the depth of feeling with which a cognitive belief is experienced, and with the question of integration or dissociation of such feelings in the structure of the self. Quite another aspect of this problem is the *deepening* of religious faith in persons who have not experienced doubt, but who have rather experienced semi-mystical confirmation, or even transfiguration, of their beliefs. Of this, we shall hear more in later chapters. In general, however, it should be noted that I am addressing myself to these problems as a psychologist interested in inner experience, and not as a philosopher interested in discerning the truth about the outer cosmos (if there can be such a true difference).

Speaking as a psychologist, then, what I find primarily in this group of subjects in both these ways of resolving the crisis in belief (i.e., in the atheistic resolution and in the repudiation of a transitory atheism in favor of a return to religion) is an acceptance of emotional polarities as being genuine oppositions which necessitate a choice between them. This slavery to the antinomies shows itself wherever repudiation is necessary to the maintenance of some way of living, whether it be in matters of private philosophy, religious belief, ethnic group-membership, affairs of the heart, allegiances to opposed scientific theories, esthetic preferences, or psychodynamic mechanisms. Rebellion is a form of submission, suppression of impulse is a form of expression, the refusal to choose is a form of choice, disbelief is a form of belief. Essentially what I think we have observed in these crises is not resolution at all, in the sense of establishment of a higher-level integration, but rather perpetuation of the conflict through acceptance of polarities as real, and deferment of the decision to a later point in life. The women who had indeed settled the crisis in belief (we shall hear of them shortly) communicated quite a different sense of selfhood from the cases we have considered, and they had much greater serenity and spontaneity, and freedom of both feeling and thought, in their make-up. I need hardly say that in the assessment of the strength of any personality it is most important to know what is settled and what is unsettled, which crises are past and which are present or still ahead.

13

Believing for Oneself

To FIND seven atheists or confirmed agnostics in a sample of fifty mature and well-educated women is probably unusual; certainly among the younger generation of women at this same college the percentage of announced doubters or disbelievers is much smaller. An actual count of the declared atheists or agnostics in the senior class of the college showed only 2½ per cent as opposed to the 14 per cent observed in their elders. But perhaps age has something to do both with atheism or agnosticism and with a truly personal and deeply experienced religious belief; most of the undergraduates appeared conventional in their patterns of belief, accepting religion largely for its social utility, while only about one-third of the alumnae could be so classified. More than half (27 out of 50) of the older women were deeply religious, and the content of their beliefs was highly various and often quite idiosyncratic. In this chapter we shall consider some of these varieties of self-evolved or self-reaffirmed beliefs, and their correlates in personality make-up.

Five main varieties of belief may readily be distinguished in this group of 27 women: a) transitory disbelief, with eventual return to a new form of religious affirmation with formal church affiliation; b) inner constancy of deeply experienced belief without a period of radical doubt; c) conscious and self-determined disbelief in any orthodox religious dogma, but with deep religious experience and formal church affiliation; d) change of sectarian affiliation based on conviction; e) idiosyncratic religious belief without church affiliation.

By way of communicating some concrete imagery of persons included in this broad category, a few excerpts from interviewer reports, both psychiatric and philosophic, will be given.

CASE NO. 1

Excerpt from the philosophy interview

A central theme in the esthetic preferences, and in the life as well, of this unmarried subject is expressed in her statement that she likes "either the very old and traditional and classical, or the very modern." In politics she is a conservative of the Winston Churchill variety, with great respect for individual rights and for law. Senator McCarthy was anathema to her, for example, chiefly because "he seems really to be against the law and the Constitution."[1] She is a Republican and a Presbyterian by choice, though a Congregationalist by social necessity: there is no Presbyterian Church in her community. The town in which she lives is indeed *her* community in a more special sense than it is anyone else's; she lavishes all her generous nurturant impulses on the village, and is a sort of unofficial city manager. She listed membership in some fifteen town committees, and, having used up all of the space on the Biographical Data Form given over to lists of committee memberships, she chose to list the remaining names in the space which was intended for the listing of children's names. She is not a committee woman in the usual sense of the term, however; she pointed out that *her* committees are committees that have responsibility for doing things, such as making sure that the state paves the town's roads properly, or working out an efficient sewer arrangement, or taking care of monuments in town, and so on. She is treasurer of many local groups, and appears to be quite canny in the use of money. She is independently wealthy.

Her present way of life is one of considerable personal freedom, for she does really as she likes; it contrasts markedly with the extremely formal and rigid social requirements which marked her early years. She never went alone on the streets, for example, until she was 31 years old; it was unthinkable that she should drive a car herself, the proper role of a lady being to direct the chauffeur; and one should not fraternize except with one's social and financial equals, of whom, unfortunately, there were very few.

When this subject was in college, she was something of a social isolate. She was then, and is now, somewhat lumpish and unshapen, and is not physically attractive. She says that she knows that the other girls thought of her as peculiar, and when she meets her classmates now she senses a rejection of her. However, she is returning in these latter years to a sense of participation in the college community, a part of her gen-

[1] The study was done in the summer of 1954.

eral pattern of freeing herself from the extreme imprisoning of her individuality which marked her youth.

The subject is strongly religious in the ethical sense; i.e., she believes deeply in rules of right conduct, especially those relating to honesty in personal relations. She doesn't much like the Congregational Church because it is "too shifty. They'll let you believe anything." She considers herself basically a Presbyterian, and regrets the fact that she is unable to attend a Presbyterian Church.

She likes to travel, and every year goes on a long journey to foreign places. She travels with a 76-year-old woman whom she likes very much: "with her, it's nothing given and nothing taken." Last year they went to Guatemala together. She says she didn't notice "the Communism," but what she did notice was the extreme poverty, and she thought something should be done about it.

This woman is an unusual combination; the traditionalist and formalist here meet with the innovator and breaker-down of barriers. She is, like her preferences in art, very classical and very modern.

CASE NO. 2

Excerpt from the philosophy interview

S is a Quaker, as her parents were and as her husband is. She is very active in the particular Quaker meeting of which she is a member, being the clerk, which is virtually the only office there. In telling of her function as clerk, she said that in Quaker business discussions there is no vote taken on matters of controversy, and it is the job of the clerk to get and communicate the sense of the meeting. This works, she says.

S says, "What I enjoy most about being a Quaker, and I do enjoy it, is the intellectual part as well as the religious." She mentioned some of the tenets of the Society of Friends: that there is something of God in everyone, that for this reason one should never kill another person, even in the name of society or one's nation or in the interests presumably of justice. She says there is no racial or religious prejudice among Quakers; she personally has no feelings of prejudice of any kind, and she has been surprised to discover that her children, who go to a public school, are becoming prejudiced against Catholics. She is inclined to think it may be some passing local irritation in the school system itself.

S speaks of the absence of ostentation and display in the Quaker religion. She finds it very simple, and most congenial to her. She likes the custom of sitting silently in meeting, and of speaking only if one feels like it. She has never spoken in meeting.

Concerning the prevalence of racial prejudice, especially in some of the social circles in which she moves and the clubs she belongs to, she remarked that she always speaks her mind if the issue comes up, and that she would resign if any organization of which she is a member were to adopt the principle of excluding Jews, Negroes, etc.

Concerning loyalty oaths, she said, "Quakers don't take oaths, period."

She herself is not a pacifist, nor is her husband; he was a military officer during the war. She thinks it is unnecessary for Quaker youths to refuse to register for the draft; they should register, she thinks, and seek a non-combat assignment on grounds of principle.

S reads a very great deal, and likes "long books rather than short ones." She particularly likes history, mentioning the Golden Warrior series and Prescott's works on the Conquest of Mexico and Peru. Gibbon she intends to read before she dies, she said.

S's tastes in reading are quite catholic. She thinks of herself as having read almost everything. This includes Sears and Roebuck catalogues, she remarks. She has read a good deal of poetry, and last year re-read all of Browning. She didn't like it on second reading. She likes few of the modern poets, Dylan Thomas being an exception. She mentioned "The Screwtape Letters" as being especially enjoyable to her. In the Bible she likes the Psalms best, and knows most of them by heart. She likes them, she says, because "they are poetry and were written in the open air on a hillside."

S talked at some length about mystical experiences, saying that she had done several papers on this topic. She spoke especially of Indians in Haiti who use peyote to induce mystical communion. Elsewhere she had spoken admiringly of the description in Prescott of the battle fought by the Indians in Mexico City against the invading Spaniards. She also spoke of the Jamaicans and their religious trances, which are preceded by a physical frenzy. In this connection she spoke again of the Quaker silences. She thinks everyone should be silent at special times.

S was quite unusual in bearing and demeanor, and in her manner of talking. She spoke in a very low and even tone, and everything she said seemed to come up from depths. She was completely lacking in social front.

CASE NO. 3

Excerpt from philosophy interview report:

S belongs to the Episcopalian Church, as did her parents, but she does not believe in religious dogma of any kind. "God exists in all things, and is the principle of organization of the entire universe. The intelligibility of experience induces awe, and that is the essence of worship and reverence for God. As for spirit conceived of as something distinct from matter rather than as matter's form, it does not exist; there are no spirits in the usual sense. There is no human existence apart from the human body and brain; we die as individuals, and never live again. The knees are not to be used for praying on; contemplation of things is what prayer should properly be."

These opinions S delivers in very terse and epigrammatic fashion, almost in dots and dashes; a full sentence rarely escapes her lips.

S generally votes Democratic, although she can hardly be said to have any political affiliation; as in religion, she accepts no dogma. She is an unstereotyped liberal, a small-d democrat to the core. She represents herself as totally disenchanted, but hopeful. She goes to considerable lengths to avoid pious utterance, whether in relation to religion or political values.

CASE NO. 4

Excerpt from philosophy interview report:

S is unorthodox so far as religious dogma is concerned—"God is an anachronism, and there is certainly nothing remotely resembling Heaven or Hell, angels or devils, or resurrection in any form"—but she describes herself as very much attracted by "the cult of Christianity if not the creed." This recently led her to become confirmed in the Episcopalian Church—and she says that she would really like to join the Catholic Church—"the symbolism is much more profound." She is entirely pessimistic concerning human nature—"Our basic aim is to devour one another" and she feels that eventually human kind will destroy itself. Furthermore, she thinks this conclusion is not far off. She takes a dim view of the achievements of science, although she thinks it is "as entertaining as art, really." Her interest is in scientific *theory*, not in "gadgets."

S takes the role of debunker, and has a sharp wit to make her cynicism stick. She debunks and scorns even the things that she most admires. She spoke some harsh words about Greek literature, art, and science, though in other contexts it seemed evident that she greatly admired the Greeks.

CASE NO. 5

Excerpt from psychiatric interview report:

A very thoroughly resolved and integrated person who has made a career of questioning herself and learning from her own experiences. . . . She realizes that the fact that she is single may conceal some unresolved point, but she doesn't think so; I get the impression that she has devoted much time and thought to this point. She's highly effectively sublimated and knows it.

Excerpt from philosophy interview report:

This S seems to have a more deeply felt inner need for religion than do most of these subjects, who are usually content to be fairly conventional in their final views, even when they are serious believers. The quest for religious meaning has been a central theme in her life, and has led her to become, as she says, "a Hindu without congregation." As she explains Hinduism, it is a religion which frees the individual from conflict by resolving such opposites as good-evil, sickness-health, birth-death, body-mind, in higher syntheses, so that these things are finally seen as being aspects of truly unified functions. She feels that Christianity always accepts these opposites as real contradictions, and tries to get rid of one or the other side of the contradiction in order to feel peace in the soul; but, she says, although by some sort of "technical discipline" you can reduce the salience of one of the opposites (she used the example of patience and impatience, and training oneself not to be impatient), in spite of the control which is thus achieved there remains a hidden subterranean conflict which may revive itself at crucial times. In Hinduism, however, she feels that one goes entirely beyond moral considerations to a condition in which good and evil are perfectly natural and morally indifferent. She says she has talked with Christians about this, and they usually cannot understand it. "But I've never heard a good explanation from a Christian as to how it is that a benevolent and merciful God permits evil to exist, and by Christian standards the world is full of evil," says she. She also points out that the best-organized wars have been fought by Christian nations after twenty centuries of enlightenment. Finally, she says that Hinduism can perfectly understand and embrace Christianity, but Christianity is bound to reject Hinduism, and that fact in itself is proof enough that Hinduism as a religion is superior.

In speaking of the Christian error of fighting evil, S used an analogy from dairy farming. When you plant a field with clover, and weeds spring up, you make a mistake if you go about pulling up the weeds; it is better to feed the clover, so that it will win the field for itself. So also is it better to cultivate the good, she says, and leave the rest to natural processes of growth. A Hindu parable by an erstwhile Congregationalist.

From this interview material one gains the following impressions of subjects who are classified as experiencing deeply a personally evolved or personally reaffirmed religious belief:

1) They seem to be rather creative individuals who sound their own depths and who are willing to embark on perilous self-examination and scrutiny of important questions in the interest of inner truth.

2) They are individualists, being original not only in their way of

thinking but in their way of being themselves. Insofar as they belong to easily recognized categories of belief, they belong with a difference: a non-pacifist Quaker, a Hindu without congregation, a recently confirmed Episcopalian who states that "God is an anachronism."

3) They are notably self-reliant, and they seem to have a quite well-integrated even though idiosyncratic personal identity.

The assessment variables that are correlated significantly with mem-

TABLE 13.1 *Assessment Variables Associated Significantly with Personally-Determined Religious Belief*

Summary Description of Cluster	Names of Variables	*r*
	Barron Ratings: (scale)	
	Autonomy	.38
	Introception	.39
	Internalized morality	.35
Inner-directedness, independence, growth-orientation	Originality	.34
	Capacity for further growth	.36
	Movement towards autonomy	.29
	Valued college for: new philosophy of life	.46
	Measures:	
	Independence of judgment	.42
	Ratings:	
	Self-insight	.43
	Life *diversified*	.30
	Complexity	.41
	Social perceptivity	.37
	Gratification of needs	.37
	Extent of life space	.40
	Self-awareness	.35
	Ability to accept anxiety	.34
Ego-strength, basic soundness as well as richness of personality, psychological health	Awareness of others	.39
	Affection towards parents	.46
	Happiness in childhood	.38
	Likeableness	.43
	Social insecurity	—.29
	Repression of childhood memories	—.31
	Staff role nomination: care of children	.32
	Staff role nomination: marriage counselor	.45
	Staff role nomination: companion	.36
	Naturalness	.29
	Emotional life ordered to reality	.29

TABLE 13.1 (*Continued*)

Summary Description of Cluster	Names of Variables	*r*
	Measures:	
	CPI: Flexibility	.31
	Ratings:	
	Aesthetic appreciation	.48
	General intellectual capacity	.36
	Value placed on intellectual activity and achievement	.32
	Meets this college's expectations: intellectually	.39
Positive valuation of intelligence, aesthetics	Meets this college's expectations: aesthetically	.45
	Meets this college's expectations: morally	.41
	Meets this college's expectations: ideologically	.44
	Organizes experience: intellectually	.34
	Organizes experience: aesthetically	.30
	Organizes experience: practically	—.35
	Tender-mindedness	.32
	Measures:	
	CPI:Hr (motivation for high-level academic achievement)	.36
	Ratings:	
	Orientation to status	.31
	Achievement of security through mastery, control, manipulation	.35
High social status, desire for status, community leadership potential	Staff role nomination: citizens' committee leader	.35
	Staff role nomination: labor-management mediator	.30
	Staff role nomination: representative, state legislature	.38
	Staff role nomination: refugee camp	.40
	Staff role nomination: warden, women's prison	.31
	Measures:	
	CPI: Social Status scale	.33
Absence of authoritarianism or implicit anti-democratic trends	*Ratings:* Authoritarianism	—.33
	Measures: F scale	—.28

bership in this group are shown in Table 13.1. (The correlation coefficients are biserial r's.)

It is noteworthy that in some ways the subjects who hold to a personally evolved religious belief are similar to the group of atheists and agnostics, while in other ways they are distinctly different. The ways in which they are similar are in their relatively high valuation of the thinking processes and of intellectual achievement, and in the absence of ethnocentrism or authoritarianism in their make-up; the ways in which they are different are in their robust psychological health, their genuine independence, originality, and growth-orientation, and in their relatively high degree of desire for positions of community leadership and status, as contrasted with the degree of social isolation and preference for going-it-alone which marked the radically skeptical group.

From the correlational data shown in Table 13.1 and from the clinical impressions gained from interview material, the following formulation of the underlying psychological process in the evolvement of a really personally-integrated religious belief is suggested.

To begin with, there is a good deal of psychological strength in these subjects, whatever their troubles may be. They are able to take account equally of the inner and the outer in experience; while they are highly introceptive and have much self-insight, they are also socially perceptive and are able to use techniques of manipulation and mastery in relation to the environment in order to achieve security and to attain gratification of the needs which the culture itself defines as gratifiable. They are both self-aware and aware of others. Their life experience is broad as well as deep. While they have had happy childhoods and feel very affectionate toward their parents, they at the same time are capable of experiencing considerable anxiety, for they do not utilize repression to deal with unpleasant memories or affects, but rather face things as they are, including their feelings and impulses. They are complex rather than simple psychodynamically, and they admit new experiences into their perceptual systems even at the cost of insoluble contradictions. The ability to do this is based in part on one's faith that one can finally achieve a synthesis, that reality ultimately makes sense and that one can oneself discern that sense. Most important, as a result of this pattern of attributes, the person has great capacity for further growth, which involves somehow being able to leave oneself behind, to shed old coats, to molt, to metamorphose, to find a new order of selfhood in obedience to internal demands for change.

This capacity for self-renewal is related to the whole problem of precocity and retardation in the formation of the self; it is of the greatest importance in the psychology of individual development. It involves the way in which a person places himself in the time span which is defined by *himself as process*. The most distinctive characteristic of the self is its unceasing growth and change within the matrix of sameness given by memory. Memory seems to make the self timeless even while it presents to reflection the evidence for the irreversibility of all that has occurred.

The extent to which a person acts in the present seems to me an index of whether the self is perceived as continuing to evolve or perceived as static and essentially no longer alive. My guess is that perception of the self in relation to time is most crucial in determining attitude towards biological death, as well as the very experience of dying, which surely must show as much variation among people as does their experience of living.

What this means in terms of religious belief is that belief is not dogma, not a set of forever-prescribed particularities, not static abstraction at all, but a formative process with faith as its foundation and vision as its goal—faith in the intelligibility and order of the universe, leading through necessary difficulties of interpretation and changing meanings to moments of spiritual integration which are themselves transient.

14

Independence of Judgment

Oₙₑ of the psychological measures that proved to be significantly associated with the evolvement of a deeply felt personal philosophy was, as we have seen in the preceding chapter, independence of judgment. This measure itself was developed by a special study of the personality correlates of independence of judgment in an experimental social situation. The specific content of the test itself, as well as details of the experiment, are of considerable psychological interest and are of direct relevance to much of the research on creativity which shall concern us later in this volume. In this chapter we shall present the results of the study of independence, and as we did earlier in discussing test results and scale development we shall attempt to include an appropriate amount of technical detail.

The experiment itself is the work of Solomon Asch of Swarthmore College. He designed a group-interaction procedure in which individual subjects were put under considerable implicit pressure from their peers to agree with an erroneous group opinion. Asch studied several hundred subjects with this technique or experimental variations of it, and he has drawn a number of general conclusions concerning basic processes in the interaction between individuals and groups.

Here, however, we shall be concerned only indirectly with social process and the forces at work in the situation; our main interest is in personality differences between groups of subjects who responded in very different manners to the experimentally produced conflict.

THE PROTOTYPICAL EXPERIMENT

The basic experimental technique employed in this series of studies has been to place an individual in a relation of radical conflict of judgment with all the other members of a group and to express quantitatively certain aspects of his mode of resolution of the conflict. Disregarding for the moment the many experimental variations of the technique which were explored, we may describe the prototypical situation as this: there are from 8 to 16 ostensible subjects, only one of whom, however, is naïve; the rest conspire with the experimenter to produce the crucial conflict situation. The apparent experimental task is to judge which of three lines of variable length meets a standard line; or, to state it otherwise, to match the length of a given line with one of three other lines which are themselves not equal to one another. The subjects announce their judgments publicly, one at a time. The naïve subject is so placed that he will always be one of the last respondents. On the critical trials, the hired majority give a prearranged false answer. On such trials, to agree with group opinion is to *yield;* to give the correct response is to be *independent.* Since there are 12 critical trials, the experimental variable, Yielding, may take a value from zero to 12; zero Yielding is known as Independence.

Approximately 25 per cent of all subjects studied showed independence; at the other extreme of the distribution, 25 per cent of all the subjects yielded from 8 to 12 times. These two quartiles, numbering 92 subjects, were selected for intensive study and comparison.

All the subjects in the present study were male college students. They were drawn randomly with respect to major field of interest. They averaged slightly under 20 years in age, and they were generally at the third-year level of college training.

Two main sorts of descriptive tasks were taken as the aim of this investigation: (1) a description of Independent and Yielders, considered as groups, in terms of common traits; (2) a description of group differences on variables which recommended themselves on specific theoretical grounds as being related to the criterion behavior. They will be reported on in that order.

DIFFERENCES IN SELF-CONCEPTION

A simple way to begin the task of describing groups of persons whom you do not know individually is to ask them to describe themselves. Such a self-description, of course, may not correspond closely to the description that would be given by a thoroughly objective observer, but at the very least it reveals something of the subject's self-conception.

The procedure employed here has already been described: the Gough Adjective Check List, which, in the form used, consisted of 279 common, personally descriptive adjectives, listed in alphabetical order. The subject is asked to check those adjectives which he believes would correctly characterize himself, and, having been guaranteed anonymity, he is encouraged to be as candid as he possibly can in his self-evaluation. He is permitted to check as many or as few adjectives as he wishes.

The self-descriptions of Independent subjects were now compared with those of Yielding subjects by the standard item-analysis technique. The percentages of subjects in each group checking a given adjective were determined, their differences found, and the significance of the difference computed. From this analysis (based on N's of 43 in each group) the adjectives shown in Table 14.1 emerged.

TABLE 14.1 *Self-descriptions of Independents and Yielders*

	Checked more frequently by Independents	Checked more frequently by Yielders
at the .01 level:	artistic emotional original	determined efficient kind obliging optimistic patient
at the .05 level:	demanding excitable forgetful fair-minded idealistic logical mischievous moody rational reckless tactless	affected appreciative considerate dignified enthusiastic friendly helpful humorous mannerly modest stable tactful wise

The self-descriptions of the Independents seem to involve these factors:

(1) a certain positive valuation of intellect and cognitive originality, as well as a spirit of open-mindedness (logical, rational, original, idealistic, fair-minded);

(2) a high degree of personal involvement and emotional reactivity (emotional, excitable, moody);

(3) a lack of social ease, or an absence of the commonly valued social virtues (tactless, reckless, forgetful, mischievous).

The Yielders, on the other hand, most consistently attribute to themselves:

(1) ease and helpfulness in interpersonal relations (kind, obliging, appreciative, considerate, enthusiastic, friendly, helpful, tactful);

(2) personal effectiveness and planfulness in achieving some goal (determined, efficient, patient, wise);

(3) personal stability and healthy-mindedness (stable, optimistic, humorous, modest, dignified).

Some of them, however, confess a certain lack of spontaneity in this (12 Yielders checked "affected," as against 4 Independents). But the self-described "affected" Yielders are still a minority of the Yielders; the adjectives with which almost all of the Yielders characterize themselves are "helpful," "kind," and "obliging."

PERSONAL STABILITY

As we have indicated, Yielders tended, to a significantly greater degree than did Independents, to describe themselves as personally stable and healthy-minded. With regard to such a dimension, however, it seemed advisable to use, in addition to the Adjective Check List, a standardized test in which the testimony of the subject regarding himself had already been thoroughly studied against some objective, behavioral criterion. Such a test is the Minnesota Multiphasic Personality Inventory. The unique virtue of the Multiphasic, from this point of view, is that self-testimony is not accepted at face value; it is evaluated in terms of known nontest correlates, empirically established, of the test behavior. The most thoroughly studied dimensions are those relating to psychological morbidity.

Independents and Yielders were first compared on all of the usual clinical and validity scales of the test. No significant group differences were found.

Several other kinds of comparisons were made, using various MMPI indices and special scales designed to measure pathological trends. One such comparison consisted of scoring the records on the General

Maladjustment Scale devised by Welsh.[1] A similar index was obtained by evaluating each profile for the total amount of deviation from the mean on all of the clinical and validity scales. Still another measure consisted of summing the scores on F, Sc, Pa, and Ma; this was taken to be an index of subclinical psychotic trends (based on an unpublished cluster analysis of the MMPI by Alvin Scodel of Ohio State University).

None of these measures revealed a significant difference between Independents and Yielders. On the basis of these results, one would conclude that the two groups are about equal in personal stability, in spite of the greater tendency of Yielders to characterize themselves by adjectives which usually are taken to be related to stability.

INDEPENDENCE AND A LIKING FOR COMPLEXITY

Certain theoretical considerations led to the hypothesis that Independents would be more likely than Yielders to be able to deal comfortably with complex, apparently contradictory phenomena. In order to remain independent in this experiment, the subject must come to terms with the troublesome fact that he is suddenly at odds with his fellows in a situation where, by ordinary standards of community of experience, he ought to be in agreement with them. Only a person who can live with complexity and contradictions and who has some confidence that order lies behind what appears to be confusion would be able to bear this kind of phenomenal discord. There is a strong temptation to resolve the confusion in a simple way, by denying the most easily denied of the contradictory facts. Order is thus achieved by a process of exclusion of phenomena, and, in this case, at the cost of correct judgment.

We shall be getting a bit ahead of our story at this point, since the development of a test measure of relative preference for simplicity or complexity is described in detail in a later chapter. Suffice it to say now that these studies have shown that persons may be ordered reliably on a dimension defined by their preferences for relative degrees of complexity and simplicity in figures. The dimension itself was

[1] Welsh, G. S. & Dahlstrom, G., *Basic Readings in the MMPI in Psychology and Medicine* (University of Minnesota, 1957).

identified by Welsh[2] through a factor-analytic procedure, and a factor-test was developed by Welsh and the present writer. It is a scale of the Welsh Figure Preference test and consists of 62 line drawings in black ink on 3x5 inch white cards. The subject is asked to indicate whether he likes or does not like each drawing. The test is so scored that liking the complex figures and disliking the simple ones earns the subject a high score.

The correlates of this factor, as we shall see later, ramify through many areas of human behavior, including interpersonal relations and personal psychodynamics, politics and economics, religion, relations to authority, attitude toward sensual experience, social conformity and adherence to tradition, and originality. A liking for the complex figures is related negatively to rigidity, constriction, social conformity, subservience to authority, politico-economic conservatism, and ethnocentrism; it is related positively, however, to originality, verbal fluency, expression as opposed to repression of impulse, and to cathection of intellectual activity.

It seemed a reasonable hypothesis that a preference for the complex figures would be associated with independence of judgment as well. The test (known now as the Barron-Welsh Art Scale) was therefore given to the subjects in this study. The means and sigmas of the scores on this measure for the two groups are presented in Table 14.2.

Since an hypothesized relationship was under test, the one-tailed test of significance was appropriate. As the table shows, the hypothesis that Independents would prefer complex figures to a greater extent than Yielders would do so was confirmed at the 1-per-cent point.

TABLE 14.2   *Relationship of Preference for Complexity to Independence of Judgment*

	N	Mean	Sigma
Independents	46	20.41	12.85
Yielders	44	16.75	13.89

$t = 2.54$ (88 d.f.)
Significant at the 1-per-cent point

Thus independence of judgment in this particular experimental situation must be included in the general constellation of factors

[2] Welsh, G. S., *A Projective Figure Preference Test for Diagnosis of Psychopathology; 1. A Preliminary Investigation*, Unpublished Ph.D. thesis, University of Minnesota, 1949.

which go along with preference for complex figures. It is of some interest that the adjectives with which Independents describe themselves, such as "artistic" and "original," denote qualities which in other samples have been shown to be related to a preference for complexity. This provides some basis for belief in the accuracy of the self-descriptions given by the Independents on the adjective list.

A CRITERION-SPECIFIC QUESTIONNAIRE

What very often happens when one makes a psychological analysis of a significant bit of behavior is that a sort of theoretical "apperception-mass" is activated, and the process of analysis actually consists in classifying the many concrete images that come to mind. While this may eventuate in a formal and general hypothetical statement for which a rigorous test can be found, it often happens that the theoretical formulation remains tentative and couched in concrete imagery which hardly deserves the name of scientific hypothesis. Such guesses may nevertheless be quite valuable, and to a certain extent can be put to the test by the construction of questionnaires that embody the psychologist's hunches.

Such techniques, while they seem to call for self-report, need not do so naïvely. The guess that an item represents, for example, may be that a certain kind of person will in the testing situation assent to a certain kind of sentence; it need not matter whether the subject is reporting correctly on his own experience or actual opinions, since the guess made by the psychologist takes the situational context into account. Items may be written with different degrees of clarity or ambiguity of meaning, and it is possible to embody considerable projective elements in a seemingly objective questionnaire.

With these considerations in mind, we brought together some 200 sentences or items, each of which was thought to relate to the personality variables determinative of independence of judgment. Most of these items were written anew, but others were culled from such sources as Murray's "Explorations in Personality," the E, F, and PeC scales of the California Public Opinion Study, and scales developed at the Institute of Personality Assessment and Research to measure such variables as Originality and Personal Soundness.

With Asch collaborating, this list was then cut down to 84 items, each one representing a clearly formulated guess by the experimenters concerning the personality characteristic that ought to go along with independence of judgment.

The questionnaire was then administered to the subjects along with the rest of the tests reported here, and the answer sheets were scored on the a priori Independence scale, each response in the hypothesized Independent direction contributing a single point to the total score. The results are presented in Table 14.3.

TABLE 14.3 *Relationship of Scores on A Priori Independence Questionnaire to Independence and Yielding in the Experiment*

	N	Mean	Sigma
Independents	43	43.58	8.06
Yielders	42	38.97	9.35

$t = 2.439$ (83 *d.f.*)
Significant at the 1-per-cent point

As the table shows, the test as a whole discriminated the groups in a statistically significant manner, suggesting some validity for the overall theoretical formulation. In order to discover what particular items discriminated most effectively, an item analysis (43 Independents vs. 43 Yielders) of the scale was carried out.

Of 22 items that showed differences significant at the .05 point or better, 20 were in the hypothesized direction, again indicating the general correctness of the theory. The discriminating items are given below, with the Independent direction of response in the parentheses after the items.

At the .01 level:

1) What the youth needs most is strict discipline, rugged determination, and the will to work and fight for family and country. (False)

2) Some of my friends think that my ideas are impractical, if not a bit wild. (True)

3) Kindness and generosity are the most important qualities for a wife to have. (False)

4) I have seen some things so sad that I almost felt like crying. (True)

5) I don't understand how men in some European countries can be so demonstrative to one another. (False)

6) I must admit that I would find it hard to have for a close friend a person whose manners or appearance made him somewhat repulsive, no matter how brilliant or kind he might be. (False)

7) A person should not probe too deeply into his own and other people's feelings, but take things as they are. (False)

8) I prefer team games to games in which one individual competes against another. (False)

9) I could cut my moorings—quit my home, my family, and my friends—without suffering great regrets. (True)

At the .05 level:

10) What this country needs most, more than laws and political programs, is a few courageous, tireless, devoted leaders in whom the people can put their faith. (False)

11) I acquired a strong interest in intellectual and aesthetic matters from my mother. (False) (Contrary to hypothesis)

12) Human nature being what it is, there will always be war and conflict. (True) (Contrary to hypothesis)

13) I believe you should ignore other people's faults and make an effort to get along with almost everyone. (False)

14) The best theory is the one that has the best practical applications. (False)

15) I like to fool around with new ideas, even if they turn out later to be a total waste of time. (True)

16) The unfinished and the imperfect often have greater appeal for me than the completed and polished. (True)

17) I would rather have a few intense friendships than a great many friendly but casual relationships. (True)

18) Perfect balance is the essence of all good composition. (False)

19) Science should have as much to say about moral values as religion does. (True)

19) The happy person tends always to be poised, courteous, outgoing, and emotionally controlled. (False)

21) Young people sometimes get rebellious ideas, but as they grow up they ought to get over them and settle down. (False)

22) It is easy for me to take orders and do what I am told. (False)

At this point it might be well to set down some of the notions that guided the investigator in the construction of this questionnaire and that to a certain extent have been borne out by the results. These notions are:

1) Independents value creative work, in others and in themselves. They are receptive to new ideas, even apparently impractical ones, and are more interested in the originality or aptness of an idea or theory in describing reality than in its possible practical applications. (Relevant items are numbers 2, 14, and 15.)

2) Independents place particular value upon the person as an individual, and respond more to the inward integrity of another person than to superficially pleasing characteristics. (Items 3, 6, 17, 20.)

3) Independents are independent. They are not fond of taking

orders, or integrating with the group, or getting along with everyone, and they don't subscribe to the notion that rebellion in youth is to be indulged because, after all, young people *will* be rebellious before settling down sensibly. (See items 22, 8, 13, 21.) They do not particularly value strict discipline or tireless and devoted leadership as an alternative to law. (Items 1 and 10.)

4) Independents tend to be in communication with their own inner life and feelings and are intraceptive rather than extraceptive. They have empathy. (Items 4, 5, 7.)

5) Independents like some uncertainty and do not respond favorably to polish and perfection. They prefer imperfections and contradictions which challenge the understanding and call for imaginative completion by the observer. (Items 16 and 18.)

It should be noted at this point that the questionnaire is oriented almost exclusively toward the virtues of Independents, or at least toward the qualities that Independents would consider virtues. The virtues of Yielders are not to be found here, nor are the more unpleasant characteristics of Independents. Indeed, it is evident from the design of the experiment itself that the kind of social conformity known as Yielding is achieved at the cost of abandoning the evidence of one's own senses, which would seem to be carrying a good thing (i.e., agreeableness) rather too far. It is clearly better to be independent; and good or bad behavior is what the experiment seems designed to elicit.

This is all by way of pointing out that the experimenters approved of Independence as opposed to Yielding. There is nothing irregular about this, since it is the rule rather than the exception that scientific investigators take sides on the questions that they study. Since this particular question is intimately bound up with social values, however, the experiment becomes especially sensitive to bias; it deserves special scrutinizing for errors in design which would result in incorrect conclusions. The criterion-specific questionnaire probably contains such bias in its construction, a fact that would be kept in mind in interpreting the results.

15

Simplicity and Complexity in Personality

A_T the outset of this series of inquiries we suggested that psychological health, when most elegantly embodied in any individual, reflected true simplicity of expression of a highly complex set of cognitions, feelings, and intentions. The relationship between simplicity and complexity in personality is itself a complex one. Perhaps we shall not be able to arrive at a simple expression of the relationship, but we may be able to advance the matter somewhat by considering the research results that emerged from a first attempt to study objectively the correlates of preferences for the simple as opposed to preferences for the complex.

This investigation began with the construction of a new sort of psychological test, consisting, as we have said, of several hundred line drawings in black ink on 3x5 inch white cards. Its author, George S. Welsh, then of the University of Minnesota, intended it as a nonverbal psychiatric diagnostic instrument—essentially, a nonverbal form of the Minnesota Multiphasic Personality Inventory. He sought, therefore, to develop scales to measure such variables as Hysteria, Depression, Schizophrenia, Paranoia, and so on. The subject was asked to indicate for each figure whether he liked it or did not like it, and thus to sort the drawings into two groups according to his preferences.

The effort to develop a diagnostic instrument is still in progress, but did not immediately meet with success. In seeking to understand the nature of the preferences being expressed, however, Welsh carried out a factor analysis of various scales defined on the basis of his own judgment as to the stimulus-character of the drawings: e.g., bilaterally symmetrical figures, three-dimensional figures, figures with many projections, figures with few projections, ruled-line drawings, free-hand drawings, angular figures, curved figures, and so on.

From this analysis, two factors emerged: an acceptance-rejection factor (expressing the general tendency of the subject either to like or to dislike the figures), and a second, bipolar factor, orthogonal to the first, whose poles, as determined by inspection of the figures, seemed to be simplicity (combined with a rather obvious, bilateral symmetry) and complexity (usually associated with a much less obvious kind of balance, or even asymmetry).

This latter factor bears a close resemblance to that earlier identified by Hans Eysenck, and named by him the *K* factor. Eysenck has demonstrated for a number of stimulus classes (colors, odors, paintings, polygons, poetry) the existence not only of a general factor of esthetic appreciation, but of a secondary, bipolar factor as well. The second factor presents the same polar opposition noted by Welsh, one pole being represented by preference for the simple polygon, the strong, obvious odor, the poem with the obvious rhyming scheme and the definite, unvarying, simple rhythm, and the simple, highly unified picture; at the other pole is preference for the more complex polygon, the more subtle odors, the poem with a less obvious rhythm and a more variable and loose rhyming scheme, and the complex, more diversified picture.

THE BARRON-WELSH ART SCALE

A measure of this secondary, bipolar factor in the Figure Preference Test was constructed in much the same incidental manner as that in which the factor had been discovered. It had happened that several artists were included in the control sample that Welsh used for comparison with psychiatric patients, and these artists all clustered together at the complex-asymmetrical pole of the factor. The present writer, in search of measures of artistic discrimination for inclusion in a battery of assessment procedures, recalled this finding and was led to wonder whether the factor was not significantly related to ability to discriminate the good from the poor in artistic productions. In any case, the Figure Preference test clearly consisted of stimulus material which might yield such a measure. The most straightforward way of checking on this seemed to be to give the entire 400-item test to a sample of artists and nonartists and then to construct, by means of the item-analysis technique, a scale that would embody the differences between artists and nonartists in their preferences for the figures; and finally, of course, to cross-validate the scale on new samples of artists and nonartists. This was accordingly done, and a highly reliable and valid scale resulted.

Inspection of the items in the scale quickly revealed that the secondary, bipolar factor that had emerged from the factor analysis was reproduced in the later empirically derived measure. The artists *liked* figures which were highly complex, asymmetrical, free-hand rather than ruled, and rather restless and moving in their general effect. (Several artists, in reacting to them, had described them as "organic.") The figures that were *liked* by people in general, however, were relatively simple, often bilaterally symmetrical, and regularly predictable, following some cardinal principle that could be educed at a glance. These figures were described by artists as "static," "dull," "uninteresting."

This convergence of the results of factor-analytic and external-criterion methodologies seems especially worth noting. Factor analysis not only revealed the psychological unity in perceptual preferences with which we are here dealing, but in addition provided the clue to an extremely important external correlate which could be used for straightforward empirical scale derivation. The scale is now properly designated as an Art Scale, but can be equally properly construed as a measure of the factor found by Eysenck and by Welsh. It has both psychological unity and external predictive power. Most of the remainder of this paper will be devoted to what has been called "construct validity," an extension of the investigation to correlates of the scale in areas of behavior that theory would suggest as relevant. First, however, we shall review briefly some findings concerning the relationship of these figure preferences to preferences in paintings and to self-descriptions.

In the sample of 40 male graduate students already described, scores on the test proved to be distributed bimodally, so much so that there were two distinct groups defined by these figure preferences. When the four middlemost cases of the distribution were excluded, there was an interval of 20 points on a 62-unit scale that was not occupied by any case, 18 cases falling on each side of this interval.

It was evident from an inspection of how scores were arrived at that one of these groups preferred, as did the artists, those figures that were asymmetrical, highly complex, free-hand rather than ruled, and restless and moving in their general effect. The other group preferred the symmetrical, relatively simple, and decidedly "balanced" figures.

The 18 subjects who preferred the symmetrical and regularly predictable figures will hereafter be referred to as Group S, and the 18 who preferred the asymmetrical, irregular, and unpredictable figures will be called Group A.

Comparisons of the groups thus defined will be limited here to the results of a few fairly clear-cut techniques, involving little specialized psychological knowledge.

PREFERENCES FOR PAINTINGS

The subjects in this study had been asked to indicate the degree of their liking for each of 105 postcard-size reproductions in color of paintings by a large number of European artists, widely varied both as to time and place of origin, and representing many styles of painting as well as different choices of subject matter. Each painting was to be placed in one of four groups: Like Best of All, Like Much, Like Just Moderately, and Like Least of All. The subjects were asked to place approximately twice as many items in each of the two middle categories as in each of the two extreme ones.

An item was now defined to be a characteristic preference of a group if that item was placed in a given category significantly (.05 level of confidence) more often by that group than by the other. When this sort of analysis was carried out, it was found that no item was "characteristic" of a group in more than one category. It did happen, however, that some items appeared as characteristic of one group in the category "Like Best of All" while appearing as characteristic of the other group in the category "Like Least of All." Such extreme discordances in esthetic preferences between Groups A and S are of special interest. In Table 15.1, they are set off from the rest of the paintings in the "Liked Best of All" and "Liked Least of All" categories for the two groups.

The first thing that strikes the eye about this set of paintings is that

TABLE 15.1

Liked Best of All by Group S	
Veneziano	Portrait of a Young Lady
Botticelli	Virgin and Child
Corot	The Woman with the Pearl
Fra Lippo Lippi	The Adoration
Leonardo da Vinci	John the Baptist
Ecole Francaise, 16th century	Elizabeth of Austria
Gainsborough	Blue Boy
Raeburn	Boy with a Rabbit
Clouet	Portrait of Francis I
Ecole Francaise, 16th century	Francis I

(Paintings above were "liked least" by Group A)	
Rembrandt	Portrait of Hendriche Stoffels
Rembrandt	Portrait of Himself in Old Age
Sanzio	Portrait of Balthazar Castiglione
Rembrandt	His Portrait by Himself
Utrillo	A View of Anse
Rembrandt	The Syndics
Gauguin	The Seine at Paris

it consists largely of portraits. Of 17 paintings in the group, 12 are portraits, 3 are religious scenes, and 2 are landscapes.

Considering how portraits usually get to be painted, one is not surprised to note in addition that the subjects are generally of aristocratic bearing and mien, richly and fashionably clothed. The ladies portrayed are pure and noble—not by character only, but by birth. The gentlemen are clearly persons of substance, accustomed to homage and given to command. (The imperious Francis I is represented twice, the portraits being by different artists.)

The paintings with a religious theme are the Virgin and Child, the Adoration of the Infant, and Leonardo's St. John the Baptist. The landscapes are tranquil and pleasant ones, somewhat formal and "cultivated."

The dominant note in this set of paintings is one of religion, authority, and aristocracy, personified in the courtly, high-born, and holy personages depicted.

Now, let us examine the paintings that are placed at the opposite pole by Group S, as shown in Table 15.2.

First, we note that all of the "abstractions" (five in a group of 105) are placed by these subjects in the Like Least of All category. (Four

TABLE 15.2

Liked Least of All by Group S	
Picasso	The Bust Before the Window
Picasso	Still-life by Candle-light
Modigliani	The Woman from Burgundy
Gris	The Breakfast
Modigliani	Marcelle
Gris	Woman with a Book
Toulouse-Lautrec	The Clowness
Vuillard	In Bed
(Paintings above were "liked best" by Group A)	
Cézanne	Women Bathing
Cézanne	The Black Marble Clock
Léger	Composition in 3 Profiles
Renoir	Woman with the Veil
Cézanne	Onions and Bottle
Lautrec	Jeanne Avril

of these same five abstractions are liked "Best" by Group *A*.) In addition, the Modigliani women (who clearly are not faithful representations of "real" women), are similarly liked "Least" by Group *S* but "Best" by Group *A*.

What seems to be expressed here is a strong rejection of the esoteric, the radically experimental, and the "unnatural." (Supernatural themes, however, win approval if naturally represented and peopled by recognizably human beings.)

Rejected along with the unnatural and the radically experimental are ladies of low birth and ignoble pursuits. In this group we find the prostitute painted by Toulouse-Lautrec, the nudes in the Cézanne painting, "Women Bathing," Renoir's "Woman with the Veil" (an impressionistic suggestion of intrigue, assignation, and so on), and Vuillard's young woman "In Bed."

In summary, Group *S* approves good breeding, religion, and authority, and rejects the daring, the esoteric, the "unnatural" and the frankly sensual.

Table 15.3 lists the paintings liked best by Group A. We note immediately that in this set are represented the products of such "modern" art movements as Primitivism, Expressionism, Impressionism, and Cubism. These were revolts against traditional ways in art, expressed in radical experimentation in design, a search for the primitive and the naïve, a rejection of the directly representational in favor of the deriv-

TABLE 15.3

Liked Best of All by Group A	
Picasso	The Bust Before the Window
Picasso	Still-life by Candle-light
Modigliani	The Woman from Burgundy
Gris	The Breakfast
Modigliani	Marcelle
Gris	Woman with a Book
Toulouse-Lautrec	The Clowness
Vuillard	In Bed

(Paintings above were "liked least" by Group S)

Renoir	Bathing Woman
Van Gogh	The Bridge
Vlaminck	The House with the Weatherboard
Daumier	The Amateur of Etchings
Dunoyer de Segonzac	Staddle
Toulouse-Lautrec	Two Waltzes
Gauguin	Women of Tahiti
Gauguin	And the Gold of Their Bodies
Degas	The Ironers

ative and the abstract, and a choice of subject matter that affirmed the importance of the commonplace. Here sensuality and the instinctual life receive at least their due. Like many revolutionary movements, these delighted in being extreme, and one senses at times a certain histrionic and theatrical element accompanying the honest quest for new ways of expressing reality (and new realities to express).

It is evident from Table 15.4 that the members of Group *A* do not like religious themes in paintings. Of the eight religious scenes in the 105 paintings, six are placed in the Like Least category: Leonardo, Botticelli, Angelico, Grunewald, and Fra Lippo Lippi alike fall before this categorical rejection of the religious.

Further, the members of Group *A* do not like portraits of lords and ladies. Three different portraits of Francis I are relegated to the "Like Least" category, in company with Lucrezia Crivelli, Ann of Cleves, Elizabeth of Austria, the young aristocrat who served as the model for Blue Boy, and Whistler's Mother. (It is ironic that the eccentric and self-consciously non-conformist Whistler should be remembered to common fame largely by courtesy of the American commercialization of Mother's Day, for a painting which he intended as an innovation in design, and which he titled "Arrangement in Grey and Black.")

TABLE 15.4

Liked Least of All by Group A	
Veneziano	Portrait of a Young Lady
Botticelli	Virgin and Child
Fra Lippo Lippi	The Adoration
Corot	The Woman with the Pearl
da Vinci	John the Baptist
Ecole Francaise, 16th century	Elizabeth of Austria
Gainsborough	Blue Boy
Raeburn	Boy with a Rabbit
Clouet	Portrait of Francis I
Ecole Francaise, 16th century	Francis I
(Paintings above were "liked best" by Group S)	
da Vinci	The Virgin, Child, and St. Anne
Redon	Flowers
Lucientes	Lady with the Fan
Whistler	Mother
Grunewald	The Annunciation
da Vinci	Portrait of Lucrezia Crivelli
Holbein	Portrait of Ann of Cleves
Watteau	Embarkment for Cythera
Goya y Lucientes	The Manikin
Ingres	The Odalisque
Corot	Landscape
Ecole Francaise	Francis I
Angelico	The Annunciation

The women in the portraits disliked by Group *A* have in common that they are rather aloof and distant. Even the odalisque in Ingres' painting is remarkably unsensual in appearance. This is in strong contrast to the women in the paintings liked best by Group *A*, who are considerably more informal and relaxed, and whose sexual role receives more emphasis.

In summary, Group *A* approves the modern, the radically experimental, the primitive and the sensual, while disliking what is religious, aristocratic, traditional, and emotionally controlled.

GROUP DIFFERENCES IN SELF-DESCRIPTION

We have seen that the two groups defined by figure preferences show consistently different preferences in paintings as well, and that the two sets of preferences taken together seem to suggest quite different perceptual attitudes bearing on (1) predictability, stability, balance, symmetry, and governance by a simple general principle; and

(2) acceptance or rejection of tradition, religion, authority, and sensuality. How do persons with such different attitudes differ in seeing themselves?

A partial answer to this question is provided by an item analysis of the Gough Adjective Check-List, which was used in the study. Each subject had been asked to indicate (by a check mark) what adjectives in the list were, in his opinion, descriptive of himself. There were 279 adjectives in all. Table 15.5 records the adjectives that differentiated the groups, listed in the order of their discriminating power.

TABLE 15.5

	Group S	*Group* A
At the .05 level:	contented	gloomy
	gentle	loud
	conservative	unstable
	unaffected	bitter
	patient	cool
	peaceable	dissatisfied
		pessimistic
		emotional
		irritable
		pleasure-seeking
At the .10 level:	serious	aloof
	individualistic	sarcastic
	stable	spendthrift
	worrying	distractible
	timid	demanding
	thrifty	indifferent
At the .15 level:	dreamy	anxious
	deliberate	opinionated
	moderate	temperamental
	modest	quick
	responsible	
	foresighted	
At the .20 level:	conscientious	

In these self-descriptions, as in the characteristic art preferences, these two groups clearly separate themselves from one another. It seems not too much to say that they hold different views of themselves and of the world.

The polarity noted in these three domains of figure preferences, art preferences, and adjective self-descriptions are summarized in Table 15.6.

TABLE 15.6

Group S

In Figure Preferences
Preferring what is simple, regularly predictable, following some cardinal principle that can be educed at a glance.
In Art Preferences
Preferring themes involving religion, authority, aristocracy, and tradition.
In Adjective Self-Checks
Contented, gentle, conservative, patient, peaceable, serious, individualistic, stable, worrying, timid, thrifty, dreamy, deliberate, moderate, modest, responsible, foresighted, conscientious.

Group A

In Figure Preferences
Preferring what is complex, irregular, whimsical.
In Art Preferences
Preferring what is radically experimental, sensational, sensual, esoteric, primitive, and naïve.
In Adjective Self-Checks
Gloomy, pessimistic, bitter, dissatisfied, emotional, pleasure-seeking, unstable, cool, irritable, aloof, sarcastic, spendthrift, distractible, demanding, indifferent, anxious, opinionated, temperamental, quick.

FURTHER RESULTS

At the conclusion of the series of four assessments, all the subjects were rated by the staff on 40 variables that previous personality researches had indicated as being of general importance. We are thus in a position to see how the simplicity-complexity dimension is manifested in many different areas of behavior, by correlating the Figure Preference measure with other variables. For the most part, we shall restrict ourselves to relationships obtaining in this one sample of 40 subjects. However, the scale was also given, together with some questionnaires, to a sample of some 100 male undergraduates in two Pennsylvania colleges, and the correlates of Complexity in that sample will be described. Data are also available from the assessment study of 80 other subjects (Ph.D. candidates and medical school seniors) who took a revised form of the test.

For ease of reporting, we shall adopt the technique of drawing a composite picture of two ideal, modal persons, the simple and the complex, on the basis of the correlational results. The statistical support for the portrait will be cited as we go along. Several cautions must be observed in interpreting such material, however. For one thing, since the picture is based entirely on group relationships, it will fail in some respects to do justice to unique patterning of the variables in individual cases. Like the average man, the composite simple or complex person would be hard to find.

In addition, one must be particularly cautious in evaluating the "goodness" and "badness" of the correlates of this dimension. It is important to bear in mind that, in terms of the total constellation of factors making for personal effectiveness and professional promise, simple persons and complex persons were equally represented among subjects who were rated as possessing that combination of attributes in high degree. This equal representation held also among the group of subjects with low ratings. One must conclude that both simplicity and complexity have their effective and ineffective aspects; they simply result in different sorts of merits and liabilities.

As we have indicated, in order to facilitate the reporting of the data, we shall adopt two conventions, one with regard to the scale and the other with regard to the designation of the subjects. The Barron-Welsh Art Scale will hereafter be referred to as a measure of the variable *Complexity*, since it is that feature of the scale which is of interest here, and since the scale is so scored that preferences like those of artists (hence, preference for the complex) earn the subject a high score, while preferences like those of people in general (i.e., preference for the simple) earn a low score. The designations *Complex person* and *Simple person* will be employed to indicate a modal high scorer and a modal low scorer, respectively, on this particular test.

THE CORRELATIONAL COMPOSITE

This description begins with personal tempo, which is usually a rather easily observed, surface attribute, complicated though its ramifications may be in the personal character. It is "surface" in the sense that it is what we are first presented with when we meet another person; we take in almost automatically such attributes as flow of speech, speed of response, rate and intensity of expressive movement, and expansiveness or constriction in interaction with the environment.

It will be recalled that on the Adjective Check-List our Complex subjects had described themselves as "quick" and "temperamental." The Simple subjects, on the other hand, had characterized themselves as "deliberate" and "dreamy." These self-descriptions would seem to be borne out by the staff's ratings of subjects on such variables as Personal Tempo, Verbal Fluency, and Constriction. The correlations with Complexity are, respectively, .50, .29, and —.42. Thus, the Complex person is more intensely expressive, expansive, and fluent in speech than the Simple person. The Simple person, on the other hand, is seen as being more natural and likeable, and also as more straightforward and lacking in duplicity. (Complexity correlates —.44 with Naturalness, —.27 with Likeability, and +.56 with Deceitfulness, as rated by the staff.) This picture of easy and uncomplicated simplicity is further supported by staff ratings of such factors as Good Judgment, Adjustment, and Abundance Values, all of which go with preference for the simple figures. (The r's with complexity are —.39, —.31, and —.34, respectively.)

"Adjustment" had here been defined as "getting along in the world as it is, adequate degree of social conformity, capacity to adapt to a wide range of conditions, ability to fit in." As we shall see later, this kind of adjustment is not an unmixed blessing; the "unadjusted" complex person, who does not fit in very well in the world as it is, sometimes perceives that world more accurately than does his better-adjusted fellow.

The negative correlation with Abundance Values, combined with the positive relationship of Complexity to Deceitfulness, merits some comment. The term "Abundance Values" was defined as "Sense of security and optimism regarding the future, absence of fears of deprivation, of being exploited, and of being cheated." Deceitfulness was identified with "duplicity, lack of frankness, guile, subterfuge." Again, one recalls the adjective self-descriptions of the Complex people: gloomy, pessimistic, bitter, dissatisfied, demanding, pleasure-seeking, spendthrift. There is certainly some suggestion here of early deprivation, of pessimism concerning the source of supply, which is seen as untrustworthy and which must be coerced, or perhaps tricked, into yielding. It is as though the person had reason to believe that he would not "get what was coming" to him unless he made sure that he did, by whatever device might be available. It is this lack of infantile *trust* that leads to adult duplicity and craftiness. One aspect of complexity then (and perhaps a penalty sometimes attaching to it) is, to render it in the common phrase, a sort of "two-facedness," an inability to be wholly oneself at all times. The more simple, natural, and likeable person finds it easier to be always himself. As compensation, the complex person may possess the capacity to be ironic or sardonic, which can be valuable attitudes.

The preference for Complexity is clearly associated with originality, artistic expression, and excellence of esthetic judgment. Originality was one of the three criterion variables around which the assessment research program was organized, and every subject was rated by the faculty members of his department on the degree of Originality he had displayed in his work. The Complex person is seen as more original, both by the assessment staff and by the faculty of his department. The correlation with the criterion ratings on Originality is .30.

Complexity is also related to Basic Good Taste as measured by a test that presents various alternative arrangements of formal design elements and asks the subject to choose the most esthetically pleasing combination. This test, constructed by Sanford E. Gerard, is scored a priori in terms of known principles of composition. The correlation with Complexity is .44.

The subjects were also given a mosaic construction test devised by Gordon Turney, and known as the Turney Designs. In this test, the task is to construct a mosaic design in rectangular form from several hundred one-inch square solid-colored pieces of pasteboard (20 different colors being represented). The designs were then rated by members of the Art Department of the University, in terms of the artistic merit of the productions. The ratings thus obtained correlate .40 with Complexity.

To be purely speculative for the moment, one might wonder whether there is not some relationship between the more enduring and intense oral stage of development in our Complex subjects suggested by some of the data, and their evidently greater originality and sensitivity to the esthetic character of objects. Fowler[1] has shown that oral character traits are significantly associated with textural responses to shading on the Rorschach, and psychoanalytic writers, particularly Rank, have emphasized the relationship between femininity and artistic productiveness in men. A tendency toward somewhat slower social development in the earlier years in original people has appeared in several of our later studies. Perhaps a person must have more com-

---

[1] Fowler, C., *Personality Correlates of the Differential Use of Shading on the Rorschach Test*, Unpublished bachelor's thesis, Bennington College.

merce with himself and his feeling states and less with the environment during childhood if he is later to have sufficient communication with his own depths to produce original thought. In this view, originality evidenced in maturity is to some extent dependent upon the degree to which the person in early childhood is faced with a complicated relationship to the maternal source of supply, combined with his capacity to persist at and eventually to achieve some mastery of this earliest problem situation. The agrument would be that this primitive experience of phenomenal complexity sets a pattern of response which results in slower maturation, more tentativeness about the final form of organization, a resistance to early crystallization of the personality, and finally, greater complexity in one's view both of the outer and of the inner worlds.

Perhaps such speculation is unwarranted, however, and in any case it is clear that a great many other factors are involved in determining originality. What can be said is that originality and artistic creativeness and discrimination are related to the preference for complexity.

The Complex person's greater flexibility in thought processes is shown by a correlation of −.35 with rated Rigidity, defined as inflexibility of thought and manner; stubborn, pedantic, unbending, firm."

That repressive overcontrol may sometimes be associated with the preference for simplicity has already been indicated by the correlation of −.42 of Complexity with Constriction, and by another correlation of .50 with Impulsiveness. It is shown also in the relation of the Complexity measure to psychiatric variables that are scaled on the Minnesota Multiphasic Personality Inventory. With Hysteria, for example, Complexity correlates −.30, while with Schizophrenia it correlates +.37, and with Psychopathic Deviate +.36. Thus Complexity goes along both with lack of control of impulse (the *Pd* scale) and with the failure of repression which characterizes the schizophrenic process. This is by no means to suggest that any of these graduate students showed schizophrenic tendencies of a pathological degree, but it is reasonable to suppose that the *Sc* scale of the MMPI has in it the correlates of the sort of free-floating symbolic activity and frank confrontation and expression of the unconscious that is often so startlingly present in schizophrenic patients. The *Hy* scale, on the other hand, picks up the tendency of the subject to repress aggressive and erotic impulses, or to render them innocuous by rationalization, reinterpretation, or gratification in a substitutive manner which will not cause conflict. At the risk of being over-simple, we might say that preference for the complex in the psychic life makes for a wider consciousness of impulse, while this sort of simplicity, when it is preferred, is maintained by a narrowing of that consciousness.

That the perceptual decision in favor of admitting complexity may make also for greater subjectively experienced anxiety is indicated by the correlation (.34) of Complexity with Overt Anxiety as measured by the Welsh Anxiety Index on the MMPI. To tolerate complexity one must very often be able to tolerate anxiety as well, this finding would seem to say.

The negative correlation with Hy, and the positive correlation, of about the same magnitude, with Sc would seem to fit well with a finding of Eysenck's that his own measure of the Complexity-Simplicity dimension, the K test, correlates in this same direction with his Hysteria-Dysthymia factor.

The person who prefers complexity is socially nonconformist. Staff ratings of Conformity correlate —.47 with Complexity, while the self-ratings of Ss on Conformity correlate —.53. Related to this is a correlation of —.29 between Complexity and Submissiveness, which was here defined as "deference, willingness to be led, compliance, over-ready acceptance of authority." In addition, Complexity correlates positively (.36) with the F scale of the MMPI. The F scale consists of items that are psychologically heterogeneous, the defining property of the scale being that all items in it have a low probability (about .1) of being answered in the scored direction. Thus, the higher the F score, the more likely it is that the subject holds a set of socially dissident and deviant opinions.

RESPONSES TO AN ATTITUDE QUESTIONNAIRE

In the study described in the previous chapter, Asch and the present writer collaborated in the construction of a criterion-specific questionnaire, which consisted of 84 items which were especially selected, or written anew, to test particular hypotheses concerning personality differences between Independents and Yielders. The results of an item analysis of the Independence questionnaire against the criterion of high or low score on Complexity are shown in Table 15.7.

Since all these subjects were undergraduate students in Pennsylvania colleges, and their average age was 19, it is of some interest to

TABLE 15.7

Answered True by High Scorers on Complexity

1. The unfinished and the imperfect often have greater appeal for me than the completed and the polished.
2. I could cut my moorings . . . quit my home, my parents, and my friends . . . without suffering great regrets.
3. Politically I am probably something of a radical.
4. I think I take primarily an esthetic view of experience.
5. I would enjoy the experience of living and working in a foreign country.
6. Many of my friends would probably be considered unconventional by other people.
7. Some of my friends think that my ideas are impractical, if not a bit wild.
8. I enjoy discarding the old and accepting the new.
9. When someone talks against certain groups or nationalities, I always speak up against such talk, even though it makes me unpopular.

Answered True by Low Scorers on Complexity

1. I don't like modern art.
2. Disobedience to the government is never justified.
3. Perfect balance is the essence of all good composition.
4. Straightforward reasoning appeals to me more than metaphors and the search for analogies.
5. It is a pretty callous person who does not feel love and gratitude toward his parents.
6. Things seem simpler as you learn more about them.
7. I much prefer symmetry to asymmetry.
8. Kindness and generosity are the most important qualities for a wife to have.
9. When a person has a problem or worry, it is best for him not to think about it, but to keep busy with more cheerful things.
10. It is the duty of a citizen to support his country, right or wrong.
11. Barring emergencies, I have a pretty good idea what I'll be doing for the next ten years.
12. I prefer team games to games in which one individual competes against another.
13. An invention which takes jobs away from people should be suppressed until new work can be found for them.

---

compare their characteristics with the correlates of Complexity noted in the sample of California Ph.D. candidates. By grouping items, we may summarize the personality differences between the Complex and Simple persons in the Pennsylvania sample somewhat as shown in Table 15.8.

The general pattern is certainly similar to that shown by the correlations we have been reporting. In Pennsylvania as in California, preference for simplicity is associated with social conformity, respect for custom and ceremony, friendliness toward tradition, somewhat cate-

TABLE 15.8

The Complex person

1. Is artistic (4).
2. Has unconventional friends, occasionally is visited by an impractical, not to say wild, idea, and would rather be creative and neurotic than normal and ordinary (6, 7, 10).
3. Is politically somewhat radical, and can be militantly opposed to racial prejudice (3, 9).
4. Is aware of present imperfections, would welcome and has faith in future developments (1, 2, 5, 8).

The Simple person

1. Doesn't like modern art (1).
2. Particularly values kindness and generosity in a wife (as opposed to implied alternative values), and feels that the proper filial sentiments toward one's parents are love and gratitude (8, 5).
3. Feels that a citizen should support his country, right or wrong, and that disobedience to the government is never justified. Somewhat allied to this, he prefers a team effort to individual competition (2, 10, 12).
4. Prefers symmetry to asymmetry, considers perfect balance the essence of good composition, and prefers straightforward reasoning to metaphors and the search for analogies (7, 3, 4).
5. Has clear plans for the future, and considers that things seem simpler as you learn more about them (11, 6).
6. Believes that a person with a problem or worry should not think about it, and that inventions which take jobs away from people should be suppressed until new work can be found for them (9, 13).

gorical moral judgment, an undeviating patriotism, and suppression of such troublesome new forces as inventions that would temporarily cause unemployment. This last item is almost prototypical of the simple person's orientation toward repression as a psychic mechanism. In the California sample, it was shown in the negative correlation of Complexity with Hysteria and the positive correlations with Psychopathic Deviate and Schizophrenia. Its derivatives appear in many other characteristic attitudes as well, such as acceptance or rejection of sensual experience, of conventional religion, of paintings of unclad ladies, and so on. For "invention," write "impulse," and it is not hard to see an analogy to the common clinical formulation of the function of repression in the hysterical character.

The correlates of preference for complexity in this undergraduate sample are, again, much like the correlates of the corresponding preference among the Ph.D. candidates. Complexity goes along with artistic interests, unconventionality, political radicalism, high valuation of creativity (even at the expense of "normality," as the item puts it), and a liking for change.

It seems evident that, at its best, preference for simplicity is associated with personal stability and balance, while at its worst it makes for categorical rejection of all that threatens disorder and disequilibrium. In its pathological aspect it produces stereotyped thinking, rigid and compulsive morality, and hatred of instinctual aggressive and erotic forces which might upset the precariously maintained balance.

There is a passage in Hugo's *Les Miserables* which is remarkably coincident with these observations. It occurs at that point in the narrative when Javert, the single-minded and merciless representative of the law, has turned his own world upside-down by allowing Jean Valjean, the outlaw whom he had so relentlessly pursued, and whom he finally had in his grasp, to escape. He says to himself, in this surprising moment, "There is something more then than duty." At this, "he was startled; his balances were disturbed; one of the scales fell into the abyss, the other flew into the sky . . ."

> . . . To be obliged to acknowledge this: infallibility is not infallible, there may be an error in the dogma, all is not said when a code has spoken, society is not perfect, authority is complicate with vacillation, a cracking is possible in the immutable, judges are men, the law may be deceived, the tribunals may be mistaken . . . to see a flaw in the immense blue crystal of the firmament!
>
> . . . Certainly it was strange, that the fireman of order, the engineer of authority, mounted upon the blind iron-horse of the rigid path, could be thrown off by a ray of light! that the incommutable, the direct, the correct, the geometrical, the passive, the perfect, could bend!
>
> . . . Until now all that he had above him had been in his sight *a smooth, simple, limpid surface; nothing there unknown, nothing obscure; nothing which was not definite, coordinated, concatenated, precise, exact, circumscribed, limited, shut in, all foreseen;* authority was a plane; no fall in it, no dizziness before it. Javert had never seen the unknown except below. *The irregular, the unexpected, the disorderly opening of chaos,* the possible slipping into an abyss; that belonged to inferior regions, to the rebellious, the wicked, the miserable. [Italics added.]

This passage brings together many observations made intuitively by Hugo and arrived at in a more pedestrian manner in this research. A precise simplicity is seen to be related to authority, dogma, tradition, morality, constriction, and repression. The opposite of all these things is typified by the flaw in the crystal, by the irregular, by disorderly chaos, by such qualities as are to be found in the inferior regions, where reside the rebellious, the wicked, and the miserable. The emphasis here is pathological, and the dichotomy absolute, but if we extend the range into normal behavior and admit the many shortcomings of the typology, there is considerable agreement between Hugo's intuition and this set of correlations.

We would suggest that the types of perceptual preference we have observed are related basically to a *choice of what to attend to* in the complex of phenomena that makes up the world we experience; for the world *is* both stable and unstable, predictable and unpredictable, ordered and chaotic. To see it predominantly as one or the other is a sort of *perceptual decision*. One may attend to its ordered aspect, to regular sequences of events, to a stable center of the universe (the sun, the church, the state, the home, the parent, God, eternity, etc.), or one may instead attend primarily to the eccentric, the relative, and the arbitrary aspect of the world (the briefness of the individual life, the blind uncaringness of matter, the sometime hypocrisy of authority, accidents of circumstance, the presence of evil, tragic fate, the impossibility of freedom for the only organism capable of conceiving freedom, and so on).

Either of these alternative perceptual decisions may be associated with a high degree of personal effectiveness. It is as though there is an effective and an ineffective aspect of each alternative. Our thinking about these various aspects is as yet based only upon clinical impressions of our subjects, but it is perhaps worth recording while we go on with the business of gathering more objective evidence.

At its best, the decision in favor of order makes for personal stability and balance, a sort of easy-going optimism combined with religious faith, a friendliness toward tradition, custom, and ceremony, and respect for authority without subservience to it. This sort of decision will be made by persons who from an early age had good reason to trust the stability and equilibrium of the world and who derived an inner sense of comfort and balance from their perception of an outer certainty.

At its worst, the decision in favor of order makes for categorical rejection of all that threatens disorder, a fear of anything that might bring disequilibrium. Optimism becomes a matter of policy, religion a prescription and a ritual. Such a decision is associated with stereotyped thinking, rigid and compulsive morality, and hatred of instinctual aggressive and erotic forces which might upset the precariously maintained balance. Equilibrium depends essentially upon exclusion, a kind of perceptual distortion which consists in refusing to see parts of reality that cannot be assimilated to some preconceived system.

The decision in favor of complexity, at its best, makes for originality and creativeness, a greater tolerance for unusual ideas and formulations. The sometimes disordered and unstable world has its counterpart in the person's inner discord, but the crucial ameliorative factor is a constant effort to integrate the inner and outer complexity in a higher-order synthesis. The goal is to achieve the psychological analogue of mathematical elegance: to allow into the perceptual system the greatest possible richness of experience, while yet finding in this complexity some overall pattern. Such a person is not immobilized by anxiety in the face of great uncertainty, but is at once perturbed and challenged. For such an individual, optimism is impossible, but pessimism is lifted from the personal to the tragic level, resulting not in apathy but in participation in the business of life.

At its worst, such a perceptual attitude leads to grossly disorganized behavior, to a surrender to chaos. It results in nihilism, despair, and disintegration. The personal life itself becomes simply an acting out of the meaninglessness of the universe, a bitter joke directed against its own maker. The individual is overwhelmed by the apparent insolubility of the problem, and finds the disorder of life disgusting and hateful. His essential world-view is thus depreciative and hostile.

16

The Disposition Toward Originality

THERE has been a marked tendency in psychological research on originality to focus attention upon the single original act in itself, rather than upon the total personality of the originator. This is understandable, for the birth and development of the original idea is usually more immediately interesting and dramatically vivid than the birth and history of the man who had the idea. Newton's apple and Archimedes' tub and the well of Eratosthenes are thus naturally the circumstances with which we associate the remarkable insights of these original geniuses. We do not often ask ourselves whether these men were for the most part disposed to express or to suppress erotic impulses, or whether their emotions were fluent or turgid, or how subject to intense anxiety they were, or how much given to violent action. We tend to disembody the creative act and the creative process by limiting our inquiry to the creator's mental content at the moment of insight, forgetting that a highly organized system of responding lies behind the particular original response that, because of its validity, becomes an historical event.

There is good reason for believing, however, that originality is almost habitual with persons who produce a really singular insight. The biography of the inventive genius commonly records a lifetime of original thinking, though only a few ideas survive and are remembered to fame. Voluminous productivity is the rule and not the exception among individuals who have made some noteworthy contribution. Original responses, it would seem, recur regularly in some persons, while there are other individuals who do not ever depart from the stereotyped and the conventional in their thinking.

If, then, some persons are regularly original while others are regularly unoriginal, it must be the case that certain patterns of relatively enduring traits either facilitate or impede the production of original acts. Rather than focusing on the immediate conditions that have triggered the original response, the study to be reported in this chapter was concerned with the underlying disposition toward originality which it may be presumed exists in those persons who are regularly original. The research was directed first of all toward identifying individuals who performed consistently in a relatively more or relatively less original way. When this had been done, the more original were compared with the less original in terms of personality organization. Independent evidence concerning the personalities of the subjects was obtained both through the use of standardized paper-and-pencil tests and through employment of the living-in assessment method, with its emphasis upon observation of the subjects through several days of informal social interaction, situational tests, group discussions, psychodrama, and the like. The observers were of course kept in ignorance of the scores earned by the subjects on tests of originality.

THE RELATIVITY OF ORIGINALITY

It is a basic assumption of this study that acts are original only in relation to some specified commonality. The original must be defined relative to the usual, and the degree of originality must be specified statistically in terms of incidence of occurrence. Thus the first criterion of an original response is that it should have a certain stated uncommonness in the particular group being studied. A familiar example of this in psychological practice is the definition of an original response to the Rorschach inkblots, the requirement there being that the response should, in the examiner's experience, occur no more often than once in 100 examinations.

In the present study, we propose to deal with a relatively low order of originality, its limits being set by the nature of the sampling of subjects. The subjects are 100 captains in the United States Air Force, and originality as discerned here is originality in relation to the usual responses of only 100 persons. Furthermore, these 100 persons are not themselves especially selected for originality in relation to the population in general. Nevertheless, as we shall show later, some of the 100 captains are regularly original in comparison with the remainder, while others are regularly unoriginal in relation to the entire group. Apart from their military status, the sample may be described as a group of normal, healthy young men, of average intelligence, socio-economically of the lower-middle class in their pre-army background, and similar to young men in general in terms of the usualness and the unusualness of their responses to the tests of originality employed in this experiment.

A second criterion that must be met if a response is to be called original is that it must be to some extent adaptive to reality. The intent of this requirement is to exclude uncommon responses that are merely random or that proceed from ignorance or delusion. An example of the application of this second criterion may be taken from the scoring of one of the measures of originality used in this experiment: the measure is a count of the number of uncommon *and correct* anagram solutions to the test word "generation." Many subjects did not hesitate to offer solutions that were incorrect, and that were usually unique. In such instances, the application of the second criterion of originality was straightforward and decisive. Not all of the tests called for such purely cognitive responses with unambiguous denotative meaning, however. In the case of inkblot tests, for example, we come closer to the problems involved in evaluating fantasy or works of art, and verification cannot be had by recourse to a dictionary. Instead, when the experimenter himself cannot "see" the form pointed to by the subject, he must have recourse to other psychologists who have given many Rorschachs and who can be considered fairly open to suggestions as to what the blots might reasonably look like. Consensual verification is thus sought for such imaginings. Poor forms, or uncommon responses that did not sufficiently respect the inkblot reality, were not credited as original in this study.

THE MEASUREMENT OF ORIGINALITY

Eight test measures were accepted here as indicative of originality. They are described below. The first three of these measures are taken from the creativity battery developed by J. P. Guilford and his associates in the Project on Aptitudes of High-Level Personnel at the University of Southern California. These three tests had significant loadings on the Originality factor in the Guilford researches. Of the remaining five measures, two are derived from commonly used projective techniques, the Rorschach Psychodiagnostic and the Thematic Apperception Test; another is a commonly used anagram test, and the remaining two tests were devised by the writer.

1. *Unusual Uses.* This test calls upon the subject to list six uses to which each of several common objects can be put. It is scored for infrequency, in the sample under study, of the uses proposed. Odd-even reliability in this sample is .77.

2. *Consequences B.* In this test, the subject is asked to write down what would happen if certain changes were suddenly to take place. The task for him is to list as many consequences or results of these changes as he can. The responses are scored according to how obvious the imagined consequences are, the less obvious responses receiving the higher scores. Interrater agreement is .71.

3. *Plot Titles B.* Two story plots are presented, and the subject is asked to write as many titles as he can think of for each plot. The titles are rated on a scale of cleverness from 0 to 5. The number of titles rated 2, 3, 4, or 5 constitutes the cleverness score. Interrater agreement in this study was .43.

4. *Rorschach O+.* This is a count of the number of original responses given by the subject to the 10 Rorschach blots and adjudged by two scorers, working separately, to be good rather than poor forms. Standard Rorschach administrative procedure was followed. Interrater agreement was .72, and only those responses scored by both scorers as O+ were credited.

5. *Thematic Apperception Test: Originality Rating.* Two raters, working independently of one another, rated the T.A.T. protocols of the 100 subjects on a nine-point scale, using approximate normal curve frequencies for each point along the scale. Interrater agreement was .70. The subject's score was the average of the two ratings.

6. *Anagrams.* The test word "generation" was used, and the anagram solutions were scored for infrequency of occurrence in the sample under study. If the subject offered a solution that was correct and that was offered by no more than two other subjects, he received one point for originality. Total score is therefore the number of such uncommon but correct solutions.

7. *The Barron Word Rearrangement Test: Originality Rating.* In this test, the subject is given 50 words that were selected at random from a list of common nouns, adjectives, and adverbs. He is told to make up a story that will enable him to use as many as possible of the listed words. His composition is rated for originality on a nine-point scale, just as the T.A.T. was. Interrater agreement in this instance was .67.

8. *The Barron Movement-threshold Inkblots.* This is a set of 26 achromatic inkblots constructed locally. The subject is asked to give

only one response to each blot. Responses were weighted according to their frequency of occurrence in the sample under study, the more infrequent responses receiving the higher weights. Score is the sum of the weights assigned to the subject's responses on all 26 blots. Odd-even reliability was .43.

It is worth noting that all eight of these tests are free-response tests. The respondent is not presented with alternatives devised by the test maker; instead, he must summon from within himself his own way of solving problems, seeing the blots, interpreting the pictures, or putting together the words or letters. There is considerable latitude allowed for self-expression and for idiosyncratic interpretation.

Furthermore, diverse media are presented for the respondent to express himself through. The two inkblot tests allow for original visualization, or original perceptual organization of visual forms. The T.A.T. and the Word Rearrangement Test permit originality of verbal composition to show itself. Consequences and Unusual Uses call for bright ideas in more or less discrete form. Plot Titles evokes epigrammatic or sloganistic originality, while Anagrams requires a combination of word fluency and ease of perceptual reorganization.

If originality is indeed a dimension, and if some persons are regularly original while others are regularly unoriginal, we should expect the intercorrelations of these measures to be positive and to be statistically significant; we should not, however, expect the coefficients to be very high, for it is reasonable that the dimension of originality would have its variance apportioned to several media of expression. Even regularly original persons can be expected to be outstandingly original in only one or two ways. The extent to which these expectations are confirmed in the present study may be seen from Table 16.1, in which the Pearsonian correlation coefficients of all eight test measures with one another are given. (With an N of 100, a Pearsonian r is significant at the .05 level if it is .20 or greater; an r of .26 is significant at the .01 level.)

As Table 16.1 shows, the correlations of the eight measures with one another tend to be positive and to be significantly different from zero. The inkblot tests alone appear to bear little relationship to the other measures; indeed, they do not even correlate significantly with one another. If the two inkblot tests are excluded, however, two-thirds of the intercorrelations of the remaining six measures are significant at the .05 level, and all are positive. The table thus provides satisfactory evidence of the expected coherence or regularity of the manifestations of originality, with considerable reservations, however, concerning the relevance of inkblot originality to the dimension here being measured.

TABLE 16.1 *Interrelations of Eight Originality Measures*

Test Measures	1	2	3	4	5	6	7	8
1. Unusual Uses	—	.42	.37	.08	.17	.29	.06	.17
2. Consequences B	.42	—	.46	−.02	.21	.21	.16	.09
3. Plot Titles B	.37	.46	—	.17	.26	.17	.16	.07
4. Rorschach O+	.08	−.02	.17	—	.21	.03	−.05	.17
5. T.A.T. Originality	.17	.21	.26	.21	—	.36	.41	.02
6. Anagrams	.29	.21	.17	.03	.36	—	.33	.38
7. Word Synthesis Originality	.06	.16	.16	−.05	.41	.33	—	.09
8. Movement-threshold Originality	.17	.09	.07	.17	.02	.38	.09	—

Since it is quite possible that originality is simply a multifactorial dimension in which certain factors bear little relationship to other factors but yet are positively related to the underlying dimension as a whole, it would probably be premature to exclude the inkblot measures from this battery of tests of originality. Considerable doubt must be entertained concerning their validity, however, and another piece of evidence reinforces the doubt. The staff psychologists who conducted the three-day living-in assessments were particularly interested in two theoretically central variables which they sought to rate on the basis of their observations: one of these variables was Originality (the other was Personal Stability). The correlations between this final overall rating on Originality and the eight test measures of originality are shown in Table 16.2. Also given in this table are the correlations of the eight measures individually with a variable that is the sum of the standard scores earned by each S on each of the eight tests; in other words, each test measure is correlated with a composite of which it is itself a part. The correlations thus show the relative contributions of each test to the total score on the battery of tests.

Table 16.2 provides evidence that the test battery is in substantial agreement with the staff psychologists who gave ratings on Originality without knowledge of the test scores. The correlation of .55 between the test composite and the observers' ratings is encouraging evidence that inexpensive, objective, and efficient measurement of originality is possible.

Again, however, the inkblot measures have relatively little rela-

TABLE 16.2 *Relationship of Eight Test Measures to Rated Originality and to Composite Test Originality*

Test Measures	9	10
1. Unusual uses	.30	.60
2. Consequences B	.36	.59
3. Plot Titles B	.32	.62
4. Rorschach O+	.18	.38
5. T.A.T. Originality	.45	.59
6. Anagrams	.22	.62
7. Word Synthesis Originality	.45	.51
8. Movement-threshold Originality	.07	.46
9. Staff Rating: Originality	—	.55
10. Composite Test Originality	.55	—

tionship to these composite variables. The staff rating of Originality correlates significantly with six of the eight measures (well beyond the .01 level of significance with five of them); but neither Rorschach Originality nor Movement-threshold Originality is significantly related to the staff rating. As would be expected, these measures also have the least contribution to make to the test composite.

In spite of this situation, both inkblot measures were retained in the battery for purposes of identifying regularly original and regularly unoriginal subjects. The reasoning was as follows: On the face of it, uncommon responses to inkblots are original acts within the definition of originality being employed here. Tendencies toward uncommon visual perceptions are of course not readily recognized in ordinary social situations, since they have to be verbalized to be socially visible. Hence the failure of inkblot tests to correlate with the staff rating of Originality, based on observations of social behavior alone, should be discounted. The lack of a verbal component in perceptual originality, and its conspicuous presence in the other originality tests, may also account for the relative independence of the inkblot tests in the test composite. Finally, if the inkblot measures contribute only error variance to the composite, their retention will result in failure of some true relationships to appear, but this will be an error on the conservative side; and if they do in fact contribute true variance not contributed by any other test, they may add appreciable validity to the picture of the personality correlates of originality. They were therefore retained for the purpose of identifying regularly original and regularly unoriginal subjects.

A dual criterion was now established for calling a given subject regularly original: (a) he had to be at least one standard deviation above the mean on the test composite; (b) he had to be at least two standard deviations above the mean on at least one of the eight measures. Fifteen regularly original subjects were thus identified; more than half of them were at least two standard deviations above the mean on two or more of the eight tests.

For comparison purposes, the 15 lowest scorers on the final distribution of summed standard scores were selected; all of these subjects also met the criterion of being at least two standard deviations below the mean on at least one of the eight measures. They will be referred to as the regularly unoriginal subjects.

SOME HYPOTHESES SUGGESTED BY PREVIOUS WORK

The existence of a very general attitude toward experience, of a sort that disposes toward complexity of outlook, independence of judgment, and originality, has been suggested by the results of the studies reported in earlier chapters. To recall some of those findings: individuals who refused to yield to strong pressure from their peers to concur in a false group opinion described themselves, on an adjective check-list, as "original" and "artistic" much more frequently than did subjects who yielded to such group pressure. In addition, the independent (nonyielding) subjects showed a marked preference for complex and asymmetrical line drawings, as opposed to simple and symmetrical drawings. This preference for the complex and asymmetrical had been shown previously to be highly correlated both with the choice of art as a vocation[1] and with rated artistic ability among art students. Furthermore, in a sample of Ph.D. candidates in the sciences, preference for the complex and asymmetrical figures proved to be significantly related to rated originality in graduate work. This same relationship was found among graduating medical school seniors who were rated for originality by the medical school faculty. Other evidence indicated that the opposed preferences, for complexity or for simplicity, were related to a generalized experiential disposition: the preference for complexity is associated with a perceptual attitude that seeks to allow into the perceptual system the greatest possible richness

[1] Barron, F., & Welsh, G. S., "Artistic Perception as a Factor in Personality Style: Its Measurement by a Figure Preference Test," *Journal of Psychology*, 1951, 33, 199–203.

of experience, even though discord and disorder result, while the preference for simplicity is associated with a perceptual attitude that allows into the system only as much as can be integrated without great discomfort and disorder, even though this means excluding some aspects of reality.

From all these considerations, certain hypotheses as to the characteristics of original persons were derived and put to the test in the present study. The hypotheses, and the ways in which they were tested, or partially tested, are described below.

Hypothesis 1: That original persons prefer complexity and some degree of apparent imbalance in phenomena.

Test 1. The Barron-Welsh Art Scale of the Figure Preference Test. Preference for complex-asymmetrical figures earns the subject a high score.

Hypothesis 2: That original persons are more complex psychodynamically and have greater personal scope.

Test 2. Psychiatric interviewer rating on "Complexity and Scope as a Person." The subjects receiving high ratings are those who were diagnosed by a psychiatric interviewer, on the basis of a two-hour interview, as having a "more complex personality structure and greater potential for complex ego-synthesis." Ratings were on a nine-point scale with approximate normal curve frequencies being assigned to each point along the scale.

Hypothesis 3: That original persons are more independent in their judgments.

Test 3a. The Independence of Judgment Scale. On this inventory scale, which was developed against the criterion of actual behavior in the Asch group pressure experiment in previous studies, high scores indicate similarity to persons who manifest independence.

Test 3b. A modification of the Asch group pressure experiment.[2] This is a situational test in which subjects are put under pressure from their peers to agree to certain apparent group judgments. High scores indicate yielding to such pressures; regularly original persons should therefore have lower scores.

[2] This version of the group pressure experiment retains the prototypical psychological situation used by Asch, but introduces novel methods of experimental control and greatly expands the kinds of judgments on which group pressure is brought to bear. The new technique was designed by Richard S. Crutchfield, and arose out of discussions in 1952 at the Institute of Personality Assessment and Research concerning the problems posed in adapting the Asch technique to a living-in assessment situation in which there could be no confederates of the experimenter. Crutchfield has reported its details in his presidential address, "Conformity and Character," before the Division of Personality and Social Psychology, American Psychological Association, New York City, September 4, 1954. (*American Psychologist,* 1955, 10, 191–198.)

Hypothesis 4: That original persons are more self-assertive and dominant.

Test 4a. Dominance-submission ratings in a psychodramatic situation especially designed to elicit such tendencies in the subjects. Ratings were on a nine-point scale.

Test 4b. The Social Dominance scale of the California Psychological Inventory. This is a thoroughly studied and validated scale for the measurement of dominance in real-life social situations.

Test 4c. Staff rating on Dominance, based on three days of observation of social behavior. Dominance was defined for the raters as follows: "Self-assurance, ascendance, and self-confidence in dealing with others; forceful, authoritative, resolute, not easily intimidated." A five-point rating scale was used.

Test 4d. The Self-assertiveness scale of the California Psychological Inventory.

Test 4e. The Phallicism scale of the Personal Preference Scale.[3] This scale is intended as a measure of the derivatives and residuals in the adult personality of propensities that were highly cathected in the phallic stage of psychosexual development. High scores indicate an emphasis on personal power and desire for recognition.

Hypothesis 5: That original persons reject suppression as a mechanism for the control of impulse. This would imply that they forbid themselves fewer thoughts, that they dislike to police themselves or others, that they are disposed to entertain impulses and ideas that are commonly taboo, and in general that they express in their persons the sort of indiscipline that psychoanalytic theory would ascribe to a libidinal organization in which derivatives of the early anal rather than of the late anal stage in psychosexual development predominate.

Test 5a. An index of suppression-expression on the Minnesota Multiphasic Personality Inventory is obtained by adding the T scores on the Lie, Hysteria, and K scales and subtracting from that sum the sum of T scores on Psychopathic Deviation and Hypomania. On this index, regularly original subjects should obtain lower scores.

Test 5b. The Policeman Interest scale of the Strong Vocational Interest Blank. While this is bound to be a somewhat derivative measure of the personality tendency toward suppression of outlawed impulse, it does at least reflect the similarity of the subject's interests to those of persons who are regularly employed at maintaining law, order, and civil discipline—who, in short, seem vocationally suited to policing. Regularly original subjects should earn low scores.

Test 5c. The Early Anal and the Late Anal scales of the Personal Preference Scale (Grygier revision).[4] If the scales are valid and the hy-

[3] Krout, M. H., & Tabin, J. K., "Measuring Personality in Developmental Terms," *Genetic Psychology Monograph*, 1954, 50, 289–335.

[4] The form of the Personal Preference Scale used in this study is a revision made by Tadeusz Grygier. The revision consisted chiefly of the addition of items to certain scales, including the Early and Late Anal scales.

pothesis is correct, regularly original subjects should score higher on Early Anal and lower on Late Anal than do regularly unoriginal subjects.

Test 5d. The Impulsivity Scale of the California Psychological Inventory. Since high scorers are those who express impulse readily, the regularly original subjects should earn higher scores than the regularly unoriginal subjects.

Test 5e. Staff rating: Impulsivity. Again, regularly original subjects should receive higher ratings.

The group comparisons specified in these predictions are presented in Table 16.3. As that table shows, 12 of the 15 predictions proved correct. A fairly conservative criterion of confirmation was adopted: significance at the .05 level when the two-tailed test was applied. The theoretical formulation suggested by the previous work on complexity-simplicity and on independence of judgment is substantially confirmed by these results.

ORIGINALITY AND REJECTION OF CONTROL

The five major hypotheses in this study have been stated in terms derived directly from previous observations. There is another way of looking at them, however, which permits the results to be considered in somewhat other terms and in a broader context. Since the hypotheses have already been stated and to some extent justified, it may be appropriate in discussing these results to venture somewhat beyond the literal meaning of the findings to date.

We have spoken here of the disposition toward originality, with originality being so measured as to be equivalent to the capacity for producing unusual adaptive responses. But unusualness of response may be considered a function as well of the objective freedom of an organism, where this is defined as the range of possible adaptive responses available in all situations. (This we shall discuss more fully in Chapter 21.) As the response repertoire of any given organism increases, the number of statistically infrequent responses, considered relative to the population of like organisms, will also increase. Thus the ability to respond in an unusual or original manner will be greatest when freedom is greatest.

Now freedom is related in a very special manner to degree and kind of organization. In general, organization in company with complexity generates freedom; the more complex the level of integration, the

TABLE 16.3 *Tests of Hypotheses*

Hypotheses	Originals (N = 15)		Unoriginals (N = 15)		t	P
	M	SD	M	SD		
1. Preference for complexity						
Test 1. Barron-Welsh Art Sacle	19.40	12.28	12.67	10.69	2.16	.02
2. Complexity as a person						
Test 2. Psychiatric rating: "Complexity as a person"	6.40	1.82	4.00	1.67	3.58	.001
3. Independence of judgment						
Test 3a. Independence of Judgment Scale	9.60	1.67	8.00	2.94	1.74	.05
Test 3b. Group pressure situation*	5.00	1.87	8.60	1.80	3.93	.001
4. Self-assertion and Dominance						
Test 4a. Psychodrama: Dominance rating	41.13	11.70	38.40	7.78	0.72	.23
Test 4b. CPI: Social Dominance Scale	36.60	3.74	28.87	4.75	4.74	.001
Test 4c. Staff rating: Dominance	34.40	7.10	25.40	4.06	4.05	.001
Test 4d. SCPI: Self-Assertiveness Scale	15.73	1.44	15.07	2.74	0.78	.22
Test 4e. PPS: Phallicism Scale (VIK)	13.20	2.37	9.13	4.27	3.08	.01
5. Rejection of suppression; tendency towards expression of impulse						
Test 5a. MMPI: $(L + Hy + K) - (Pd + Ma)$	43.47	26.24	58.87	12.30	1.78	.045
Test 5b. SVIB: Policeman Interest Scale	44.67	9.87	55.00	10.81	−2.61	.01
Test 5c. PPS: Early Anal Scale (IVB)	20.33	4.57	17.87	2.90	1.66	.06
Late Anal Scale (VB)	23.53	4.59	26.80	4.85	−1.81	.05
Test 5d. CPI: Impulsivity Scale	23.13	7.86	16.60	6.08	1.98	.03
Test 5e. Staff rating: Impulsivity	32.27	6.41	27.80	5.42	4.74	.001

* For the test of this hypothesis, only eight Ss in each group (eight Originals and eight Unoriginals) were available. This occurred because half of the subjects in the study were used as controls in the Crutchfield experiment, and hence made the judgments without being under pressure to conform to group opinion.

greater is the repertoire of adaptive responses. But the tendency toward organization *may* operate in such a fashion as to maintain a maladaptive simplicity. We are familiar in the political sphere with totalitarian states which depend upon suppression to achieve unity; such states are psychodynamically similar to the neurotic individual who suppresses his own impulses and emotions in order to maintain a semblance of stability. There are at hand enough case histories of both such organizations, political and private, to make it clear that the sort of unity and balance that depends upon total suppression of the claims of minority affects and opinions is maladaptive in the long run.

Suppression is a common way of achieving unity, however, because in the short run it often seems to work. Increasing complexity puts a strain upon an organism's ability to integrate phenomena. One solution of the difficulty is to inhibit development of the greater level of complexity and thus to avoid the temporary disintegration that would otherwise have resulted.

Originality, then, flourishes where suppression is at a minimum and where some measure of disintegration is tolerable in the interests of a higher level of integration which may yet be reached.

If we consider the case of a human being who develops strongly the disposition toward originality, we must posit certain personal characteristics and personal history which facilitated the development of such a disposition. In our hypotheses, the term "dominance" was used to describe one trait of the regularly original individual. Dominance may be translated as a strong need for personal mastery, not merely over other persons, but over all experience. It initially involves self-centeredness (which in its socialized form may come to be known as self-realization). One aspect of it is the insistence on a high degree of self-regulation, and a rejection of regulation by others.

For such a person, the most crucial developmental crisis in relation to control of impulse comes, if we accept the psychoanalytic formulation of stages of psychosexual development, at the anal stage of socialization. What our hypotheses have suggested is that there is a positive rebellion against the prohibition of unregulated anal production, and a carrying of the derivatives of anal indiscipline into adult life. The original person, in adulthood, thus often likes things messy, at least at first. The tendency is toward a final order, but the necessary preliminary is as big a mess as possible. Viewed developmentally, the rejection of externally imposed control at the anal stage is later generalized to all external control of impulse, with the tendency toward socially unlicensed phallic activity, or phallic exhibitionism in its more derivative forms, being simply another expression of the general rejection of regulation of impulse by others, in favor of regulation of impulse by oneself.

The disposition toward originality may thus be seen as a highly organized mode of responding to experience, including other persons, society, and oneself. The socially disrated traits that may go along with it include rebelliousness, disorderliness, and exhibitionism, while the socially valued traits which accompany it include independence of judgment, freedom of expression, and novelty of construction and insight.

17

Intelligence Quotient, Personality, and Originality

THAT homely yearning for simplicity which we have been discovering in ourselves and in the great majority of people who have taken our preference tests has not escaped the bosoms of educators any more than of the parents of the children they teach. One sign of it is the immense popularity of the notion that intelligence can not only be measured, but can be expressed in a simple number, with a base of reference something like a dollar—the I.Q., one hundred units of which can be counted upon to indicate that the Lord dealt out to his servant an average number of talents, to be buried or used according to his character and personal worthiness, for better or for worse.

The enduring vogue of the I.Q. is certainly testament to our natural desire to keep the story simple, and psychologists and teachers have been the worst offenders in supporting this popular simplification. The fact is, of course, that intelligence is a complex set of interrelated aptitudes and abilities, some of them verging closely upon the temperamental rather than being limited to what we usually think of as intellective.

In this chapter we shall consider the results of a study designed especially to discover some of the determinants, other than a simple one-number estimate of intelligence, that are important in the production of the sorts of original perceptions and problem-solutions we discussed in Chapter 16. In brief, we shall first report relationships observed in that sample of military officers between the composite test measure of originality and certain other aspects of personal and intellectual functioning, and then we shall consider the statistically significant correlates of originality both when intelligence is partialled out statistically and when it is systematically varied through special selection of subjects.

The study, as we have seen, employed a wide variety of psychological tests in the usual living-in assessment setting. Both because of the nature of the sample and because of the method employed for discovering significant relationships, several restrictions upon the generalizability of the results must be recognized. For one thing, correlation coefficients between the measure of originality and several hundred other variables were computed in a search for significant associations, and the observed correlations have not as yet been checked in any other sample that is this similar to the general population (simply because we changed tack and decided to work particularly with highly creative individuals whose life was devoted to creative endeavor). The military officers, of course, were not selected with a view to discovering the traits of original persons; they had not engaged themselves in work that called for a high order of original thought, nor was originality an important value in their lives. In brief, the correlations to be reported may not reflect anything concerning the way in which highly creative people differ from the norm. The results therefore are germane to the question of how originality varies with other personal characteristics only if originality be considered as a variable that is distributed continuously throughout the general population.

In spite of these strictures inherent in the design of the study, there is some reason to believe that the results are generalizable to the problem of creative process in the highly original person. In the preceding chapter, we saw that originality in free-response performance tests is sufficiently consistent across tests to be considered a dimension, and that in addition the test dimension itself is related to personality variables which were hypothesized on theoretical grounds to be characteristics of highly original persons. Thus the testing of theory in that respect suggests that generalizable relationships may be discovered in this sample, and perhaps in fact that it particularly favors the finding of valid relationships.

ASSESSMENT OBSERVATIONS AND VARIABLES

Observations made by staff members during the assessment period were put in summary form and prepared for statistical analysis mainly through two techniques: a Q-sort deck of 76 statements descriptive of personal functioning, and the adjective check-list consisting of 300 common, personally descriptive adjectives. Both techniques were used by staff members at the conclusion of each assessment period to describe each assessee.

The Q-sort statements were sorted on a nine-point scale, while the adjectives were checked simply as characteristic or not characteristic of the given subject. A composite Q-sort description of each subject was obtained by averaging the placements of the items by four staff members. The composite adjective description consisted of all adjectives which had been checked as characteristic of the subject by at least three of ten raters.

These descriptions were given without knowledge of the objective test performances of the subjects. No rater knew any subject's score on the Originality Composite at the time the descriptions were made.

Scores on the Originality Composite were correlated also with nearly 200 other assessment variables, most of which had proved upon inspection to be normally distributed. Space limitations prohibit the listing of all these variables here, but the nature of most of them are indicated briefly in Table 17.1. A full description of each variable,

TABLE 17.1 *Sources of Variables*

The Concept Mastery Test: total score
The Wesman Personnel Classification Test: Verbal and Numerical subtests and
    total score
The Minnesota Multiphasic Personality Inventory: 14 scales
The Rorschach Psychodiagnostic: 20 scores
The Personal Preference Survey: 10 scales
The Strong Vocational Interest Blank: 46 scales
The Idea Classification Test: total score
Charades: four ratings and five scores
Staff ratings: 30 traits
The Barron M-threshold Inkblots: threshold for human movement and volume
    of human movement
The Barron-Welsh Art Scale
Improvisations: 20 ratings
The Gottschaldt Figures Test: total score
The Bennett Mechanical Comprehension Test
The Minnesota Paper Form Board
The Chapin Social Insight Test
The Special IPAR Composite Personality Inventory: 19 scales
The California Personality Inventory: 20 scales
Form 60 of Berkeley Public Opinion Survey Scales: 3 scales

---

together with statistics descriptive of the variable's distribution in this sample, may be found in another more technical report.[1]

DIFFERENCES IN STAFF DESCRIPTIONS OF HIGH AND LOW SCORERS

The 25 highest scorers on the Originality Composite were compared with the 25 lowest scorers on both the Q-sort descriptions and the composite adjective descriptions. The Q-sort items that showed statistically significant differences are given in Table 17.2.

TABLE 17.2

High Scorers

At the .001 level:
1. Verbally fluent, conversationally facile.
2. High degree of intellect.
3. Communicates ideas clearly and effectively.
4. Highly cathects intellectual activity.
5. Is an effective leader.
6. Is persuasive; wins others over to his point of view.

At the .01 level:
7. Is concerned with philosophical problems and the meaning of life.
8. Takes an ascendant role in his relations with others.

Low Scorers

At the .001 level:
1. Conforming; tends to do the things that are prescribed.
2. Is stereotyped and unoriginal in his approach to problems.
3. Has a narrow range of interests.
4. Tends not to become involved in things.
5. Lacks social poise and presence.
6. Is unaware of his own social stimulus value.

At the .01 level:
7. Slow personal tempo.
8. With respect to authority, is submissive, compliant, and overly accepting.
9. Lacks confidence in self.
10. Is rigid, inflexible.
11. Lacks insight into own motives.
12. Is suggestible.
13. Is unable to make decisions without vacillation, hesitation, and delay.

[1] MacKinnon, D. W., Crutchfield, R. S., Barron, F., Block, J., Gough, H. G., & Harris, R. E., *An assessment study of Air Force officers: Part I. Design of the study and description of variables.* Lackland Air Force Base, Texas: Air Force Personnel and Training Research Center, April 1958. (*Technical Report* WADC-TR-58-91 [I], ASTIA Document No. AD 151 040.)

Adjectives that were applied differentially (at the .05 level or better) by the assessment staff to high and low scorers are given in Table 17.3, with the frequencies (i.e., number of cases out of 25 to which the adjective was applied) stated in parentheses after the adjective. Frequencies for high scorers are given first.

TABLE 17.3

High Scorers	
Interests wide (12–1)	Logical (9–2)
Clever (9–1)	Rational (9–2)
Imaginative (9–1)	Shrewd (9–2)
Planful (9–1)	Civilized (8–2)
Poised (11–2)	Loyal (8–2)
Resourceful (12–3)	Mature (8–2)
Reflective (9–3)	Versatile (7–0)
Quick (9–3)	Efficient (14–3)
Enterprising (11–4)	Initiative (13–3)
Energetic (10–4)	Organized (10–4)
Determined (10–2)	Fairminded (13–6)
Talkative (10–2)	
Low Scorers	
Dull (0–8)	Apathetic (1–8)
Commonplace (1–11)	Rigid (1–7)
Simple (1–11)	Unassuming (5–12)
Slow (1–10)	Conventional (7–13)

From these *Q*-sort and adjective descriptions one is led to believe that considerable validity inheres in the originality measure. In brief, high scorers are seen as intelligent, widely informed, concerned with basic problems, clever and imaginative, socially effective and personally dominant, verbally fluent, and possessed of initiative. Low scorers are seen as conforming, rigid and stereotyped, uninsightful, commonplace, apathetic, and dull.

However, the marked relationship of originality to verbal fluency and to rated intellect raises a question concerning the extent to which this list of traits is determined by intelligence quite apart from originality. Perhaps these are in large part the traits of intelligent people, rather than of people who are not only intelligent but original as well. What we should like to know is the correlation between personality variables and the part of the variance in originality that is *not* associated with variance in general intellectual ability.

It is, of course, reasonable to expect that intelligence and originality will co-vary positively. If one defines originality as the ability to re-spond to stimulus situations both adaptively and unusually, and if one defines intelligence simply as the ability to solve problems, then at the upper levels of problem-solving ability the manifestation of intelli-gence will be also a manifestation of originality. That is to say, the very difficult and rarely solved problem requires by definition a solu-tion that is original.

It seems desirable, therefore, to partial out the effect of intelligence upon the correlations between the Originality Composite and other assessment measures. The Concept Mastery Test was here accepted as a good measure of general intelligence, though clearly with most em-phasis upon the verbal comprehension factor in intelligence.

The product-moment correlation coefficient between the Concept Mastery Test and the Originality Composite in this sample is .33, a relationship significantly different from zero at the .01 level. When the Originality Composite is correlated with the other assessment measures and its relationship to the Concept Mastery Test is partialled out, the statistically significant partial r's shown in Table 17.4 are discovered. (In this table the variables are grouped, and the groups named, simply in a way that makes sense subjectively to the present writer; these are not clusters established statistically.)

With the effect of verbal intelligence thus removed, the forces de-termining original response emerge in an interesting pattern. One cluster of variables that are in fact uncorrelated with intelligence consists of responsiveness to color on the Rorschach, high scores on the scale purporting to measure undercontrol of impulse, and high scores on the CPI Impulsivity scale. Perhaps the rating of motility in Charades (defined as amount of motoric activity by the subject when attempting to convey a title to his teammates) is better grouped with this cluster too. What may be involved here is the tendency of the individual to discharge tension, through motor avenues of discharge, as immediately as possible, and hence to be relatively more under what in psychoanalytic terms would be called the domination of the pleasure principle rather than the reality principle.

Another cluster, that which is here labeled "energy, fluent output, involvement," would seem to indicate a higher level of drive, as well as ease of expression of the drive in work. This might well be a generic factor which shows itself interpersonally in the form of dominance and striving for power. The behavior apparently is effective as well,

TABLE 17.4   *Variables Significantly Associated with the Originality Composite When Concept Mastery Test Scores Are Partialled Out*

	Partial *r*'s
Disposition toward integration of diverse stimuli:	
1. Rorschach: *W*	.52
2. Rorschach: number of different determinants used	.37
3. Idea Classification Test: number of classes discerned in sets of varied objects and property	.31
Energy, fluent output, involvement:	
4. Improvisations: degree of participation	.35
5. Word Fluency Test: total output	.41
6. Charades: motility	.39
7. Charades: fluency	.28
8. Staff rating: fluency of ideas	.49
9. Staff rating: drive	.42
Personal dominance and self-assertion:	
10. Improvisations: dominance	.37
11. Staff rating: dominance	.37
12. CPI: Dominance scale	.29
13. Personal Preference Scale: Active Phallic	.47
Responsiveness to impulse and emotion:	
14. CPI: Impulsivity scale	.39
15. Ego-control Scale: undercontrol	.40
16. Rorschach: sum *C*	.38
Expressed femininity of interests:	
17. SVIB: Masculinity	−.31
18. MMPI: Femininity (*Mf*)	.33
19. PPS: Feminine Identification	.30
General effectiveness of performance:	
20. Charades: overall performance	.39
21. Improvisations: total effectiveness	.34
22. Staff rating: Overall effectiveness in command functions in the Air Force	.36
23. Staff rating. Overall effectiveness in staff function in the Air Force	.37

judging from the correlations with various ratings of effectiveness of performance.

The group of variables titled "disposition toward integration of diverse stimuli" suggests an openness in the more original subjects to a variety of phenomena, combined with a strong need to organize those phenomena into some coherent pattern. This might best be described as a resistance to premature closure, combined with a persistent effort to achieve closure in an elegant fashion. In brief, everything that can be perceived must be taken cognizance of before a configuration is recognized as a possibly final one.

The relationships noted between originality and femininity of interest pattern may conceivably be explained in terms of some of the dynamics suggested above, although they lend themselves also to a quite different sort of speculation. In a sense, the recognition by men of impulses or interests that are considered more appropriate in women, or at least more characteristic of women than of men in this culture, may be seen as one aspect of the more basic disposition to allow more complexity and contradictions into consciousness; this assumes, of course, an initial biological bisexual disposition in both men and women. Thus the more original men would permit themselves to be more aware of tabooed interests and impulses, and would seek to integrate these superficially discordant phenomena into a more complex total pattern.

Another possible explanation is that some degree of cross-sex identification is important for creativity in men, and perhaps women as well. The creative act is a kind of giving birth, and it is noteworthy that as an historical fact intellectual creativity has been conspicuously lacking in women, whose products are their children. At the risk of making too much of a linguistic parallel, it might be said that nature has literally arranged a division of labor. Men bring forth ideas, paintings, literary and musical compositions, organizations of states, inventions, new material structures, and the like, while women bring forth the new generation. Perhaps it is also true that women who do the kind of creative work usually done by men may themselves have some degree of reversal of the usual sexual identifications, being relatively more masculine in interests and impulses than the generality of women; at any rate, such an hypothesis seems worth investigating.

However, it may be that the present finding requires no very high-flown explanation, since this sample of military officers was on the average more masculine (in terms of scores on the tests mentioned) than men-in-general, and high scores on femininity in these subjects represented quite unremarkable deviations in the feminine direction.

CORRELATES OF LARGE DISCREPANCIES BETWEEN ORIGINALITY AND INTELLIGENCE

Data gathered in a larger sample of officers, most of whom did not take part in living-in assessment, permit another approach to the question of what personality traits go along with originality in the absence (in this instance, the conspicuous absence) of the usually co-varying verbal intelligence. In this study, 343 officers of the rank of captain, 100 of whom comprised the sample discussed previously, were scored on four of the eight measures used in the Originality Composite. The four measures were: Unusual Uses, Consequences B, Plot Titles B, and Word Synthesis Originality. The Concept Mastery test was also administered to these 343 officers. In addition, the officers themselves filled out the adjective check-list under instructions to give a candid and accurate picture of themselves.

Two groups were now selected for comparison with one another: all the subjects (15 in number) who were one standard deviation above the mean on the abbreviated four-measure Originality Composite while being one standard deviation below the mean on the Concept Mastery test, and all the subjects (23 in number) who were one standard deviation above the mean on the Concept Mastery test while being one standard deviation below the mean on the Originality Composite. The two groups will be referred to respectively as O_h-I_l and I_h-O_l. The adjectives that each group applied to itself significantly more often (at the .05 level of confidence) are given below.

O_h-I_l: affected, aggressive, demanding, dependent, dominant, forceful, impatient, initiative, outspoken, sarcastic, strong, suggestible.

I_h-O_l: mild, optimistic, pleasant, quiet, unselfish.

When these extreme groups are compared, the impulse-control dimension emerges most clearly as a determinant of originality. Subjects who are relatively original in spite of being relatively unintelligent show a lack of ego-control. They describe themselves as persons whose needs demand immediate gratification and whose aggressive impulses are out in the open. They are willful, obstreperous, and extreme individuals. One would not be inclined to select them as companions for a long trip in a submarine. By contrast, their relatively unoriginal but more intelligent fellows seem very much on the pleasant side, although perhaps a bit *too* bland and unwarlike, all things considered.

When one compares these self-descriptions with the staff descriptions of subjects who are *both* original and intelligent, it appears that intelligence represents the operation of the reality principle in behavior, and is responsible for such characteristics as the appropriate delay of impulse-expression and the effective organization of instinctual energy for the attainment of goals in the world as it is. To use another of the distinctions proposed by Freud in his theory of the functioning of the mental apparatus,[2] primary process thinking to the exclusion of the secondary process marks the original but unintelligent person; secondary process thinking which carries ego-control to the point where the ego is not so much strong as muscle-bound marks the intelligent but unoriginal person; and easy accessibility of both primary process and secondary process marks the person who is both original and intelligent.

SOME SPECULATIONS

If these conclusions from the observed results be permitted for the moment, a speculative formulation suggests itself. The effectively original person may be characterized above all by an ability to regress very far *for the moment* while being able quite rapidly to return to a high degree of rationality, bringing with him the fruits of his regression to primitive and fantastic modes of thought (a variant of the phenomenon termed "regression in the service of the ego" by Lowenstein and Kris). Perhaps when the cortex is most efficient, or intelligence greatest, the ego realizes that it *can afford to allow* regression— because it can correct itself. A basic confidence in one's ability to discern reality accurately would thus facilitate the use of the powers of imagination.

Another way of putting this (and heuristically, I think, a better way) is to say that when the distinction between subject (self) and object is most secure, the distinction can with most security be allowed to disappear temporarily. In such an individual there might therefore occur some transitory phenomena of the sort that in truly pathological form are characteristic of the very weak ego (such as hallucinations, sense of oneness with the universe, visions, mystical beliefs, superstitions: phenomena which we shall discuss later and at length in Chapter 20). But in the highly creative individual the basis for these phenomena is precisely the opposite of their basis in mentally ill individuals. In paranoia, for instance, the fundamental ego-failure is the chronic *inability* to distinguish between subject and object, between

---

[2] Freud, S., "Formulations regarding the two principles in mental functioning," *Collected Papers*, Vol. IV (London: The Hogarth Press and the Institute of Psychoanalysis, 1950).

inner and outer sources of experience, so that introjection and projection appear as characteristic mechanisms. In the creative person, this distinction may indeed have been attained with great difficulty and may have been won out of childhood circumstances that are ordinarily pathogenic, but once attained it is then *maintained* with unusual confidence. Thus the creative genius may be at once naïve and knowledgable, being at home equally to primitive symbolism and to rigorous logic. He is both more primitive and more cultured, more destructive and more constructive, occasionally crazier and yet adamantly saner, than the average person.

18

Unconscious and Preconscious Influences in the Making of Fiction

"THE WORLD as it is" . . . "the reality principle" . . . "adamantine" sanity . . . these reassuringly solid phrases may furnish just the firm ground one needs to embark on a consideration of the role of the unconscious, that realm of chaos and shadows, in creative activity. Let us consider first of all what we mean by "realistic thinking" and what part it plays in science, psychoneurosis, psychotherapy, and artistic creativity.

To see things as they are when they are not as we would like them to be is the sternest task to which as rational beings we are called. In the service of this stern necessity, conscious thought and reflection have arisen. The marks of consciousness and rationality are attention, discrimination, memory, judgment, logic, and experiment. To be able to doubt methodically while suspending judgment, to explore alternative explanations in the light of certain canons of evidence and criticism, is the essence of the scientific attitude. Pristine common sense is the everyday form of this attitude; the physical sciences and mathematics are its most rigorous and pure embodiment.

It is no news that many scientists, and especially the very best, are odd people. As we have suggested elsewhere, they are in the very forefront of the direction in which evolution is taking us, and as such they exemplify in their work such qualities as dryness of judgment, meticulous attention to details, distinctions and small differences, radical questioning of common assumptions, a distrust of the unfortified senses, and a preference for the abstract and the quantitative as against the metaphorical, the poetical, the qualitative, and the immediately natural. We are all of us children of Adam, however, if I may so show my hand, and even the most scientific of scientists usually has a streak of irrationality a yard wide up his back, which makes his oddness complete. The distinguished historian of science, A. C. Crombie, has given us in his monumental presentation of the history of the scientific revolution literally hundreds of accounts of how superstitions, whims, bizarre images or convictions lead finally to scientific advances and important break-throughs.

The point of all this is that Necessity may be as stern as she wishes, and when we are called to the task we must go, but we rarely go quietly. There is something in the human mind that does not like things as they are, something that will make up its own little world in whatever way seems to that individual piece of mind to be an improvement. Even that most dedicated of realists, Sigmund Freud, whose work is recognized in the title of this chapter, found himself near the end of his life composing the most improbable romance, "Moses and Monotheism," the burden of his thesis being that Moses was really an Egyptian, a claim which has left historical scholars aghast and which it is fair to say arose more from a lively imagination than from dry and discriminating research. The opening sentence of that entertaining monograph reads as follows: "To deny a people the man whom it praises as the greatest of its sons is not a deed to be undertaken light-heartedly—especially by one belonging to that people." We have already learned from Freud the realist, in his brilliant paper on "Negation," to be wary of sentences containing denials, and to read "not so" as "so." Perhaps the heavy-hearted elucidator of the Oedipus riddle had a light-hearted holiday at last when he removed, not the greatest of its sons, but the father of its laws, from the people to whom he belonged.

The greatest of art bears a peculiarly two-faced relationship to external reality and the private universe of meaning that the individual artist has created. It is two-faced not merely in the sense of "the mask," as the Irish poet, William Butler Yeats, described his world of symbols, but Janus-like, facing backward and forward simultaneously. Goethe has the heavenly chorus sing at the conclusion of *Faust:*

> All things transitory
> but as symbols are sent;
> Earth's insufficiency
> *Here* grows to event.

The symbol presents a reality transcended. It is the medium through which a superior vision of reality is attained; it amplifies the poor real world through the act of imagination. This extension of reality is at the heart of the poetic view of things. The 16th-century Spanish poet Calderón has his hero in "La Vida es Serena" declare "Life, it seems, is but a dream, And even dreams are dreams." Yeats himself, in a poem titled significantly "The Circus Animals' Desertion," in which he laments a period in which his reverie failed him and his poetic fount seemed to have gone dry, gives us these lines: "Players and painted stage took all my love/And not the things that they were emblems of."

Symbols, dreams, play, light-heartedness—these are the stuff of a part of mind that gives little service to syllogism, evidence, judgment, classification, prediction, law, and stern necessity. But stern necessity calls: let us consider the way in which unconscious and preconscious forces may influence the making of fiction. What we shall begin with is a brief review of the psychoanalytic theory of the unconscious and the preconscious; then we shall consider their role in the making of fiction; and we shall conclude with an attempt to appraise the role of psychic conflict in generating, particularly through the mechanism of symbolization, novel imaginings that are the raw material out of which the work of art is made.

Freud conceived the "mental apparatus," which might just as well be called the mind, both topographically and dynamically. The topography does not, of course, have anything to do with the anatomy of the central nervous system, but is concerned solely with hypothetical spatial arrangements in a formal theoretical system, irrespective of their possible situation or neurological correlates in the body. The mental apparatus, then, like all Gaul, is divided into three parts: the unconscious, the preconscious, and the conscious. The theory claims that all mental acts belong first to the unconscious. Unconsciousness is described by Freud as "a regular and inevitable phase in the processes constituting our mental activity; every mental act begins as an unconscious one, and it may either remain so or go on developing into consciousness, according as it meets with resistance or not." Between the unconscious and the preconscious there occurs a kind of testing process, which is called "the censorship." The mental act in the unconscious has two alternative fates open to it: upon being scrutinized by the censorship it may be rejected, not allowed to pass into the second phase, in which event it is said to be "repressed" and must remain unconscious. If, however, it passes this scrutiny it enters upon the second phase, the preconscious, and becomes *capable of entering consciousness*. The rigorous censorship exercises its office at the point of transition from the unconscious to the preconscious. Once in the preconscious, the thought may now, without any special resistance and given certain conditions, become the object of consciousness.

The core of the unconscious consists of "instinct-presentations" having the sole aim of discharging the energy with which they are invested. In other words, they are the mental representation of impulses, or drives, or physiologically-based excitations which seek discharge. A tension or imbalance exists, and the tendency of the organism is to regain balance and stability by a discharge of energy.

These ideational representations of drives that—because of the nature of the external world as well as of the organization of consciousness—are denied discharge become related to one another by laws quite different from those that govern logical thought. For one thing, they are exempt from mutual contradiction; quite opposite feelings about the same object may exist simultaneously in the unconscious. Time, place, and custom have no effect upon them. Moreover, they are continually seeking short-cuts to discharges of their energy, and this they achieve by such mechanisms as displacement, condensation, substitution, and symbolization. These mechanisms are exhibited most clearly in dreams. Several persons whom the dreamer knows in his waking state may be condensed into a single dream personage; one person may be substituted for another, and feelings displaced from the original object of them to another object; situations that trouble the dreamer in his waking life may undergo a symbolic transformation which serves to make them almost unrecognizable.

Our studies of the psychology of literary creation persuade us that ideas from the unconscious play a large part in furnishing the material out of which the work of art is made. Art differs from dream and neurosis, however, in that its elaboration requires conscious effort, criticism, judgment, and a sense of form that is quite alien to the chaos of the unconscious. What appears to happen is this: the censorship momentarily suspends its function and an unconscious idea passes into the preconscious. This idea at first seems vague and appears to have no relationship to other conscious content. Often it finds its first fleeting representation simply as a momentary visual or verbal image.

It then somehow begins to pull along with it various associated ideas, feelings, and symbols from the unconscious, which then enter into relationship to one another in the preconscious, as well as with other ideas already in the preconscious. The complex of ideas thus elaborated may finally come to conscious expression almost fully formed, or, more commonly, they come in fragments, and it is the task of conscious thought to relate them to one another. The real work, of course, comes in making out of this material a communication, i.e., giving it a social reality, which involves discrimination, selection, technique, purpose, and understanding both of the material itself and of an audience of at least one other person who can appreciate it.

Most fictions, including many that are published in book form, are not works of art and do not possess social reality in the sense of which I have spoken of it. The world of the psychotic, and to a lesser degree of the neurotic, is a private world, and the creator of it is bound to feel alone in it. Probably the feeling of isolation is the most poignant aspect of neurotic suffering, rather than the effects that we designate as "symptoms."

One of the creative writers who took part in our research was the poetess Muriel Rukeyser, and she has given us permission both to say so and to use as an example in the present context her own already published description of the genesis of her poem "Orpheus."[1] This magnificent poem presents Orpheus resurrected; the torn body is magically restored to integrity. The poem began many years before it came to words; it began in an image of disintegration which came to Miss Rukeyser as she walked along a crowded street in New York City. The people whom she saw suddenly in her vision became all jumbled together, dismembered, their bodily organs torn from their own bodies and attached to others, their identity itself destroyed. The image came to her for one horrible moment, then disappeared; but

---

[1] "The Genesis of *Orpheus*," in *Mid-Century American Poets*, edited by John Ciardi, Twayne Publishers, Inc., New York, 1950.

she was shaken and changed by it. For several years thereafter it re-
curred occasionally, and it always was an experience of horror and
terror. By a process too complex for me to describe here, it somehow
became assimilated to the image of the body of Orpheus, torn by the
stones of the Thracian women and left strewn on the mountain top.
Finally came the act of reconstruction, reconciliation, transcendence:
the poem came to her, which to her was itself the resurrection, Orpheus being the archetype of the poet. Rilke has expressed beautifully
in one of his sonnets to Orpheus this quality of erotic transcendence:

> But you, divine one, unto the last still singing,
> although attacked by the flouted Maenads' throng,
> beautiful god, above the shrieks rose ringing
> among the destroyers, your ordered upbuilding song.[2]

In the records of our research we now have many such accounts of
symbolic transformation, the essence of the act of poetic and artistic
creation. An account of that research requires a volume of its own.
Without attempting to do justice to the richness of that material here,
I shall nevertheless give a few examples of what I mean by symbolic
transformation as shown by experiments and tests in the research on
writers, and shall describe also such results of the research as bear
directly upon the psychometric data presented from other studies in
the preceding several chapters.

The first experiment that I shall describe in this connection is one
that I developed from a study of originality in dreaming. In that
study, I secured the cooperation of some 150 individuals who agreed
to report all their dreams every day for three weeks, writing down
the dreams as they had experienced them just as soon as they woke
up. From these protocols, which describe the so-called "manifest
content" of the dream, it was possible to obtain estimates of the relative originality of the dream. Raters who read the protocols independently agreed highly among themselves in this sort of judgment.
Moreover, originality in dreaming proved to be related to a number
of other factors in cognitive functioning as determined by tests. However, a serious problem presented itself: might not the real act of
originality be shown not in the content of the dream as the dreamer
experienced it consciously, but in the act of transformation from the

---

[2] Sonnet 26, I, in *Sonnets to Orpheus*, Rainer Maria Rilke, with English translations
by C. F. MacIntyre. University of California Press, Berkeley and Los Angeles, 1960.
Reprinted by permission of the translator.

so-called "latent content" which Freudian theory insists is there and which it is the business of the dream to disguise?

In trying to find a way to answer this question, I hit upon the following idea: have everyone dream a dream whose latent content is identical for each. This could be done, or at least closely approached, by suggesting to each subject the same complex during a deep hypnotic trance, and then suggesting as well that he would be amnesic for all suggestions and would while asleep that evening have a dream about the events described. The implanted complex which the hypnotized subject was directed to remember as an incident that had actually occurred to him was as follows:

> Last Sunday evening on your way home you found a red purse in which there was a $100 bill. In the purse was the name of its owner, a neighbor of yours. Since it was late at night you took the purse home, planning to return it to its owner the next day. But then you were tempted, and took the $100 out of the purse. You then placed it in a drawer of your desk. In the middle of the week you opened the drawer and much to your surprise discovered that the purse was gone. You were at once fearful that the person who had found the purse would return it to its owner and implicate you. And you were also troubled by having yielded to temptation in taking the $100 bill, feeling very guilty. You have not been able to sleep well since this happened, and you have spoken to no one about the incident. You have been trying to forget the whole affair, but it is troubling you very much and tonight you will have a dream about it.

I will give just one example of a dream built upon this implanted complex, although many examples from our research files, all wildly different, might be given. The following was a dream reported by one of the student writers, a young woman:

> Strangely enough, I didn't want to go to sleep last night. I was frightened of it and continually saw strange figures and designs running before my eyes—mostly red squares, circles, straight black lines, all of them falling quickly down. It was very depressive, and a sense of foreboding settled—almost that to go to sleep would be evil. I opened my eyes once trying to shake away the evil. The skis in the corner, black and evil, seemed to be coming at me. I rolled over. I tried day dreams but I couldn't concentrate. My rebelling psyche wouldn't allow sleep. I tried concentrating on numbness, but my limbs only assumed a dull ache, particularly in my right hand, which throbbed, a similar sensation when in a dream trying to run away from something but unable to run fast enough.

Somehow, sleep.

And then sharp awakening. I sat up in bed with a quick vengeance, eager to shake off an oppressive, weighing force. Such a strange dream. I can't understand it.

Running, running happily, laughing breathlessly, down a long road; something under my arm, a small red object without any definite shape, more a shade of a color. Suddenly, a large deserted mansion loomed up in front of me. I hurried quickly inside and climbed, climbed blocky, heavy steps. A long time. But at the top a closet, open. The red shade had grown to gigantic proportions, almost the size of a trunk. I pushed it in the closet, but not really pushed—despite its size it was very light and almost dropped into the closet. I started gathering things from the red trunk, some strange objects. Suddenly the door slammed hard against its frame, and frightened I rushed down the stairs. As I walked down, I seemed to change clothes, or rather new things seemed to replace the old. I was richly clothed by the time I reached the bottom. But then a great sense of fright fell about me and I began to run— quickly through a meadow. Someone chased me—a stout figure with long, flowing hair. Soon, more stout figures pursued. Back in the mansion I hurried up the stairs, but there were few this time. The closet door was open and there was nothing there, only space. I could hear rumbling of voices, pounding, pounding, louder and louder. And then a mass of grey or rather haze rushed at me and I started back hurriedly into the closet—back, back. And then space, falling, falling, falling . . .

Even from this one example it is apparent that the technique is a powerful one for studying the nature of symbol formation; the complete set of protocols from this experiment and from the experimental situation that will be described in Chapter 20 demonstrate vividly the enormous variation among individuals in their ways of experiencing the world. Social conversation and everyday concerns are designed to conceal this variation and to increase the comfortable feeling that we are all more or less alike. That is why the sudden breakdown or the unexpected divorce or the inexplicable crime surprises or startles us. There is a widespread tacit pact not to reveal oneself, not to speak of the extremes of emotion, or terror, anger, pride, death-wish or glory-wish, or even "the great joy," as Thomas Mann calls the moment of illumination when the vast expanse of life and time, and the arrays of the dead, and the passing moments, are suddenly realized and one's own passing life is self-blessed.

Creative writers are, of course, not so disposed to silence in these matters. After all, their business is to tell, if not to tell outright. In one of the specially designed interviews for this study, an attempt was made to obtain their testimony concerning depth of feeling, range and oscillation of emotion, tendency to "go too far." As a group they showed themselves unusually open to feelings of awe, despair, devastation, oneness with the universe, mystical communion, premonition, divination, and other such unlikely states.

Concerning the general relationship of emotional conflict to creativity, much more needs to be said. To get some perspective on the dynamics involved, we must consider the problem in some of its formal aspects.

To begin with, conflict, taken in the most general sense, describes a state of affairs in which one force, or a complex of forces acting in relative unity, meets another force or complex of forces similarly organized. Forces in the stars and forces in the atom are prototypical physical examples in which conflict may produce explosion and enormous destruction. Conflict is one aspect of all natural phenomena; it is an indispensable part of life, of change, of the development of new forms. Forces change one another, just as people, who are forces, do; and we are changed by what we change. Conflict would cease only if the universe itself in its totality came to a state of perfect equilibrium, in which case it would be dead. Life itself, in this interpretation, is a vehicle for the maintenance of disequilibrium. As Henri Bergson said in his book *Creative Evolution*, "Life is a stone thrown uphill against the downward rush of matter," or as Freud put it in *Beyond the Pleasure Principle*, a bit cheerlessly, I thought, and inaccurately, "Life is a detour on the road to death." Both were referring to the physical theory that the material universe is tending toward a state in which there will be no motion and no conflict. In this view, life itself is a force that offers challenge to the inanimate.

Conflict is thus a universal in all of nature and is in some sense disembodied; genuine emotional conflicts can be lively things and often we can thank our lucky stars when we get a good one to grapple with. They can have in them the makings of something better.

Conflict is in many instances generative of new solutions rather than a disabling form of stasis. The real question is this: can an internal dialogue take place between conflicting forces in such a fashion that the speakers do not simply repeat themselves but that occasionally something new gets said?

Let us consider for a moment the more common case, in which the dialogue is forever repeated and the opposing forces in the conflict, quite undeterred by tedium, reassert their position over and over again in an intrapsychic equivalent of the cold war. Freud gave the name "repetition compulsion" to the universal human tendency to get into the same jam time after time. Usually the situation that is repeated is one which in its most primitive form occurred in early childhood. As the brain develops, however, and the capacity for complex symbolization increases, the situations tend to get fancier and fancier so far as content is concerned, so that in extreme cases, such as the delusional system of a paranoid schizophrenic, the entire cosmos becomes involved, complete with men from outer space armed with ray guns, and private conversations with divine personages and the celebrated dead. A well-worked-out psychoneurosis may be equally elegant, however, and I think it not too much to suggest that many events of great importance in world history had their beginnings in infantile disasters or conquests which individuals of unusual personal force caused to find re-enactment, with the world itself as stage.

Whether the re-enactment is momentous for others or hardly noticed at all by them, the point is that these repetitions are essentially static in character and have the smell of death about them. Forces in the unconscious are blind, they are locked in upon themselves, they do not change one another because essentially there is never a mutual confrontation. Moreover, the histrionics in which they involve the individual and those with whom he himself is involved in the external world are generally grade B or C melodramas. If viewed from the outside and if viewed without sympathy, they are like nothing so much as the kind of television film that is regularly re-run. Psychoneurosis in this view is the most tedious thing under the sun, and banality is its essence.

What "depth psychotherapy" attempts to do is to alter the deadly stasis of unconscious conflict by bringing the conflicting forces into consciousness, where they will have a chance to look at one another and hear what the other has to say. The hard necessity in depth therapy is to permit regression to occur, a little bit at a time, concurrently with efforts at increasing the strength of the ego, so that the patient may allow to come back into consciousness some painful feeling or severely tabooed impulse which had earlier been repressed. When this happens, the conflict can come out into the open, elements in it can be discriminated and criticized, and genuine confrontation with consequent decision may ensue.

This sort of constructive meeting of opposing forces may occur without psychotherapy, of course. People were working hard at knowing themselves long before Freud cast into the form of a theoretical system and a technique of therapy his own particular way of getting to know *himself*. Socrates long ago took self-knowledge as his goal, and judging from the Platonic dialogues he seems to have progressed well. Many of the philosophers and artists of the world have exemplified in their persons the same process. The artist transforms material from the unconscious into a social communication; he gives it a reality involving discrimination, selection, technique, purpose, and understanding both of the material itself and of its potential audience. In saying this, let me make it plain, I am not saying that the artist is usually neurotic or that his neurosis is being expressed in his art. Artists indeed seem to have more than their share of troubles, at least troubles of a certain sort, but we certainly need not say that because a person is troubled he has a psychoneurosis. Could it not be that individuals of unusual sensibility and symbolic scope are at once more prone to despair, disgust, forlornness, and rage at the tragedy, to use Yeats' vivid expression, of consciousness "harnessed to a dying animal" and yet at the same time more capable of transcending these universal human bonds through metaphor and through identification with natural processes? Fear, anger, guilt, and despair are perfectly natural and appropriate emotions for all of us at times, and people who experience life most intensely are likely to feel such emotions most extremely (as well, let it be said, as joy, love, and freedom of spirit). So, if they are artists, they will seek to express their image of life and their relation to it in the cultural language of which they have most command, and thus invite others to test the reality of their perceptions and, in a sense, to join them. Whatever is neurotic in them then becomes a part of the content, symbolically expressed, of their creative activity, and not simply a part of themselves that inhibits construction. Many creative people offer to psychoanalysis when it is proferred them a fundamental objection which for them is perhaps right. Although by not accepting it they may thus be left with their woes, there is yet the chance that as they struggle with their problems they may out of their distress make a testament to their belief in the ultimate intelligibility and significance of not only their own lives, but the lives of others. And for this, of course, there are great rewards.

But one need not be an artist or philosopher or even just a singularly valiant person to do the work of getting a conflict out into the open. An individual who decides to enter upon a psychoanalysis formally, i.e., with benefit of couch and analyst (or, to put it another way, makes a systematic practice of going to bed twice, and at least once by himself, on certain days) has usually already begun the work himself. Moreover, when the analysis is, as they say, terminated, he almost invariably continues it by himself, using the techniques he has learned. These consist usually in paying attention to small signs in himself that something is going on within him that he doesn't quite know about, letting his feelings and ideas come out even when they don't seem sensible, and paying attention to his dreams and reveries. It certainly is not easy, but it can be done. I might add, however, that psychoneurosis, in addition to being essentially stereotyped, is also rather shiftless and usually avoids work whenever possible, so that it is not a bad idea to have a schedule of appointments and some monetary inducement for keeping them.

19

The Creative Writer

THE MAIN body of findings that I shall discuss has emerged from work with a group of 56 professional writers and 10 student writers, and the method of work germane to this comparison has been characterized chiefly by reliance upon our usual psychological tests, interviews, and experiments. Although all these writers were actively engaged in creative work, they did differ widely among themselves in the goals of their work and in the audiences they reached. Thirty of them were writers of wide renown who are generally considered important artists in the field of writing; their names were obtained by asking three faculty members in the English Department and one in the Drama Department at the University of California to nominate writers of a conspicuously high degree of originality and creativeness. Twenty-six others are successful and productive writers who were not nominated as outstandingly creative, but who have clearly made their mark in the field of writing. While I intend to present some comparisons between these two groups, I wish to make it quite clear that I am not suggesting that one group is creative and the other is not. Apart from the fact that my life would be in danger if I were to do so, I must say quite honestly that some of the writers nominated as outstandingly creative appeared to me to be less creative than many of those who were not so nominated, and among the writers who were not mentioned by the nominators (and hence by this exclusion defined simply as representative of their craft) were persons of a high order of creative ability. In brief, the central body of data from which we have drawn generalizations in this particular study comes from the testing and interviewing of 66 persons whose main aim in life was to create meaningful patterns with words.

The True-False verbal scale developed from responses of subjects in the Asch study, some sample items of which are given in Chapter 14, has continued to prove quite valuable as a predictor of creativity not only in the study of writers, as you shall hear, but in studies of research scientists, architects, mathematicians, and creative women. These results are to be reported in a volume now in preparation by the entire staff of the Institute of Personality Assessment and Research.

The average score of the general population on the Independence of Judgment Scale is 8.12; the group of representative successful writers scored 11.69, the student writers scored 15.2, and the distinguished creative writers scored 15.69. While the distinguished creative writers and the student writers were not significantly different from one another, both differed significantly from representative successful writers at the one per cent confidence level, and they in turn obtained significantly higher scores for independence of judgment than do people in general.

This sort of general trend obtains for a number of other measures as well. Representative writers tend to fall about midway between the general population and distinguished writers, with student writers being much more like the latter than like the former, probably reflecting patterns of identification and of life style as much as of ability proper. This was true, for instance, of the Originality scale: distinguished writers scored 67.3 and representative writers scored 61.58, where the mean of the general population is set at 50, and the standard deviation at 10. Another scale that showed this pattern was Flexibility, distinguished writers scoring 60.5; representative writers, 55.65. In this case, student writers were markedly higher than either of the other groups, averaging 72.8. Using this sort of convention or so-called standard score format with the average at 50, scores of 70 or more are higher than those of 98 per cent of the general population, while a score of 60 places the individual higher than about 84 per cent of the generality. So, another way of putting this, which perhaps expresses the pattern better, is to say that the *average* student writer is more flexible than 98 per cent of the general population, while his elders in the field of creative writing are more flexible than about 84 per cent of the general population. However one puts it, the finding is clear: writers as a class are significantly more independent, flexible, and original than most people, and the creative writers who have achieved renown do very well for their years by being almost as flexible as their student counterparts, and a bit more independent.

When one turns to the question of psychological health in relation to creativity the picture is, as our discussion of ego-strength and the unconscious might have led us to expect, by no means a simple one. All three groups of writers earn markedly deviant scores on the scales of the Minnesota Multiphasic Personality Inventory. Since the MMPI was designed to measure the resemblance of those who take the test to certain diagnostic groups in the mental hospital setting, this finding on the face of it suggests that writers and psychiatric patients are indeed like one another in at least some respects. Again, both distinguished writers and student writers are most deviant, with representative writers falling in between them and the general population. In Figure 19.2 are shown the average scores on the California Psychological Inventory of our groups of distinguished creative writers and our representative writers, where a score of 50 is the average of the general population.

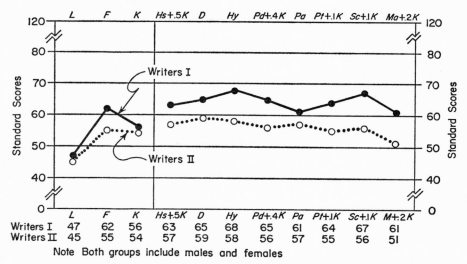

	L	F	K	Hs+.5K	D	Hy	Pd+.4K	Pa	Pt+.1K	Sc+.1K	M+.2K
Writers I	47	62	56	63	65	68	65	61	64	67	61
Writers II	45	55	54	57	59	58	56	57	55	56	51

Note Both groups include males and females

Fɪɢ. 19.1 A Comparison of Minnesota Multiphasic Personality Inventory Scores of Writers Nominated by Critics as "Highly Creative" (Writers I) with "Representative Successful" Writers (Writers II)

Distinguished writers score particularly high on scales measuring schizoid, depressive, hysterical, and psychopathic tendencies. They are also very far indeed from the general population norms in terms of femininity of interest pattern (the few female subjects were omitted from the latter calculation).

As I say, however, the picture is not simple, even in unthinking psychometric terms. In spite of obtaining such high scores on measures of pathology, all three groups of writers also obtain distinctly superior scores on the MMPI scale which we developed first of all for prediction of recovery from neurosis, and which other evidence indicates is a good measure of strength of the ego. And that very scale (*Es*), it will be remembered, bears a high negative relationship to the MMPI measures of pathology when general population norms are considered. In brief, if one is to take these test results seriously, the writers appear to be both sicker and healthier psychologically than people in general. Or, to put it in another way, they are much more troubled psychologically, but they also have far greater resources with which to deal with their troubles. This jibes rather well with their social behavior, as a matter of fact. They are clearly effective people who handle themselves with pride and distinctiveness, but the face they turn to the world is somtimes one of pain, often of protest, sometimes of distance and withdrawal; and certainly they are emotional. All of these are, of course, the intensely normal traits indicated by the peaks on their profile of diagnostic scores.

The California Psychological Inventory (which is similar in format to the Minnesota Multiphasic Personality Inventory and built in part from the True-False items of the Minnesota test, but which differs in that its purpose is to measure traits related to personal effectiveness rather than psychopathology) bears out the finding regarding greater ego-strength in these creative individuals. The CPI, it will be remembered, provides measures of such traits as personal dominance, social presence, motivation to achieve through independent work, intellectual efficiency, and the like. In Figure 19.2 are shown the average scores of our groups of creative writers and representative writers in comparison with general population norms.

As this figure shows, both these groups of writers are significantly superior to the general population in Social Presence, Self-acceptance, Capacity for Social Status, Psychological-mindedness, and Achievement through Independence. They achieve markedly lower scores in Achievement via Conformance, and also make rather low scores on Socialization, a performance which in this context I think is correctly interpreted as resistance to acculturation, for the so-called socializa-

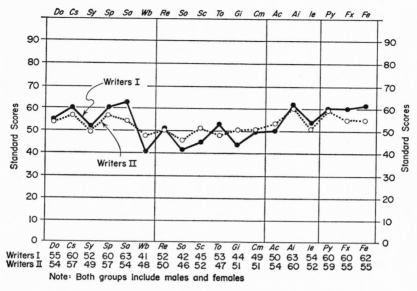

Fig. 19.2 A Comparison of California Psychological Inventory Scores of Writers Nominated by Critics as "Highly Creative" with "Representative Successful" Writers

tion process is often seen by the creative individual as a demand for the sacrifice of his individuality, which indeed it often is.

One other set of findings, which I shall mention only briefly, concerns the relationship of creative writing ability to such Jungian concepts as extraversion-introversion, feeling-thinking, judging-perceiving, and intuiting-sensing, functions which are seen in Jung's theories as polar opposites. A measure of each of these factors, the Myers-Briggs Jungian Type Indicator, was used in our studies. Both groups, distinguished writers and representative writers, show much the same pattern; they are distinctly more *introverted* than *extraverted*, more *feeling* than *thinking*, and more *intuitive* than oriented to *sense experience*. The latter finding is particularly marked. Only two distinguished writers, and only four representative writers, were not classified by the test as intuitive; overall, 89 per cent of the writers studied were intuitive, as compared with about 25 per cent of the general population.

Besides being markedly intuitive, creative writers as a class are of unusually high conceptual and verbal intelligence. This is hardly news, perhaps, but still we were surprised at the consistency with which we observed high scores on standardized tests of intelligence. One of the tests we have used is the Concept Mastery test already described. Developed by Lewis M. Terman and his associates at Stanford University, it was designed especially to provide differential measurement in the high I.Q. ranges. Normative data were available from the Terman study of gifted children with I.Q.'s in the range from 140 up. Scores made in adulthood by that highly gifted group were compared with our own highly selected group of writers who had achieved distinction, and on the basis of that comparison it appears safe to say that creative writers who produce original work in large quantities have I.Q.'s, on the average, in the neighborhood of 140 or higher.

The relationship between intelligence and creativity is also not quite so simple, as the data analysis presented in Chapter 17 made plain. And some of the studies done by other members of the Institute staff, and by the present writer at the Rhode Island School of Design, support those findings. Where the subject-matter itself requires high intelligence for the mastery of its fundamentals, as in mathematics or physics, the correlation of measured intelligence with originality in problem-solving within the discipline tends to be positive but quite low. Among artists such as painters, sculptors, and designers, the correlation between rated quality of work and measured intelligence is zero or slightly negative. Again, however, it must be remembered that commitment to such endeavors is already selective for intelligence, so that the average I.Q. is already a superior one. I would suggest a generalization based not only on my own studies and those of my colleagues at the Institute, but upon a number of other researches during the past three years at the University of Minnesota, the University of Chicago, and the National Merit Scholarship Corporation: Over the total range of intelligence and creativity a low positive correlation, probably in the neighborhood of .40, obtains; beyond an I.Q. of about 120, however, measured intelligence is a negligible factor in creativity, and the motivational and stylistic variables upon which our own research has laid such stress are the major determiners of creativity.

Among these motivational variables must be included what I shall call simply "the moral attitude." One finds in creative writers a profound commitment to larger meanings of an esthetic and philosophical sort which can find expression in the life work that the individual has chosen for himself (or, as some have put it, in the life work that has chosen him). As an aside, one may recall here Goethe's statement: "I did not make my songs, my songs made me." In brief, such individuals are involved constantly in the creation of their private universes of meaning; they are cosmologists all. I am convinced that without this intense cosmological commitment no amount of mental ability of the sort measured by I.Q. tests will suffice to produce a genuinely creative act. Without wishing to be overly dramatic in this matter, I believe it is literally true that the creative individual is willing to stake his life on the meaning of his work. We think we have observed this in the personal accounts given in intensive interviews with subjects in our own studies, and certainly the many biographies and autobiographical writings of the great artists and scientists bear the conclusion out. Indeed, as Crombie concluded from his survey of the scientific revolution, regulative beliefs of an almost metaphysical sort lie behind the most dedicated quests for new theoretical formulations.

Creative vision, whether in art or in science, has always involved an act of rejection preceding the act of construction; the structure of the world as most people see it must be broken or transcended. William Blake, a great artist both in writing and in painting, has spoken of "fourfold vision." For him, single vision is simply what ordinary physical eyesight enables us to see: the world that the consensus of opinion based on a limited use of senses would affirm as real. A tree is a tree, an inkblot is an inkblot, the sky is blue, and so on. Two-fold vision is the still-limited act of imagination; a cloud formation looks like two lions fighting, or an elephant pushing a Mack truck; the inkblot "might be" two dancers, or a bird in flight, or a monk kneeling in prayer. In three-fold vision, we do not see the mean thing-in-itself as in single vision, nor the thing as it might be if it were a little or even a lot different, as in two-fold vision, but we see the thing as symbol. Recall again the heavenly chorus at the conclusion of *Faust*:

> All things transitory
> but as symbols are sent;
> Earth's insufficiency
> *Here* grows to event.

The symbol presents a reality transcended. It is the medium through which a superior vision of reality is sought; it amplifies the poor real world by an act of imagination. The symbol, the play, the dream: these are the manifestations of three-fold vision.

Four-fold vision is still a step beyond. It is the vision of the mystic, the seer, the prophet; it is vision suffused with the most intense feeling: horror, awe, ecstasy, desolation. A passage from Blake himself illustrates it well:

> I assert for myself that I do not behold the outward creation, and that to me it is hindrance and not Action . . . "What," it will be Questioned, "When the Sun rises, do you not see a round disk of fire somewhat like a Guinea?" Oh, no, no, I see an Innumerable Company of the Heavenly host crying, "Holy, holy, holy is the Lord God Almighty." I question not my corporeal or Vegetarian Eye any more than I would Question a Window concerning a Sight. I look through it and not with it.

In this research we have attempted through a variety of techniques to understand the vision of the world that these our subjects had. Their work itself, of course, is their primary testament, and that work we studied in great detail so that in our interview on the actual process of creation we might be enabled to ask the significant questions. How often we succeeded I do not know, but I did feel in many of the interviews that we were getting close to the heart of the matter. That report must wait, however. Meanwhile, through quite another experimental technique, and with the assistance of distinguished artists in music, painting, and writing, we are enabled to study unusual vision and changes in consciousness (perhaps "expanded" consciousness) quite directly. The observations to which this further research gave rise are presented in the next chapter.

20

Unusual Realization and Changes in Consciousness

THE ADAPTIVE function of repression, and the part it plays in ego-strength, was discussed briefly in Chapter 9. There the emphasis was placed upon flexibility in the repression-mechanism itself. Almost everyone who is considered "normal" represses certain facts and affects systematically, for if we are to get on at all in the world there are certain things at certain times that it seems better not to know or to be much aware of, even though we might obtain such information if we directed our attention to doing so.

About the human body itself there are several features we tend not to notice, they seem so common. Please bear with me while I remind you of them. When we have considered these common enough facts briefly, we may then turn to certain features of the human mind that also are so commonplace that one must make a special point of thinking about them if they are to be noticed at all.

Consider, then, these characteristics of our bodies:

1) Our bodies are not closed, but open. Some of the openings seem mostly to let things in and others seem mostly to let things out, but the main function of the 11 or 12 major openings and numerous minor ones is to provide a constant interchange of materials between the system or field that we identify as ourselves and the systems or fields that we recognize as not-ourselves.

2) We generally face the way we are going. Another way of putting this is to say that our face is to the front. In terms of temporal passage, the things that have not yet happened are in front of us, and in the course of time we shall face them.

3) Like almost everything in nature, in our gross aspect we are approximately symmetrical, and generally bilateral. In a wonderful old textbook of experimental psychology by Robert S. Woodworth, the author remarks that one of the most interesting facts about the ears is that there are two of them and that they are located on opposite sides of the head. The fact of bilateral symmetry has a great deal to do with how we locate ourselves and all the not-ourselves in space and time.

I need not go on with these commonplaces, for you can yourself think of many more and of their consequences for our sense of self: our jointedness, our plasticity, the flexibility of control we have over our openings, our shape and our size and the tiny span we occupy in the scale of magnitude of the physical world, our remarkable similarity to one another, the counterphobic quality of our motility (in Samuel Johnson's dictionary, walking is defined as "a series of arrested falls"), our bony skeletons and casings, our living and moving brains, and our perishability.

I remind you of these aspects of our structure—the structural shapers of our destiny—both because I want as well to remind you of certain aspects of the structure of mind and because mind and body bear to one another a relationship which poses for psychology its ultimate and most crucial problem. I see no reason why we should not conceive of the body as a machine, and indeed I can think of no reasonable alternative conception. But protoplasm is different from all other mechanical systems in that it feels, and that in its complex human embodiment it possesses what we know as our own consciousness. This consciousness has a structure in the same sense that our body does, and some of its structural aspects do seem to derive from the structure of the body, though to say "derive from" already prejudges the question and exhibits one of the structural aspects of my own consciousness (and yours as well, I would guess), which sees a before and an after, logical antecedent and logical consequence, cause and effect. Charles Peirce, who is known to most psychologists for his essay "How to Make Our Ideas Clear," perhaps the germinal contribution to pragmatism, is up to another sort of business in a much less well-known essay, "Man's Glassy Essence." He argues there that the phenomenon of feeling cannot be shown to arise from any peculiarity of our mechanical constitution. Here are his words: "The attempt to deduce it (i.e., the property of feeling) from the laws of mechanics, applied to never so ingenious a mechanical contrivance, would obviously be futile. It can never be explained, unless we admit that physical events are but degraded or undeveloped forms of psychical events."

If you do not find this a remarkable passage, I wish you would consider it again. I cite this conclusion of the founder of pragmatism in the hope that you may be a bit upset by it, as I was. Our ordinary consciousness does not prepare us for such a notion, and the fact that Charles Peirce arrived at it in the way that he did is a mark of his creative genius. We see frequently in creative individuals such an ability to transcend the ordinary boundaries of structures of consciousness; indeed, more than an ability, an actual *desire* to break through the regularities of perception, to shatter what is stable or constant in consciousness, to go beyond the given world to find that something-more or that something-different that intuition says is there.

Let us take a look now at the features of mind that are as commonplace as those we have considered in thinking of the human body, but that ordinarily do not claim our attention. One word of qualification first, however. Structural characteristics of our body, even though we recognize them as dynamic and passing, seem to us more tangible than the structures of consciousness of which I shall speak. When I say that these are structures I mean simply that they are relatively enduring and constantly recurring psychic dispositions, and thus have a sort of permanence and distinctness and boundedness which make the word *structure* appropriate.

1) Our mind so operates that we consider the proposition logically impossible that a thing can both be and not be at the same time.

2) Space and time seem to exist independently of our perception of them, and to be separate categories of being, themselves independent of one another. In science we say that a protocol sentence is one that specifies some space-time coordinate and ascribes to a thing or event there a certain quantity or value. In common sense, anything that happens happens at some particular time and in some particular place.

3) Everything in principle has an explanation; that is, if we could but know everything, there would be no unintelligible or unaccountable-for event. In common parlance, there's a reason for everything.

4) Our mind seems to be distinct and separate from other minds, our self to belong to us alone; and like everything else, we exist in a

particular time for us, the present, and a particular place, our body. Our self is the only self we know, and no other self knows us. And while our own individual mind, if it could validly be compared with other minds, might prove to be remarkably similar to those other minds, to us it is unique, the only one.

Again, as in the case of the body, one could go on at some length with this sort of listing: the fact that attention seems to wax and wane, that mind seems to sleep and to wake, that time seems to pass moment by moment in a succession of states rather than in an unstoppable flow, that most inanimate objects seem impenetrable and unmoving, that up seems to be above down, that the inside of a thing cannot be the outside of it, and so on. These "seemings" are of course the fundaments of common sense, or, to put it another way, the basic achievements of the ego. In an older day the standard psychiatric way of determining whether or not the patient had what was called a clear sensorium was to ask the "W" questions: who are you, where are you, why are you here, when did you arrive, what is your name, what day is it, which way is out, and so on. Knowing these whys and wherefores, and being able in addition to make some simple comparisons and strike some arithmetical averages, meant that you were sane enough for most purposes.

It is no longer news that modern mathematics and physics can do very well without some of these common sense notions, and in most of the modern arts as well there are significant works that aim at breaking up the best established of our regularities of perception. Cubism and surrealism were explicit and systematic attempts to do so in the realm of visual form; Rimbaud and Joyce were fierce destroyers and creators in the realm of language. Ernst Mach in his notable work, *The Inspiration to Order*, has given in conventional language a justification of the Dadaist revolution in painting, and Norman Mailer, in the clear analytic prose of his essay "The White Negro," offers a theoretical understanding of the language of hip. With very little extension of his thesis, we can comprehend the entire Joycean adventure, from the beautiful description of the "making up of mind" in *Portrait of the Artist as a Young Man*, through the merging streams of consciousness in *Ulysses*, to the final ironic self-analysis of Shem the Penman in *Finnegan's Wake*.

Both from such explicit theoretical analyses and from the retrospective accounts by famous creators of the process whereby they arrived at unusual realizations and expressions, it seems quite evident that at the very heart of the creative process is this ability to shatter the rule of law and regularity in the mind. Remember Bergson's phrase: "Life is a stone thrown uphill against the downward rush of matter." Perhaps we may be permitted this paraphrase: Creation is a stone thrown uphill against the downward rush of habit. In saying so we must remember that without habit we cannot exist, just as without creation we would not exist. Habit and creation, or law and freedom, or gravity and turbulence, depending upon how or in what aspects we view these polarities, conduct an incessant and fruitful dialectic.

In another aspect, or from another and judgmental point of view, we may call the polarities heaven and hell, though it is not always clear which is which. In Blake's extraordinary visionary fragment titled "The Marriage of Heaven and Hell," not only does he have the two talking but he gets them to bed together. As he remarks there, rather blandly I must say, "without contraries there is no progression." In that same work he describes a condition in which "the doors of perception are cleansed," and by "doors" in that phrase I take him to mean those structural aspects of consciousness of which we are speaking, and by "cleansed" I take him to mean, to be less visionary about it, unhinged and plain removed.

Aldous Huxley, himself a person of unusual vision, has seized upon the effects of mescaline as a possible route of access to a state of consciousness innocent of such near-blinding structures, and has written beautifully of his own experiences with mescaline in two books, *The Doors of Perception* and, more recently, *Heaven and Hell*. The latter title is perhaps derived from the work of Swedenborg, the legendary scientist and mystic who has exerted such enormous influence upon literature and psychology as well as upon religion, physics, and physiology. (Among those who were intrigued by *his* vision and who have responded strongly to it have been Blake, Coleridge, Balzac, Kant, Emerson, the elder James, and Yeats, not to mention the multitude who have been in turn influenced by the strain of "Swedenborgianism" running through the work of these others.)

All these men were concerned with consciousness, its structure, and the alterations and transcendences possible to it. A number of them have testified to radical alterations in their own consciousness, produced without drugs taken into the system from without, as was true of Swedenborg as well. But many notable creators in science and in art have also used such consciousness-altering substances as hashish, cocaine, and opium, either occasionally or regularly. The names of Baudelaire, Poe, Freud, de Quincy, Sir Alexander Cushing, Gautier, and Havelock Ellis come at once to mind, and many others, including some of our most renowned contemporary writers and scientists, could be mentioned.

We have already made reference to the utilization of the relatively harmless and non-addicting drug psilocybin in relation to work in group psychotherapy at Harvard. While I did not participate in that therapeutic work, and in fact took part in the research as a whole only during the first exploratory period before any experiments or correlational analyses of test results were undertaken, I was able nonetheless to make some observations of the drug's effect upon highly creative individuals who volunteered to be subjects in the early stages of that program. Here are some examples of reports written by these subjects, usually within a day or two after experiencing the psilocybin effect.

First, a painter:

> I was most strongly aware of the effects of the drug upon my vision, not in the sense of optics but in the disarrangement of the total process of seeing, including clarity, emphasis, perceptual focus, and spatial disarrangement. I do not believe that I underwent any hallucinatory visions; all that I saw was "real," but it was different in many ways from what I have previously known.
>
> Time seemed to move pleasantly slowly . . . the music that was being played was noticeably pleasant, but then so was everything else . . . I felt very much attuned to the world as a whole and I felt in extremely high humor . . . I looked at my watch and was surprised and relieved to discover that so little time (Note: about 40 minutes) had passed. At about this time I became aware of several visual facts which I had not noticed before; an appealing parallelism between the horizontal window moldings and the horizontal branches of a tree beyond the window, a subtle play of color involving a distant red signboard and some foliage, a blue-green shutter that seemed to glow in an otherwise muted setting, the interplay of the patterns and colors of the sofa cushions, and the contrast between a symmetrical and upward-arched evergreen and the starkness of a bare branch which reached towards it. In none of these was there any distortion although I seemed to be able to accentuate or diminish apparent depth at will and there was an intriguing visual play involved in the whole process of snapping from one plane to another. . . . The first real distortion which I noticed was on the wall of the central hallway where the strongly textured wall covering seemed to

undulate slightly but appealingly. Later I felt that the living room was somewhat plastic and that when I attended to a certain aspect of the room, the room as a whole seemed to recede away from that point and the area of my attention seemed to flow or bulge outward. This apparent phenomenon was highly transitory and shifted very fluidly and readily from one kind of form to another. It was, again, not in the least unpleasant. I attempted some drawings but found that my attention span was unusually brief. . . . Interruptions, such as the model moving, did not really bother me and on at least one occasion a considerable period passed between the beginning of the drawing and its completion (if it could have been called complete even at that point); I simply picked it up and finished it when the occasion presented itself. I seemed to become unusually aware of detail and also unusually unconscious of the relationship of the various parts of the drawing. My concern was with the immediate and what had preceded a particular mark on the page or what was to follow seemed quite irrelevant. When I finished a drawing I tossed it aside with a feeling of totally abandoning it and not really caring very much. In spite of the uniqueness of the experience of drawing while influenced by the drug and my general "what the hell" attitude toward my work I cannot help but feel that the drawings were, in some ways, good ones. I was far better able to isolate the significant and ignore that which, for the moment, seemed insignificant and I was able to become much more intensely involved with the drawing and with the object drawn. I felt as though I were grimacing as I drew. I have seldom known such absolute identification with what I was doing—nor such a lack of concern with it afterward. Throughout the afternoon nothing seemed very important beyond what was happening at the moment. . . . As the afternoon wore on I felt very content to simply sit and stare out of the window at the snow and the trees and at that time I recall feeling that the snow, the fire in the fireplace, the darkened and book-lined room were so perfect as to be almost unreal.

Aspects of this painter's report that are most consistently reported by other subjects as well are these:

1. The plasticity that the forms of the visual world assume, even though ordinarily we see these forms as having sharp boundaries, as being immovable or impenetrable, and as being straight rather than curved. There was an increased fluidity and fleetingness of impression. I myself was an observer during this session, not myself under the influence of the drug, and I watched the artist as he did the drawings he described. I was impressed by their rapidity, their intuitiveness, and their conciseness of expression.

2. The emphasis upon play of light and color, as though light were alive.

3. The increased beauty of the world, in terms of subtlety, glowingness, softening of otherwise harsh outlines.

4. Total identification with the object at the precise moment of viewing it, but total unconcern once it had passed out of the visual field. What this seems to reflect is an increased importance of the momentary, the here and now. What is past is not real, what is done with is not worth remembering nor caring about.

Here are excerpts from the report written by another painter a few days after he experienced the psilocybin effect:

> The first thing I will consider will be the visual part of the experience. My vision seemed to broaden and I was able to see everything at once—to see everything totally and never really feel that I was unable to see small details. However, when focussing on a part of a particular object all details became visible—in other words I think that the details cannot be seen in the total but were never missed. . . . I was able to concentrate entirely on one object to the total exclusion of all others. The one object would seem to radiate light or glow from within. From time to time other members of the group would take on this glow, which would attract my attention and then I would narrow my gaze. This inner glow for some reason seemed to disappear when that person's revery was interrupted by someone else's comment. . . . All space seemed to be curved and the importance of verticals and horizontals diminished greatly. . . . Objects didn't seem to end abruptly but had an ability to extend themselves. . . .
>
> Color and the reality of space were actually not a new experience to me. It was very similar to the reality of both during a period of high painting excitement. . . . Space itself took on a very real quality and was related in its shape to visual concentration. When I looked at an object close at hand I felt as though I were in a cylinder of space. Space closed in around me but was open at the top. When I looked at the total the corners of the room were unimportant and seemed to curve—the space of the room was not really related to the four walls but was enclosed within them. Once again the top seemed open and the floor uneven. When I left the room and then came back into it, it seemed to have an umbrella-shaped top (mushroom-shaped) which hung below the ceiling. When I looked out of the window there always was a thorough detachment. The space was not as real. Everything was clear and sharp but not real. . . .
>
> Perhaps the most amazing thing to me was what happened to me when I wanted to express myself verbally. Most of the time I felt that there was no reason to talk. When I felt that something was important to say I first had to find the words to express the thought. I was really thinking thoughts free from the limits of verbiage. . . .
>
> Possibly the most important part of the experiment for me was my

awareness of a totality and my awareness of nothing. Thoughts took on a great reality and I could sit and enjoy myself thinking. Sometimes the thoughts were so delightful and so real that I would laugh happily over them. While the thoughts took on this reality at the peak point of the experience I felt that I was able to not think. I could sit empty and then a thought would pulse through my mind. I was never quite sure whether the thought came from—originated—with me or outside me. Many times I felt like a large receiver through which things were passing. I felt as though I were collecting information. This made me extremely happy. My laughter was about this happiness and was not in response to what other people in the room had said. . . .

There were times when I became extremely restless and walked about the room. I almost felt that I could walk away from my physical self. I would walk and then stop walking in hopes that I could continue on. This would happen once or twice but I was snapped back and never was able to stay outside for any duration—even though I think I would have liked to. This just seemed as though it should follow but never did. I was not afraid. Everything that was happening to me was good. Everything that I touched—everything that I saw.

Several times I was bothered by H. to do some drawings which seemed to be an invasion of privacy to even think of doing such a thing at that time. What was happening was more important to me than trying to record it. *Being* was the most important thing and I didn't want anything to interfere with being. I felt a communion with all things. It was difficult for me to determine whether I was reaching out to all things or whether all things were reaching out to me. I now feel it must have been a mutual reaching out because I was convinced at the highest point that the right wall loved the left wall and that all walls loved me. And that I loved them. At this very high point I seemed to be aware of everything within my view as well as those outside my view. What was behind me was as real as what was in front of me. At one point I am sure that everything came together with me. I became excited at this point—extremely excited. I tried to walk away from myself. . . .

Now I think that the most important part of what has happened to me since the experiment is that I seem to be able to get a good deal more work done. Sunday afternoon I did about six hours work in two hours time. I did not worry about what I was doing—I just did it. Three or four times I wanted a particular color pencil or a triangle and would go directly to it, lift up three or four pieces of paper and pull it out. Never thought of where it was—just knew I wanted it and picked it up. This of course amazed me but I just relied on it—found things immediately. My wife was a little annoyed at me on Sunday afternoon because I was so happy, but I would not be dissuaded.

When painting it generally takes me an hour and a half to two hours to really get into the painting and three or four hours to really hit a

peak. Tuesday I hit a peak in less than a half hour. The esthetic experience was more intense than I have experienced before—so much so that several times I had to leave the studio and finally decided that I was unable to cope with it and left for good! I now have this under control to some extent but I am delighted that I can just jump into it without the long build-up and I certainly hope it continues.
. . . all these words really don't say it.

Here are excerpts from reports by two other subjects: one a promising and original graduate student in psychology, the other a composer who has won considerable distinction. These I have edited somewhat in the sense of omitting some personally identifying references, but otherwise what is given below is a verbatim record of the subjects' reports.

First, the graduate student:

Without a doubt this was the most amazing and intense experience of my life. At first everything seemed very funny, and I laughed uncontrollably, sometimes for no apparent reason. Then the carpet started to sway and move in waves. When I closed my eyes there was a whole field of highly symmetrical three-dimensional geometric patterns that shifted and changed constantly . . . brilliantly colored geometrical patterns of fantastic beauty collided, exploded, raced by. . . . The patterns on the carpet rose up off the ground, twisted and moved about. Outside the window the branches of the trees were gigantic arms with transparent muscles, now threatening, now embracing. The bookcase was full of swimming books, the door bulged like a balloon, the carpet in the other room was full of thousands of little green snakes. The dial on the telephone was a huge pearl-studded wheel. The shapes and colors of objects got more and more intense, the outlines etched with luminous clarity and depth, anything with a polished metal surface turned into gleaming gold or silver. I felt like shouting, "Look, see how beautiful, how amazing. . . ." The music on the phonograph was transformed into Christmas bells. . . . The faces of other people became clear and beautiful and open. . . . Their faces looked bright and strong, like those of archangels. I could look at them without fear or shyness and with frank admiration and adoration. . . . People looked naked, shed of a fog of dissimulations, anxieties, hypocrisies. Everyone was true to his own self and no one was ashamed.

It is interesting that the psychologist did experience many of the visual phenomena that the two artists experienced, but that in addition he saw people differently and related to them differently. The perceptions of nonhuman visual forms and of people were similar, however, in their innocence.

Here are excerpts from a report written during the experience itself, though toward the conclusion of it, by the composer. In other words, these observations are not a recollection of the way things seemed, but a description of the world given while the composer was under the effects of the drug.

> A world of silent cathedrals.
> Thousands of magnificent cities.
> Measureless galleries.
> Warriors poised in their chariots inscribed in arabesque bas-reliefs spiraling into eternity.
>
> Objects have their own light, but they are dead.
>
> I am dead. That which men see in me is not me. They too are dead.
>
> Inconceivably, the dead themselves are alive. What has happened is this: a world of the dead, dead men and dead things, but they think, eat, reproduce and die. The dead themselves die.
>
> It is only the total volume of things and faces which is really alive.
>
> Every corner is alive in a silent intimacy (or is it dead)?
> Corners demand deathly silence.
> We live in a silent world. We are cut off and separated from reality.
>
> Truth belongs to a static face, which does not change.
> Space has won the great battle against time.
> The painters . . . above all, the sculptors and architects . . . are right.
>
> We musicians are involved in a childish game, which neither transcends nor even dies, so insignificant is it. The world is deaf and our struggles useless . . . deaf ashes, old, impenetrable and thick. . . .

With this I think it best to stop giving detailed examples from actual subject reports. However, let me add a few more observations and then make some effort to make a bit of sense out of all this.

Most of the reports I have cited have had a primarily pleasurable or even ecstatic tone to them, although the composer certainly was having a strongly dysphoric experience. About 10 to 15 per cent of the experiences do seem to be unpleasant rather than pleasant, and occasionally a positively hellish time may be had by all. The experiences which I call hellish are marked by a sense of impossible distance between people, of intrinsic solitariness of the self, of vast blackness and desolation throughout the universe, of the puniness of the shelters we have made for ourselves, the feebleness of fire against the outer coldness and blackness, and an anticipation of death or a feeling that one is already dead. The light and glow with which persons are suffused, or which come visibly from them, in the heavenly experience, seems to go out when the experience is one of hell. Or the person may seem to move in dark ugly red shadows, or to be a sickly green. Smiles become meaningless grimaces, and all human actions seem mere puppetry. In the hellish experience, time may seem impossibly slow and painful, and determinism is experienced as being a prison. By contrast, determinism is experienced under happier conditions as being perfectly natural and quite all right. The subject knows, with the preacher in Ecclesiastes, that there is nothing new under the sun, that every story is an old story and has been told an infinite number of times before, but somehow that knowledge is not disturbing. Everything is reconciled; time does not matter.

You will recognize in these observations some concrete illustrations of the age-old paradoxes that philosophy grapples with, the paradoxes that art occasionally resolves. The philosophic problems are these: the problem of the one and the many, unity and variety; determinism and freedom; mechanism and vitalism; good and evil; time and eternity; the plenum and the void; moral absolutism and moral relativism; monotheism and polytheism and atheism. These are the basic problems of human existence, and, so far as we possibly can, we arrange things so as to forget them. The requirement that the universe has put to the human brain is that of striking an average in countless dimensions simultaneously, so that the individual unit of life (i.e., you and I) may continue alive as long as possible, and thus that life on the whole may increase. But the paradox is that this striking of averages requires, from the individual point of view, a sacrifice of self. We are required to be part of universal habit, but evolution has brought us to that point of consciousness where we as individual human beings realize the preciousness of consciousness and perhaps take pride in our individual, inimitable selfhood. It does not make sense that we should be given life on the one hand and death on the other. The easiest thing to do is to forget it, and we usually succeed in doing so, with the help of our average-making brain, that remarkable machine which psychologists are now working to simulate in some material that does not feel and need not dissolve so soon. What psilocybin does is to reverse or slow down some of the averaging process, alter our experience of the passage of time, dissolve many definitions and melt many boundaries, permit greater intensities or more extreme values of experience to occur in many dimensions. We need not wonder that the Indians called the mushroom sacred and gave it a name meaning "the flesh of the god."

These observations, it seems to me, have important implications for psychology in at least four quite different areas of concern. One of these, and the one with which I myself have been least concerned although recognizing its importance, is for neurophysiology, or, to use Peirce's phrase, neural mechanics. Another is for psychotherapy, since it is evident that an experience of such intensity and emotional importance may provide a means for initiating or facilitating the process of personal growth. Still another is for the psychology of creativity. As I have indicated, certain aspects of the creative process, although by no means the creative process as a whole, are analogous to the kind of breaking of perceptual constancies that is initiated mechanically by ingestion of the drug. Finally, the whole area of psychological health and of ego-functioning may be greatly illuminated by further study of these effects.

21

Create to Be Free

WHETHER one can really separate psychology from philosophy when one deals with values and with action in the realm of values is a question that has been with us throughout this series of inquiries. What we have been trying to say is that scientific inquiry is possible if we place the philosophic positions of other people in the context of objectively discernible fact and consider philosophy of life as a psychological attribute of the persons whom we study.

This is skating on thin ice, let us admit again, and the ice gets thinner and thinner as we get closer to the great issues. Use the word theism and avoid the question the heart knows: this is method. Now we shall speak of freedom, and vast or tiny *hidden* workings are our thought. But let us see what we can do.

"Is the will free?" is a question that, as psychologists, we did put to the graduate students in our first study and to the women alumnae in the research we have reported in Chapter 13. To this question Paul said "Oh, no, I am a creature of chance." Many others said, "Oh, yes, I am a free and responsible person." So did they respectively feel, and as a matter of fact the Pauls (could there be another?) and the others acted much as though their feeling accurately reflected the behavioral reality. Paul repeated himself over and over again in behavior (as perfectly regular as the normal curve, the beautiful mathematical form that chance takes). All his seeming variety was but such a deviation as a slave's liberty might be. The "others," non-Pauls, seemed capable of genuine decision which could break patterns of compulsion. "Yes I will." "No I won't." Whether thus worded or not, there were some who felt themselves free and who in some sense seemed capable of originating patterns, of starting right then what might turn out to be without precedent. This capacity was powerfully communicated, without words, in glance or stance. No analysis, psychological or philosophical, could approach the subjective fact.

What follows here is a sort of objective analysis of the problem of freedom, construed psychologically and in such terms of naturalistic explanation as psychological theory may offer. It arose directly from meetings with the men and women, 130 in all, who spoke of these matters in answer to my questions. My method here is discursive analysis rather than the sort of statistical comparison based on crude enumeration that has served as the basis for such conclusions as earlier inquiries have offered.

UNPREDICTABILITY AS THE TEST OF FREEDOM

In Part I of his "Notes from the Underground," Dostoevski supposes a world in which "the psychologists" shall have finally catalogued all the responses of which human beings are capable, and all the functional relationships among such responses, so that, given the history of the entire series of events in the life of a person, or a complete description of his state at a given moment, all his subsequent actions would be predictable. Dostoevski supposes such a world in order to deny the possibility of its existence, for there is always, he says, an "except"—a final unpredictable, unclassifiable element, which will never behave according to rational formula and in the interest of calculated advantage. And so into the state of unrelieved order and prosperity that he has imagined, Dostoevski injects "a gentleman with an ignoble, or rather with a reactionary and ironical, countenance," who arises and, "putting his arms akimbo, says to us all: I say, gentlemen, hadn't we better kick over the whole show and scatter rationalism to the winds, simply to send these logarithms to the devil, and to enable us to live once more at our own sweet foolish will?"

Our own sweet foolish will—*this* is the last-ditch incalculable which, in the final analysis, is to save man from being a mere item in his own universal pigeon-holing scheme. The unpredictable thing is, in Dostoevski's terms, *human caprice*, which goes usually under that more solemn name, *freedom of the will*.

The essential thing is that unpredictability is made the test of freedom. Although Dostoevski states the case in somewhat more dramatic form than one usually finds it, his is actually the traditional and classical analysis of the paradox of free will and determinism. It is based upon the mistaken notion that the question of whether or not all events are absolutely predictable has some implications for the question of the freedom of human beings to choose among alternative courses of action. The free will-determinism problem has the quality of a paradox because it opposes a poignant and universal human experience (freedom of choice) to a most impelling assumption (that there is a reason for everything), and insists that *a choice* must be made between them.

It appears, of course, that if one admits that all events are absolutely predictable, then one must admit that what one is about to do a moment from now can be stated with certainty; but if this is so, then one cannot do otherwise. And if there is some possible action that one cannot do, then one is not free. One is, in fact, compelled. To deny such compulsion, it appears, one must assert that in principle not all events are predictable. Thus one seems to regain freedom to act differently a moment from now, in spite of all the psychological response-catalogues that can ever be invented.

The reply of the philosopher of science to such a position is "Freedom, my eye!" or words to that effect. In the absence of predictability, what obtains is not freedom, but chance. Free will versus determinism is a mistaken opposition. There is chance versus predictability, and there is freedom versus constraint, but freedom and predictability belong to two different universes of discourse. In the nature of the case they cannot be brought into any relationship with one another, save the mistaken opposition with which classical philosophy has so long concerned itself. There is no solution to the "problem" of free will versus determinism; there is possible, and proper, only a resolution.

Such, in brief, is the position on the question taken by the modern school of scientific philosophy. Properly stated, the arguments are as long and as complex as they ought to be to resolve so ancient an unsolved problem. However, our purpose here is not to concern ourselves with the free will problem as a vexing *philosophical* question, but to inquire into its *psychological* origins in an attempt to explain its lasting popularity, and the freshness of its appeal to each new generation upon the earth.

THE REFERENTS OF "FREEDOM"

It is necessary to begin by asking what might be meant by the term "freedom." I see two chief meanings which may be assigned to it: first, it may refer to a subjective human experience, testified to by all men: a feeling of freedom to act and to choose, or, the other side of the coin, a feeling that one is powerless to act and to choose. In this sense, freedom and compulsion are psychological phenomena of the sort that may be crudely classified as "personal feelings." In its second meaning, freedom may be defined as the range of possible adaptive responses available to organisms in all situations in which they may find themselves.

In this latter meaning, freedom in general increases univocally as the response repertoire increases. In a particular situation, it is a function as well of the constraints imposed by the situation. In effect, the situation together with the organism defines the organism's freedom at any given moment. Thus one may speak of potential freedom and actual freedom, actual freedom being freedom at the moment in a given situation, and potential freedom being some value expressing the relation of the organism's response repertoire to the population of possible situations in which the organism might be placed. In the most general case, of course, one would not speak of organisms at all, but of organizations of matter. It is meaningful to say that a clod is less free than a butterfly, and a butterfly less free than a man (in spite of appearances)—and even, in fact, to say that some clods are freer than others, for it is not necessary to be alive in order to have certain inherent response-tendencies. The existence of life itself testifies to the fact that some inanimate matter was once freer, in this sense of freedom, than other material forms.

Freedom in this sense is worth considerable thought. It can be given such thought by the human brain, the freest of all organizations. It is the happy and unique characteristic of the brain that its manifold possibilities of action may all take place inwardly, and that it may act invisibly. This capacity for inward action is a bother to tyrants and defeats the most valiant efforts at imposing constraints. This is what Spinoza meant when he said that freedom of thought is an indefeasible natural right. Spinoza's statement refers to the fact that one's brain is inside one's own skull, and that within that limited space it exercises an utterly amazing potential for varied response.

This particular instance of freedom (i.e., *indefeasible* freedom of thought, or its intrinsic solitariness), while it seems most important at times when the forces hostile to civilization are in the ascendancy, is a relatively minor and unimportant aspect of the freedom that the development of a complicated nervous system has given man. It is safe to say that our potential freedom is unimaginable. A small extension of it may be seen in the most complex of our calculating machines, and a prevision of its scope enlivens the pages of science fiction. The essence of our human freedom is this, that matter has acquired the capacity to work radical modifications in itself. Thus, among its "available responses" is the ability to act in such a manner as to increase its own flexibility, or deliberately to maximize its own response variability. One of the products of this ability in the human case is the invention and cultivation of psychotherapy, which provides a unique meeting ground of the objective and subjective meanings of freedom. Of this, more later, although much has already been said by implication in earlier chapters.

In any event, in this sense of freedom—i.e., as the range of possible adaptive responses—freedom is a characteristic of material organization, and the range of values it takes is infinite.

THE PERSONAL FEELING OF FREEDOM

We are confronted with quite a different phenomenon when we consider freedom in its other meaning, as a subjective feeling. However, there is no reason to restrict freedom in this sense to human beings, any more than in its other sense; there probably are many animals who are capable of feeling free or bound. The lower animals are different from man only in that they respond more to external constraints and external liberties, and less to internalized barriers (simply because of their limited capacity to conceptualize and hence to internalize). Still, in such animals as the ape and the dog, it is quite clear that constraints originating outside of them—for example, constraints imposed by their human masters in the interests of discipline —do become internalized and a part of themselves. And it is possible to induce something akin to an id-superego conflict in such animals, in which case they manifest anxiety and disorganization similar to what human beings do when caught up in such a conflict. I see no reason for not attributing to them precisely analogous feelings of constraint and of powerlessness to act.

Since freedom (or constraint) is a feeling, we may expect that in the psychic economy it may play all of the roles, and be subject to all of the vicissitudes, of affect in general. That is, we may expect first of all that the feeling of being free may serve as a defense, which is to say that it may be experienced consciously in the service of the ego while actually covering up an unconscious feeling quite opposite in character. Let us consider the situation first of all in relation to a sense of inner compulsion, or lack of freedom to act. It is not difficult for us to understand how it is that the feeling of being coerced, compelled, impotent, may undergo repression—it is simply too painful a feeling to be admitted to consciousness if it can possibly be kept unconscious. In most relatively efficient neuroses, the feeling of lack of freedom is suppressed almost all the time, just as the feeling of unhappiness and the sense of loneliness is suppressed. It is commonly true that patients who seek psychotherapy do so at just that moment not because of their neurosis, but because of a temporary breakdown of their usual defenses. Thus the psychoneurotic patient at the beginning of therapy is depressed, anxious, and confused, overwhelmed by feelings that may be characterized in general as psychic impotence. The inability to act is usually caused by a conflict of forces of almost equal strength, a conflict which cannot be dealt with by whatever defenses the patient had previously been wont to employ. The very urgency of the conflict most powerfully brings into consciousness the feeling of inability to act. This painful feeling brings home to the patient his need for help, and thus it is usually the initial motivating force in psychotherapy.

Apropos of this, recall here Freud's remark to the effect that psychoanalysis proper cannot begin until the crisis that brought the patient to analysis has subsided. In brief psychotherapy, only too often the patient is discharged as improved at the point where the *crisis* is successfully passed, and where if the *relationship* were to continue the neurosis itself would have to be analyzed (which would require above all an analysis of the transference and the countertransference). The aim of the superficial therapies, whether explicitly recognized or not, is to re-establish, on a somewhat more efficient basis, the same response patterns that have been the patient's chief life achievement in relation to his self. "Improvement" in this sort of psychotherapy may therefore at times be a sad thing, for the patient's initial agitated state might have served as the lever to lift him out of his neurotic pattern. Such agitation is often the first stirring of a desire for a feeling of freedom after years of unconscious bondage.

It should be said here that the feeling of lack of freedom, when it comes to consciousness under such circumstances, may be taken as a genuine expression, or a correct perception, of *real lack of freedom in the objective sense of the term*. In the individual's situation—and it must be remembered that the structure of his self is part of his situation—in that situation, his response repertoire is indeed exceedingly limited, so that he is *actually not very free*. The important point is that the feeling of being compelled arises from within, and that it is not proportionate to what we have called potential freedom; rather, it is a function of what we have defined above as actual freedom. To recall those definitions: potential freedom is the total repertoire of responses available to the individual in the whole range of situations in which he might be placed; actual freedom is given by the response repertoire in a *particular* situation. One of the most poignant aspects of neurotic suffering is the realization by the frustrated individual that "objectively" it is perfectly within his capacities for him to bring about the conditions for which he yearns. He is *potentially* free— but *actually* not, because of the structure of the self, and because he himself *is* his situation. It is, of course, not freedom of will that he lacks, objectively, but freedom of action of the self that he is.

At this point, then, freedom in the objective sense becomes relevant to freedom as a feeling. We shall try to show later that when a person attains maximum potential freedom, objectively, he no longer experiences a sense of inner constraint.

The increasing demand for psychotherapy is, I believe, due to the fact that it offers, or is seen as offering, greater freedom for the self. It is because of the nature of this inducement, so dear to mankind, that psychotherapy may be, at its worst, one of the baser forms of commerce, and at its best, one of the most heartening of human relationships.

THE FEELING OF FREEDOM AS A DEFENSE

From the foregoing, one might be led to think that the most desirable state is to feel free. This is true, but the situation, as usual, is not so simple. Very often the feeling of freedom and of power to act is the most desperate of defenses against a deep and totally unconscious sense of powerlessness and constraint. A familiar clinical example is vigorous phallic activity covering an unconscious sense of smallness. The kinds of character defenses that are classified in general as counterphobic go along most frequently with an exaggerated sense of conscious freedom, or euphoria, or power to act at will. This is seen in its most vivid and most pathological form in the manic-depressive psychosis. When the patient is in a manic state, he is perfectly happy, perfectly powerful, and perfectly free—absurdly so, of course, so that one is not surprised to find him a short time later in such a state of stupefaction and despair that he cannot speak or move at all. As in most affects, intensity of the experience is an excellent indicator that the extreme opposite is close to expression.

This brings us to a case which it would be much easier not to discuss, but which forces itself upon us for consideration. May an intense feeling of compulsion and of lack of power be a defense against the achievement of greater freedom of the self? Why, indeed, should freedom of the self be defended against, when it is presumably what all men want?

Dostoevski, again, has given this question its most dramatic statement. In the Grand Inquisitor episode in *The Brothers Karamazov*, certainly a pinnacle of world literature, Dostoevski imagines Christ as having returned to earth and to the Church He had founded. He appears and is recognized, for His grace shines among men as in the days of His life. As a crowd gathers in wonderment and love about Him, the Grand Inquisitor passes by, and, immediately understanding the situation, orders Him arrested. That evening, in the darkness of the dungeon in which Christ is imprisoned, the Grand Inquisitor himself, alone, enters with a light in his hand. He speaks sternly and bitterly to Christ and recalls to Him the temptation in the desert, during which "the cursed and dread Spirit, the spirit of self-destruction and non-existence" had put to Him the three temptations. These three temptations are interpreted by Dostoevski as temptations to Christ to offer man something less than freedom: bread, or miracle, or mystery, or authority, but not freedom. For, as the "dread Spirit" had said, "Thou wouldst go into the world, and Thou art going into the world with empty hands, with some promise of freedom which men in their simplicity and their natural unruliness cannot even understand, which they fear and dread—for nothing has ever been more insupportable for a man and a human society than freedom."

And, in the words of the Grand Inquisitor:

> I tell Thee that man is tormented by no greater anxiety than to find someone quickly to whom he can hand over that gift of freedom with which the ill-fated creature is born . . . Didst Thou forget that man prefers peace, and even death, to freedom of choice in the knowledge of good and evil? . . . In place of the rigid ancient law, Thou wouldst have it that man must hereafter with free heart decide for himself what is good and what is evil, having only Thy image before him as his guide. But didst Thou not know that he would at last reject even Thy image and Thy truth, if he is weighed down with the fearful burden of free choice? Is the nature of man such that he can reject miracle, and at the great moments of his life, the moments of his deepest, most agonizing spiritual difficulties, cling only to the free verdict of the heart? Thou didst think too highly of men therein, for they are slaves. . . .

If now as psychologists and scientists we leave aside the mystical character of freedom as Dostoevski speaks of it, and ask ourselves what arrangement of the parts of the self might produce the *feeling of freedom* which Christ is represented as offering to man, then we may get an important clue from this passage. Consider this sentence of the Grand Inquisitor: "Didst Thou forget that man prefers peace, and even death, to freedom of choice in the knowledge of good and evil?" And, again, "In place of the rigid, ancient law, Thou wouldst have it that man must hereafter with free heart decide for himself what is good and what is evil. . . ."

Here is a psychoanalytic sort of interpretation: the knowledge of good and evil refers to conscious knowledge of all the usually unconscious, internalized prohibitions and prescriptions, particularly those that relate to the most primitive and most energy-laden of our drives. Knowledge of good and evil implies the availability to consciousness both of impulses and of the forces that control impulse. It means, further, that the expression or renunciation of impulse would become a matter of conscious decision, made by the whole self, rather than a matter of the triumph of blind forces of either desire or restraint.

Another way of putting this, in terms of such theoretical constructs as psychoanalysis provides, would be to say that, in freedom, the ego would no longer relate to the superego as a child to a punishing parent, but that the superego would become entirely integrated with the ego.

The feeling of constraint, then, may be said to derive from a fearful and hating orientation of the ego to the superego—that is, from an arrangement of parts of the self that would be the inner equivalent of being constrained from without, by alien and powerful forces. Such an arrangement is learned, of course; it occurs as a result of the experience of having been constrained by others, chiefly the parents. Still, it is evident that some such specialization of parts of the self is the normal and desirable state of affairs. If discipline is orderly, rational, and loving, it will not lead to severe repression and to consequent domination by unconscious forces. The feeling of freedom and the absence of inner, irrational compulsions will then be determined chiefly by the extent to which the superego is rational and conscious, and impulse is gratified or renounced in accordance with the decision of the ego.

The existence of internalized *irrational* parents is thus a prime source of the feeling of compulsion, and indeed may *actually* restrict ability to respond adaptively—recall the phrase "the *rigid*, ancient law." If, however, the ego itself were to become the source of ethical prescriptions, having assimilated the old function of the superego, the source of the prescription would no longer be unconscious and the feeling of compulsion would vanish. This is the aim of the psycho-analytically-based psychotherapies.

It should be noted that the production of a relatively rational super-ego by loving and rational parents is still something very short of that hypothetically possible if rarely realized state in which superego and ego are one. The "client-centered therapy" whose theory and practice have been so ably developed by Carl Rogers is particularly impressive in its emphasis on the unconditional self-worth of the client and the total acceptance by the therapist of the fundamental goodness of the client. In terms of this analysis, such therapy would offer the client a loving and rational parent to internalize, but it would not have the further goal—and one that is rarely achieved in any case—of making available to consciousness once again the most primitive of impulses and the most powerful and most repressed of prohibitions.

But this latter is something of a digression. Let us return to the defensive character of compulsion, and to one of the most important of the arguments made against Christ by the Grand Inquisitor—that "nothing has ever been more insupportable for a man and a human society than freedom." Why should the majority of men find such an arrangement of the self an intolerable one?

Largely, one must answer, because of infantile fears—or, more accurately, because of fears that were very great during the period of early childhood, and that have persisted with undiminished intensity in the unconscious. Such fears were, to begin with, fears of outer forces of great power—literally, I believe, fears that one would be destroyed for expressing impulses unrestrained. In civilized society (which, unhappily, a baby does not realize it has been born into) such fears might be called, from our civilized, adult viewpoint, unrealistic. Most parents really do not mean their children any harm. The baby, however, is not yet civilized, and he invests the outer forces with every bit as much intensity of desire, and rage when frustrated, as he himself possesses. Thus he has good reason, when he is angry or insatiate, to fear the giants with whom he interacts and on whom he depends. He fears them because of the strength of his own impulses, which he experiences fully, and because the boundary between inner and outer is still fluid, so that he is not always certain who is enraged.

In the adult, such fears persist, first of all, as fear of impulses from within, and, secondly, as fear of destruction from the internalized parents. It would be easy to say, "unrealistic fears," but the fact is that persons kill themselves for their own impulses—that is, they deal out the most extreme punishment to themselves for a "crime" they were *impelled* to commit, though the crime they do in fact commit is murder of the self rather than of the other. Where impulses are so fearsome and the forces of restraint so ferocious, it seems safer not to be free—or, to put the matter in other terms, it seems safer not to know anything about the situation of the self.

But here one is reminded of a most significant quotation from the New Testament—"he who would save his life shall lose it . . ." The moral message of Christ, insofar as it is embodied in this quotation, consisted exactly of the advocacy of the wisdom of self-forgetfulness, which "objectively" in psychoanalytic terms means the establishment of a relationship of harmony and love between the ego and the superego, or the dissolution of the wall that separates what we are from what we think we should be. I cannot develop the thesis in detail here, but it seems to me that the New Testament is best understood in terms of the relationship between personified conscious knowledge—the Word made flesh, alive and changing, taking its chances, open to beauty and decay—and the ancient, rigid law and lawgiver, fixed, abstract, decided.

The constantly recurring imagery of the Son and the Father suggests that the specific content of the conflict and the disharmony which Christ sought to resolve was essentially similar to what Freud named the Oedipus complex. In terms of actual frequencies, the Oedipus situation is probably the one most generative of disruptive conflict in men, and probably most determinative of the feeling of compulsion. But let it be understood that what we have said here deals at a most general level with the relationship between impulse, its expression, and its control. The Oedipus complex is simply a special case of this relationship, though probably the most important instance so far as both frequency and intensity are concerned.

To recapitulate: freedom, or conscious knowledge of the primitive forces of id and superego, is greatly feared, even in adulthood, because of the persistence in the unconscious of the earliest and most intense of fears. Thus the prospect of freedom is intolerable. One further aspect should be touched upon. The condition of freedom, or complete consciousness, would entail complete assumption of responsibility for one's self. One could not claim to "know not what one did," for the impulse in all its nakedness would be experienced. The intention would be fully realized and, if consented to, accomplished in full knowledge. But if one follows the dictates of an internalized parent and is thereby somewhat less free to act according to one's deepest inclinations, one is at the same time not wholly responsible for the consequences. The parent is responsible, and the ego is still a child. Thus the individual may avoid judging for himself what is right and what is wrong. He is not "weighed down by the fearful burden of free choice," and he is consequently *actually less free*.

For it remains to be said that "the truth shall make one free." The essential point of this analysis is that objective freedom, in the sense of response variability, is at a maximum when a genuine feeling of freedom exists, and that such a feeling of freedom occurs in the presence of a broadened consciousness both of impulse and of ethical prescriptions. So far as the postulate of determinism is concerned (i.e., absolute predictability in principle), it should be quite evident that such a postulate is irrelevant to both the objective and the subjective meanings of freedom. If one assumes a closed system of knowledge and a perfect description of the given state of affairs, then all events are absolutely predictable, including the actions of human beings of quite different degrees of objective freedom and of subjective sense of freedom.

The acceptance of determinism as a working hypothesis is basic to psychology as a science. When it becomes more than that, as it so often does, and is elevated from modus vivendi to sentiment and then to principle for one's whole life, it is surely itself a form of self-imposed restriction upon imagination and the capacity to create. For myself, I believe there is a recalcitrant oddness at the heart of things —I had almost written at the heart of hearts—and I am pleased when my mind wanders off to think no more of this or that.

A final bow to Dostoevski's gentleman: Yes, indeed, it is time to scatter rationalism to the winds, if by rationalism is understood the mistaking of a part of mind, the intellectualizing part, for the whole. Let us conclude with four unreasonable paragraphs he might endorse:

1. Pristine common sense imprisons the human spirit; science is fortified common sense, and science as concealed metaphysic or as cosmic attitude is maximum-security confinement.

2. Reason accepts the given world, and arises in the service of adaptation to it. Its premise is determinism, and it can argue for freedom only because it considers the feeling of freedom a functionally useful deception.

3. What is reasonable in human nature is mechanical, and life is not needed for its perpetuation. If human nature is reasonable in its essence, then life is simply a means for matter to become intelligent, and the function of man is to build machines that can think and be virtually incorruptible.

4. But human nature is an emergent differing in kind from the material and from the rest of the organic universe; it is not only the newest thing in the universe, *it alone can generate novelty and resist adaptation by an act of will.* Before it, all novelty arose by chance; with it, novelty can arise by intention.

22

Violence and Vitality

Violence and vitality share a common root—the root of both is force (etymologically, in its Latin form *vis*). The various plays of force and the radical nature of the encounters of its two forms in vitality and violence will concern us in this chapter. Let us first consider in general terms the expression of force in animal instinct and the ways in which it becomes modified as a consequence of the process of socialization, adopting a coldly "rational" view.

The first instinct is to take in enough material from the outside world so that one may be sustained; that is, so that one's system may replenish itself. The system puts out energy constantly, both to maintain its individual boundaries and to perpetuate its kind; it must take in some source of energy that it does not presently contain. This source is food, which includes air, sunshine, and other organic matter.

For life as a whole, then, death must be constant and almost equal in quantity to life; organisms must die so that other organisms may live. Life therefore depends upon a quantitative superiority of the mechanisms for reproduction. On the average, each organism must reproduce itself and a surplus besides; hence the sexual function must be most powerfully motivated if life is to continue. It is of equal rank, so far as motives are concerned, as the drive to ingest. The latter is most necessary to the prolongation of individual life, and through individual forms to life itself; the latter is necessary because of the principle that life feeds upon life. It is a requirement of life that it should expand, that individual forms of it should multiply. A stasis seems theoretically conceivable; it is, in fact, the basic tendency of the supreme animal. The strongest organism will seek to limit its own reproduction out of an apparent or misguided self-interest. Because it temporarily has ascendancy and an assurance of sustenance, it finds no need for reproducing more than *one* of its own kind per unit already existing. It loses supremacy, then, purely as a function of probability arising out of life's tendency toward diversity. Prolific life produces many new forms, in such great numbers that finally there occurs some form that is better suited to be supreme. Thus are old rulers deposed; the rules of life make it certain that supremacy cannot be maintained. Death is simply a rule of life. Freud was wrong in claiming that Eros and Thanatos are equally strong forces. Life is infinitely stronger than Death, for from the beginning Death is merely a by-product of life. The tendency of matter is toward life, and the present tendency of life is toward consciousness. Consciousness itself arises in the interest of the expansion of life; the competition among organisms for food is decided ultimately by such things as attention and memory and logic. Thus forms of life arose having such traits. The unconscious is presently an anachonism. Eventually organisms must be born incapable of an unconscious; all the power of symbolism for the imaginative construction of experience must finally become conscious, together with all motives.

It may be asked, however, is not symbolism itself a diversion on the road to complete consciousness? What is symbolism but a disguised mode of representing motives that were once completely unconscious? Is not symbolism simply a step toward conscious representation of the motives of all life? Does it not decrease in the individual as motives become conscious?

It may be replied that symbols are possible because of a tremendous differentiation of matter (the structure of the human brain) and that this differentiation of structure and direction of development will not be reversed. Hence symbolic forms should continue indefinitely, though functionally they may become less important for life. It remains a question, however, whether completely conscious motives would require the complexity of determination and differentiation that symbols now have. The motives themselves might, of course, change beyond recognition, into something we cannot now conceive, into a form requiring for their representation the very mechanics that the development of symbolization has made a permanent possession of human intelligence.

The tendency of life, then, is toward the expansion of consciousness. In a sense, *a description of means for the expansion of conscious-*

ness has been the central theme of this book; it is in this evolutionary tendency that such diverse phenomena as psychotherapy, surprising or unexpected self-renewal, the personally evolved and deepened forms of religious belief, creative imagination, mysticism, and deliberately induced changes in consciousness through the use of chemicals find a common bond. Engagement as an individual in these efforts to expand consciousness is therefore, in various measure, participation in the job that life in general is now facing. It is itself a mark of vitality.

What then of violence? Analyzed coldly in terms of instinctual force, it seems evident that violence itself should provide the primal basis for all relations among individual living systems. One seeks to eat the other, and the superior force succeeds. Communities then develop from mutual recognition that selfish ends will be best served by cooperation—that two can eat better than one, or that the alien aggressor may be more effectively repulsed by a defense in common. The idea of justice, according to this conception, arises from a recognition that communities cannot be maintained unless all members hold it a superior form of interest to desist from eating one another and to cooperate in seizing the enemy and resisting his attacks. Thus murder is sanctioned only when committed against an outsider. Otherwise it would lead to disruption of the community pact and eventually to the inferior form of social organization in which everyone is the unqualified enemy of everyone else. Societies may thus be defined as a form of carefully qualified enmity.

In the interest of community organization, however, illusions (which are usually a form of self-deception in the interest of survival) must arise. The most important illusions take the form of identification, which essentially are a claim that another individual is actually oneself, to be treated by one as one would treat oneself. Such identifications in their most extreme form are extended to the entire community. In their more restricted form they pertain especially to parents, mates, and offspring, or substitutes for these (i.e., symbolic equivalents of these). Identifications arise for the same basic reason as community itself—for the more efficient securing of sustenance and for the purpose of warding off aggression, not only from outsiders, but from the very person with whom the community is made. One purpose of a pact is to reduce the number of one's enemies by, at a minimum, the number of one's allies—by those allies themselves, in fact. Community uses symbolization for this purpose. Sympathy then is based upon the complex perception of community of interest, or at least a capacity for justifying complexly one's friendships or communities.

This repelling way of putting the matter leaves quite out of account the strange force of love and the impulse to create. The analysis nevertheless has value within the framework of a purely rational psychology, if for no other reason than that it forces us to consider carefully how far objective self-interest can take us. There is a real question as to whether through simply this process of symbolization and sympathy, and eventually through attainment of the *Ultima Thule* of fully conscious rationality, aggression can be mitigated for life as a whole. Even if a species should succeed in including its entire self in a single community (as none has done yet), the reduced motive for reproduction might eventually produce a static state in the species which would ensure the succession of some other species to supremacy. The unknown quantity in all of this, as we have been arguing directly or by implication throughout, is the power of creative imagination, the main instrument of freedom.

At this writing, so far as man is concerned, it appears possible, even though the problems are extraordinarily complex and difficult, that he will extend community to include all other men. The idea is verbalized and current, and it has many advocates. All other living beings, however, have entertained to the death the notion that some infraspecies organization will attain supremacy, so that combat is entered upon even when the strength of the combatants and their equality makes it seem probable that one will die and the other nearly die, or that both will die. And life as a whole is indifferent to the success of single species, as much as to the success of single individuals. The one thing of which we can be certain is that life itself is inextinguishable. One mark of the breadth of the community that man has established is that we are able now to contemplate the idea that the very species Mankind—surely an extremely special vehicle for the expansion of consciousness—may be the final supreme form of life. This is local interest raised to the highest form it has yet attained, and it would mean the passing of violence as a form of adaptation and the total institutionalization of the remaining energy of the instinct in world law.

Religious revelation tells us much the same story as does this sort of analysis, though the terms are different. Consider the chapters of Genesis and the account it gives of the first murder:

In the relative innocence of a world but lately paradise, Cain slays Abel. The murderer, confronted by God, denies knowledge of his brother's whereabouts, for, he says, he is not his brother's keeper. When the accusation is pressed against him, however, he admits the deed. God condemns him to a life of wandering on the face of the earth, but mercifully places upon his forehead a distinguishing mark, that men may not kill him.

Thus is man's violence confessed in this early Biblical story, and its fearfulness acknowledged. The mark of Cain is a sign of human murderousness, but it carries immunity with it. The murderer within us is to be exiled, yet he is awesome because he is a murderous man.

The scene is placed in the Bible immediately after what theologians call the Fall; as we have argued earlier, biologists might well call it the Accession. Our first parents had just eaten the fruit of the Tree of Knowledge of Good and Evil, which is to say they became ethical beings, and for the first time in Nature a natural creature passed judgment. Thus, close upon the passing of innocence came murder itself, and the first ethical judgment is that murder is a crime against human nature.

An exception came quickly to be recognized. The exception is war—a large exception indeed. Its basis is the family. One may not kill one's blood relatives, but one may kill those outside the family, who are the enemies of the family. Loyalty to the family will sanction the deed.

Finally, family need not be defined by blood. Geography will suffice, or race, or economic interdependence, or religious belief. Thus the wars of families become wars of nations, and murder is countenanced once again. Man seems in war thus to triumph over his accession to conscience, and the eating of the apple was not so fateful a deed as it had at first appeared.

But in the course of the centuries fallen man has come more and more to control the world. Control is based in large part on knowledge of the workings of a machine-like universe, and the creation of new machines. Among the machines are those used for murder, private and public. Among the knowledge is knowledge of the basic structure of matter, and finally of the atom itself. New force has been released, and its release adapted to an ancient and sanctioned end: the killing of an enemy family.

The new force, however, is gigantic; its murderous power is beyond anything previously dreamt of. So great is this power that one family might destroy all others on earth, provided there could be no retaliation in kind.

Retaliation in kind, however, has come to be a certainty. This is the setting of the modern dilemma of a creature who has nibbled at the fruit of the Tree of Knowledge of Good and Evil, but who is loath to assume the responsibility given with freedom or to accept the grace of redemption. Unless consciousness can take another giant step and root out murder from the heart of man, or develop the control of violence through law to a new and extraordinary level, some other form of consciousness must become the carrier of vitality.

Technical Appendix

The main aim of this appendix is to explain as simply as possible the nature and purpose of the psychological tests and methods of analysis used in the research we have presented and discussed. It is hoped that this will be of help to the general reader who has had no formal training in psychology. In addition, references are given to the technical literature so that interested readers may pursue the topics further if they wish.

The three tests most commonly used by clinical psychologists in the United States are the Rorschach Psychodiagnostic, the Minnesota Multiphasic Personality Inventory, and the Thematic Apperception Test. Our research depended heavily upon these three devices, but we continually sought to develop new tests more directly relevant to our special interest, the study of psychological health and creativity. Although the new tests have now to some extent supplanted the old in our assessments, it seems appropriate to begin with a description of these three most widely used clinical devices, since they are not only popular, but prototypic.

THE RORSCHACH PSYCHODIAGNOSTIC

This test was developed by a Swiss psychiatrist, Hermann Rorschach. A description of its development may be found in Rorschach's monograph, *Psychodiagnostic: a diagnostic test based on perception,* which is published in Berne, Switzerland, by the Huber Company, and is available in an English translation by P. Lemkan and B. Kronenburg.

The test consists of ten inkblots, some in black and white and some containing color. These ten blots were selected by Rorschach after extensive experimentation with many other blots. They are presented to the subject one at a time, and he is asked to describe all that he can see in each blot before going on to the next one.

An inkblot can be many things to many people, just as clouds can be, or shadowy objects in the night, or a drop of oil in a puddle of water. For that matter, a person can be many things to many people, and so can the world itself: a carnival, a grim struggle, a prison, a fascinating pageant, an interval. It is not the inkblot that the psychologist cares about, at least when he is being a psychologist, but rather the interpretation placed upon it by the subject. What the subject sees or imagines, and also what he does *not* see or imagine, is what concerns the psychologist.

Psychologists often speak of *norms* for tests, by which they mean statistical averages that are arrived at by gathering information in a systematic manner so that the responses of people in general will be accurately represented. In trying to understand an individual, it is helpful to know to what extent he differs from the norm. In interpreting the Rorschach, such norms are customarily employed, sometimes informally rather than formally. The interpreter also tries to understand the unique inner life and subjective experience of the person taking the test; he does so by paying close attention to the emotional tone of responses, to sequences that may reveal strong associational patterns or ways of dealing with troublesome thoughts, and finally to the meanings of symbols.

A quite complicated scheme for scoring the Rorschach is usually employed, but this is not the place to give a description of it. In presenting the Rorschach record of Paul in Chapter 4, "An Odd Fellow," we have purposely omitted the scoring while attempting to give in the interpretation some inkling of what goes on in the psychologist's head as he seeks to construct in his own imagination a picture of how the subject functions. The validity of the usual scoring scheme is still a matter for debate among clinical psychologists, although most of them feel confident that the test as a whole is a powerful source of insight into some of the more subtle aspects of individual psychological functioning.

THE MINNESOTA MULTIPHASIC PERSONALITY INVENTORY (M.M.P.I.)

Unlike the Rorschach, the Minnesota Multiphasic is completely objective in its scoring and is explicit in its use of the normative approach to psychological measurement. It consists of 550 simple declarative sentences, which the subject is asked to consider one at a time and to say *True* or *False* to. The "normality" of the subject's response is then appraised in terms of its agreement with the consensus of opinion of normal adults. One of the sentences, for example, is "I believe there is a God," to which most people say *True*. Another is "I am a special agent of God," to which most people say *False*. Without giving away any trade secrets, we can probably suggest that saying *True* to the latter sentence is more likely to be associated with a serious form of pathology, whatever the actual truth of the matter may be. Leaving the particular example aside, the point is that the test itself, like the Rorschach, is based upon a method of *interpreting responses to a specially designed situation,* and the *mode of responding* rather than the *actual truth or falsity* of the 550 statements as they apply to the subject is what interests the psychologist.

The scoring, then, is carried out according to certain hard-and-fast rules. Let us consider a fictional example for the development of a scale to measure Hypochondriasis, which is in fact one of the variables measured by the Multiphasic. A hypochondriac is a person who is continually complaining about his health when there doesn't really seem to be very much wrong with him. Suppose that 100 hypochondriacs are asked to say *True* or *False* to the statement: "I have had a backache within the past month," and that 65 of them say *True*.

Then the same statement is presented to 100 normal adults in good health, and 12 of them say *True*. This 53 per cent difference based on a comparison of groups of this size would rarely occur just by chance—that is, if we could compare *all* hypochondriacs with *all* normal adults, we would very probably find that the observed difference is a real one. We have had occasion frequently in reporting research results to refer to "statistical significance" or "level of confidence," and generally this is what we mean: that an observed difference has only a slight likelihood (one chance in 20, or one chance in 100, or one chance in 1000) of being an error of observation, and that on statistical grounds we can specify our degree of confidence that the observed difference is a real one.

But let us return to the development of our scale to measure a person's similarity to hypochondriacs. We now have one sentence or "item" to include in such a scale. By looking at the percentage differences for another 549 items, we might find several dozen items which meet our standards for confidence that hypochondriacs differ from normal adults in their responses. We would now include all such items in a scale, and for each item that the test respondent answers in the same way as a hypochondriac does, he would get a score of 1. The total number of items for which he received a score on our Hypochondriasis scale would now constitute his "scale score."

A difficulty arises, however, if we have more than one scale in our test and if the number of items and the average scores differ for each scale. This difficulty can be solved by using *standard scores*, which in the case of the Multiphasic is accomplished by making the average score for each scale arbitrarily equal to 50. Dispersion of scores around the average can also be taken into account; in the particular test we are considering, about 68 per cent of all scale scores will fall between 40 and 60, and about 95 per cent between 30 and 70. This provides an immense convenience for the interpreter of the test results, since he can now plot a psychograph of scores on many scales (hence, *multiphasic*), all of which have the same average and the same metric for describing variation.

The actual clinical scales of the Multiphasic are these: Hypochondriasis, Depression, Hysteria, Psychopathic Deviation, Masculinity-Femininity, Paranoia, Psychasthenia, Schizophrenia, and Hypomania. In work with normal subjects and especially with creative individuals, we have found that these scale names have to be taken with a grain of salt, even when the score is quite high, such as in the top one-tenth of one per cent of the general population. Any single score must always be interpreted in terms of the context of scores and also in terms of the situational context and the emotional meaning of test-taking to the subject. The test itself does have certain built-in "validity-indicators" as well, designed to measure aspects of test-taking attitude, and recently there has been much research into the whole question of the influence upon scores of the very human wish to impute to oneself only those traits that are considered socially desirable.

The Minnesota Multiphasic Personality Inventory was developed by S. R.

Hathaway and J. C. McKinley at the University of Minnesota in the late 1930's. An early publication describing its development appeared in the *Journal of Psychology* in 1940 under the title, "A multiphasic personality schedule: I. Construction of the schedule," with Hathaway and McKinley as authors.

The reader who wishes to acquaint himself in a reasonably technical fashion with the problem of statistical inference and the establishment of confidence limits will find in *Psychological Statistics*, by Quinn McNemar, published by John Wiley & Sons, Inc., New York, an especially lucid and useful discussion of these topics. Chapters 4 and 5, titled respectively "The normal curve and probability" and "Sampling errors and statistical inference," are most relevant.

THE THEMATIC APPERCEPTION TEST (T.A.T.)

In this test, the subject is presented with a picture calculated to evoke some sort of dramatic fantasy, and he is then asked to make up a story based on the picture. In the standard form of the test, 20 pictures are used, with some slight differences in the sets for men and for women. The second ten are given to the subject on a later day than the first ten. One "picture" midway in the second set is not a picture at all, but simply a blank white card. The basic aim of the test is to stimulate the verbalization of complexes from the unconscious so that insight may be gained into determinants of behavior that the subject himself cannot report directly. At the same time, of course, one may observe the subject's skill in the use of words, his inventiveness, power of synthesis, and the like.

The pictures themselves were assembled from a variety of sources, ranging from story illustrations in popular magazines to noted works of art. From a very large initial collection, the authors of the test, Christina Morgan and Henry A. Murray, selected the final set of pictures to be used. Murray concurrently was evolving his intricate and ingenious scheme of personality needs (see *Explorations in Personality*, Oxford University Press, New York, 1938), an attempt at a comprehensive theory of personality based on individual needs and the demands and stresses (or "presses") of internal and external environments. Valiant efforts to achieve a reliable system of scoring for these needs and presses from the Thematic Apperception Test stories have been made by Murray and his colleagues and students, but the scoring is so demanding in terms of skill, time, and dedication that norms are difficult to establish and to use. Nevertheless, the experienced T.A.T. interpreter can readily discern the emergence of unusual themes, and from small signs he can often detect the presence of important conflicts revealed by the subject's stories. As with the Rorschach, the psychologist's sensitivity to emotional tone, to associational patterns, to indicators of repression, and to symbolic meaning is most important in "getting the most out of" the T.A.T. The trouble with this, as with all interpretation of fantasy material, is that one may easily get more out of it than is in it. William James once called Freud's use of symbol interpretation "a very dangerous method," and reliance upon one's intuition of the meaning of symbols is even more chancy when personal associations to the symbols are not obtained.

Even with all these reservations, however, the Thematic Apperception Test is unquestionably one of the most valuable of diagnostic devices.

A number of tests based on the same general ideas and utilizing much the same methods as these three prototypic tests have been developed at the Institute of Personality Assessment and Research for the purpose of assessing psychological health. Since some of these are described in the text, especially the Ego-strength scale, the Barron-Welsh Art Scale, and the Independence of Judgment scale, they will for the most part not be discussed here. An extension and further validation of the verbal scale to measure the Complexity dimension has recently been completed and is scheduled to appear in 1963 in *College Admissions 10*, the bulletin of the College Entrance Examination Board. An inventory scale of the *True-False* type to measure Originality has also been developed by the present writer but has not yet been published.

A comprehensive attempt to provide inventory-type measures of the positive aspects of personal functioning has been made by Harrison G. Gough of the Institute staff. He has incorporated measures developed over a period of some ten years into a single test, the California Psychological Inventory (C.P.I.). Like the Minnesota Multiphasic, it is based upon item analysis of simple declarative sentences answered *True* or *False* (in fact, many of the items are drawn from the Multiphasic item-pool) by groups of persons possessed of known attributes in terms of socially observable behavior. The Socialization scale, for example, is based on a comparison of civil prisoners, juvenile delinquents, school disciplinary problems, and the like, with normal adults and with persons selected for their exemplary social behavior. Again, as with the Multiphasic, one must be cautious about accepting the scale names at face value, especially when extremely high or extremely low scores are earned. One scale, for example, is named "Self-acceptance," but very high scores seem to be associated with a lack of the ordinary amount of self-criticality, so that the high-scoring subjects appear not so much self-accepting as self-satisfied, in the negative sense of the latter term. We have already sounded a similar warning note in regard to the Ego-strength scale, and Gough himself has been careful in qualifying interpretations based on C.P.I. scales.

In addition to Socialization and Self-acceptance, the C.P.I. provides measures of these dimensions: Responsibility, Tolerance, Flexibility, Capacity for Status, Dominance, Social Participation, Intellectual Efficiency, Motivation to Achieve through Conformance, Motivation to Achieve through Independence, Self-control, Psychological-mindedness, Desire to Make a Good Impression, and, finally, Femininity. In addition, there are scales to measure tendencies toward carelessness or falsification in responding and to identify persons who exaggerate their problems or overstate complaints.

Two other tests developed by the present writer are mentioned in the text and may be described here very briefly:

The Inventory of Personal Philosophy This is a verbal opinion inventory consisting of four sections: I. Basic Philosophical Beliefs; II. Social Attitudes and Personal Opinions; III. Valued Personality Characteristics; IV. Preferences among Persons. Section IV was contributed by Dr. Alvin Scodel. The scales include the final Complexity scale, Independence of Judgment, Extraception-introception, Liberalism-conservatism, Romanticism-classicism, and Intelligent Opinion, in addition to the four Belief scales described in Chapter 12, "The Crisis in Belief."

The Word-Rearrangement Test This is a test designed to assess the subject's ability to take a large set of disarranged or as yet unrelated words and to assemble them into sentences, paragraphs, or stories. Part I presents the subject with jumbled sentences which are to be straightened out, while Part II asks him to compose grammatical units in which at least two and preferably 50 of a total of 50 stimulus words are to be coherently combined. A full description of the test, its scoring, and its validation is given in Technical Memorandum OERL-TM-55-11, published by the Officer Education Research Laboratory, Maxwell Air Force Base, Alabama.

Finally, here are some references to published articles or monographs that describe more fully some of the tests used in our research:

Chapin, F. S. Preliminary standardization of a social insight scale. *Amer. sociol. Rev.,* 1942, 7, 214–225.

Crutchfield, R. S. Conformity and character. *Amer. Psychologist,* 1955, 10, 191–198.

Crutchfield, R. S., Woodworth, D. G., and Albrecht, Ruth E. *Perceptual performance and the effective person.* Lackland Air Force Base, Texas: Personnel Laboratory, Wright Air Development Center, April 1958. (*Technical Note* WADC-TN-58-60, ASTIA No. 151039.)

Gottschaldt, K. Uber den Einfluss der Erfahrung auf die Wahrnehmung von Figuren. *Psychol. Forsch.,* 1926, 8, 261–317; 1929, 12, 1–87.

Gough, Harrison G. *The adjective check list as a personality assessment technique.* Monograph Supplement 2, *Psychological Reports,* 1960, 6, 107–122, Southern Universities Press, Missoula, Montana.

Strong, E. K., Jr. *The vocational interests of men and women.* Stanford, California: Stanford University Press, 1943.

Terman, L. M., *et al. The gifted child grows up: Twenty-five year's follow-up of a superior group. Genetic studies of genius, Vol. IV.* Stanford, California: Stanford University Press, 1947.

Thurstone, L. L. A factorial study of perception. *Psychometric Monogr.,* 1944, No. 4.

Vitale, J. An investigation of some personality correlates during the clinical course of tuberculosis. Unpublished doctoral dissertation, Stanford University, 1953.

Wallach, H. Uber visuell wahrgenommene Bewegungsrichtung. *Psychol. Forsch.* 1935, 20, 325–380.

Welsh, G. S. An anxiety index and an internalization ratio for the MMPI. *J. consult. Psychol.,* 1952, 16, 65–72.

Bibliography

Adorno, T. W., Frenkel-Brunswik, Else, Levinson, D., & Sanford, R. N. *The authoritarian personality*. New York: Harper, 1950.

Anderson, H. H. (Ed.) *Creativity and its cultivation*. New York: Harper, 1959.

Arthur, G. *A point scale of performance tests*. New York: Psychological Corp., 1947.

Asch, S. E. *Social psychology*. New York: Prentice-Hall, 1952.

Aumack, F. L. The dramatic productions test: psychological and social validation with a Ph.D. population. Unpublished doctoral dissertation, Univ. of California, Berkeley, 1953.

Barron, F. Psychotherapy as a special case of personal interaction: prediction of its course. Unpublished doctoral dissertation, Univ. of California, Berkeley, 1950.

Barron, F. Implications of the Veterans Administration selection program for the future of assessment. Paper read at Amer. Psychol. Assn., 1950.

Barron, F. *Inventory of personal philosophy*. Berkeley, California: Univ. of California Press, 1952.

Barron, F. Personality style and perceptual choice. *J. Pers.*, 1952, 20, 385–401.

Barron, F. An ego-strength scale which predicts response to psychotherapy. *J. consult. Psychol.*, 1953, 17, 327–333.

Barron, F. Complexity-simplicity as a personality dimension. *J. abnorm. soc. Psychol.*, 1953, 48, 163–172.

Barron, F. Some personality correlates of independence of judgment. *J. Pers.*, 1953, 21, 287–297.

Barron, F. Some test correlates of response to psychotherapy. *J. consult. Psychol.*, 1953, 17, 235–241.

Barron, F. Personal soundness in university graduate students: an experimental study of young men in the sciences and professions. *Univ. of California Publications Personality Assessment and Research*, 1954, No. 1.

Barron, F. A case study of a residual. In A. Burton & R. E. Harris (Eds.), *Clinical studies of personality*. New York: Harper, 1955.

Barron, F. The crisis in belief. Paper read at California Acad. of Science, San Francisco, November, 1955.

Barron, F. The disposition toward originality. *J. abnorm. soc. Psychol.*, 1955, 51, 478–485.

Barron, F. The word rearrangement test. Maxwell Air Force Base, Alabama: Officer Education Research Laboratory, May, 1955. (*Technical Memorandum* OERL-TM-55-11.)

Barron, F. Threshold for the perception of human movement in inkblots. *J. consult. Psychol.*, 1955, 19, 33–38.

Barron, F. Ego-strength and the management of aggression. In G. S. Welsh & W. G. Dahlstrom (Eds.), *Basic readings in the MMPI in psychology and medicine.* Minneapolis: Univ. of Minnesota Press, 1957.

Barron, F. Originality in relation to personality and intellect. *J. Pers.*, 1957, 25, 730–742.

Barron, F. The needs for order and for disorder as motives in creative activity. In C. W. Taylor, *et al.*, *The second (1957) research conference on the identification of creative scientific talent.* Salt Lake City: Univ. of Utah Press, 1958.

Barron, F. What is psychological health? *California Mon.*, 1957, 68, 22–25.

Barron, F. The psychology of imagination. *Scientific Amer.*, 1958, 199, 50, 150–156+.

Barron, F. Freedom as feeling. *J. humanistic Psychol.*, 1961, 1, 91–100.

Barron, F. Psychotherapy and creativity. Paper read at the XIV International Congress of Appl. Psychol., Copenhagen, Denmark, August, 1961.

Barron, F. The psychology of creativity. *Encyclopaedia Britannica.* Chicago: Encyclopaedia Britannica, in press.

Barron, F. Unusual realization and the resolution of paradox when certain structural aspects of consciousness are altered. Paper read at Amer. Psychol. Assn., New York, September, 1961.

Barron, F. Creative vision and expression in writing and painting. In Institute of Personality Assessment and Research, University of California, *The creative person.* Berkeley, California: Univ. of California Extension, 1962.

Barron, F. The creative writer. *California Mon.*, 1962, 72(5), 11–14, 38–39.

Barron, F. Creativity. *The international encyclopedia of mental health.* New York: Franklin Watts, Inc., in press.

Barron, F., Guilford, J. P., Christensen, P. R., Berger, R. M., & Kettner, N. W. Interrelations of various measures of creative traits. Unpublished manuscript, Institute of Personality Assessment and Research, University of California, Berkeley, 1957. (Prepared in part under Contract No. AF 18 (600) −8.)

Barron, F., & Leary, T. Changes in psychoneurotic patients with and without psychotherapy. *J. consult. Psychol.*, 1955, 19, 239–245.

Barron, F., & Taylor, C. W. (Eds.) *Scientific creativity: its recognition and development.* New York: John Wiley, 1963.

Barron, F., & Welsh, G. S. Artistic perception as a factor in personality style: its measurement by a figure-preference test. *J. Psychol.*, 1952, 33, 199–203.

Bartlett, F. *Thinking.* New York: Basic Books, 1958.

Bennett, G. K., & Fry, D. E. *Test of mechanical comprehension.* New York: Psychological Corp., 1947.

Berdyaev, N. A. *The meaning of the creative act.* (Trans. D. A. Lowrie.) New York: Harper, 1955.

Bergson, H. *Creative evolution.* (Trans. A. Mitchell.) New York: Holt, 1911.

Bergson, H. *The creative mind.* New York: Philosophical Library, 1946.

Blake, W. The marriage of heaven and hell. In D. J. Sloss & J. P. R. Wallis (Eds.), *The prophetic writings of William Blake.* Vol. 1. Oxford: Clarendon Press, 1926.

Bruner, J. S. *The process of education.* Cambridge: Harvard Univ. Press, 1960.

Burt, C. The factorial analysis of emotional traits, Parts I and II. *Charact. & Pers.*, 1939, 7, 238–254, 275–299.

Chapin, F. S. Preliminary standardization of a social insight scale. *Amer. sociol. Rev.*, 1942, 7, 214–225.

Cline, V. *et al. Task: fighter*. A research report of the Human Research Unit No. 2, OCAFF, Fort Ord, California, April, 1954.

Cronbach, L. Statistical methods applied to Rorschach scores: a review. *Psychol. Bull.*, 1949, 46, 393–429.

Crutchfield, R. S. Assessment of persons through a quasi-group-interaction technique. *J. abnorm. soc. Psychol.*, 1951, 4, 577–588.

Ebin, D. (Ed.) *The drug experience*. New York: Orion Press, 1961.

Eysenck, H. J. The general factor in aesthetic judgments. *Brit. J. Psychol.*, 1940, 31, 94–102.

Eysenck, H. J. Some factors in the appreciation of poetry, and their relation to temperamental qualities. *Charact. & Pers.*, 1940–41, 9, 160–167.

Eysenck, H. J. "Type" factors in aesthetic judgments. *Brit. J. Psychol.*, 1941, 31, 262–270.

Eysenck, H. J. *Dimensions of personality*. London: Routledge, Kegan Paul, 1947.

Fenichel, O. *Psychoanalytical theory of the neuroses*. New York: Norton, 1945.

Fowler, C. Personality correlates of the differential use of shading on the Rorschach test. Unpublished bachelor's thesis, Bennington College, 1949.

Freud, S. Formulations regarding the two principles in mental functioning. In *Collected papers of Sigmund Freud*. Vol. IV. London: Hogarth Press and Institute of Psychoanalysis, 1950.

Gardner, J. W. *Excellence*. New York: Harper, 1961.

Gardner, M. *The Scientific American book of mathematical puzzles and diversions*. New York: Simon & Schuster, 1959.

Ghiselin, B. (Ed.) *The creative process*. New York: Mentor, 1955.

Ginzberg, E. *Human resources: the wealth of a nation*. New York: Simon & Schuster, 1958.

Gough, H. G. Studies of social intolerance: I. Some psychological and sociological correlates of anti-Semitism. *J. soc. Psychol.*, 1951, 33, 237–246.

Gough, H. G. *The general information survey*. Berkeley, California: Institute of Personality Assessment and Research, Univ. of California, 1954.

Gough, H. G. *California Psychological Inventory manual*. Palo Alto: Consulting Psychologists Press, 1957.

Gough, H. G., & Krauss, I. An assessment study of Air Force officers: Part II. Description of the assessed sample. Lackland Air Force Base, Texas: Personnel Laboratory, Wright Air Development Center, September, 1958. (*Technical Report* WADC-TR-58-91 (II), ASTIA Document No. AD 208 700.)

Gough, H. G., & Woodworth, D. G. Stylistic variations among professional research scientists. *J. Psychol.*, 1960, 49, 87–98.

Guilford, J. P., Wilson, R. C., Christensen, P. R., & Lewis, D. J. A factor-analytic study of creative thinking. I. Hypotheses and description of tests. *Rep. Psychol. Lab.*, No. 4. Los Angeles: Univ. of Southern California, 1951.

Guilford, J. P., Wilson, R. C., & Christensen, P. R. A factor-analytic study of creative thinking: II. Administration of tests and analysis of results. *Rep. Psychol. Lab.*, No. 8. Los Angeles: Univ. of Southern California, 1952.

Hadamard, J. *The psychology of invention in the mathematical field*. (Reprint of 1945.) New York: Dover, 1954.

Harris, R. E., & Christiansen, C. Prediction of response to brief psychotherapy. *J. Psychol.*, 1946, 21, 269–284.

Hathaway, S. R., & McKinley, J. C. *Manual for the MMPI*. Minneapolis: Univ. of Minnesota Press, 1943.

Hathaway, S. R., & Meehl, P. E. *An atlas for the clinical use of the MMPI.* Minneapolis: Univ. of Minnesota Press, 1951.

Hugo, V. *Les miserables.* New York: Modern Library, 1931.

Hutchinson, E. D. *How to think creatively.* New York: Abingdon-Cokesbury Press, 1949.

Huxley, A. *The doors of perception.* New York: Harper, 1954.

Hyman, R. *Some experiments in creativity.* New York: Behavioral Research Service, General Electric, 1960.

Innovation in science. *Scientific Amer.*, 1958, 199.

Institute of Personality Assessment and Research, University of California, Berkeley. *The creative person.* Berkeley: University Extension, Univ. of California, 1961.

James, W. *Pragmatism.* Lecture 1. *The present dilemma in philosophy.* New York: Longmans, Green, 1907.

Klein, G., & Schlesinger, H. Where is the perceiver in perceptual theory? *J. Pers.*, 1949, 18, 32–47.

Kris, E. Art and regression. *Trans. New York Acad. Sci.*, 1944, 6, 236–250.

Krout, M. Y., & Tabin, J. K. Measuring personality in developmental terms: the Personal Preference Scale. *Genet. Psychol. Monogr.*, 1954, 50, 289–335.

Kubie, L. S. *Neurotic distortion of the creative process.* (Reprint of 1958.) New York: Noonday Press, 1961.

Leary, T., & Coffey, H. The prediction of interpersonal behavior in group psychotherapy. *Group Psychother.*, 1954, 7, 7–51.

Levinson, D. J., & Sanford, R. N. A scale for the measurement of anti-Semitism. *J. Psychol.*, 1944, 17, 339–370.

Likert, R., & Quasha, W. H. *Revised Minnesota Paper Form Board Test.* New York: Psychological Corp., 1948.

McKellar, P. *Imagination and thinking.* New York: Basic Books, 1958.

MacKinnon, D. W. Genus architectus creator varietas Americanus. *Amer. Inst. Architects J.*, September, 1960, 31–35.

MacKinnon, D. W., Crutchfield, R. S., Barron, F., Block, J., Gough, H. G., & Harris, R. E. An assessment study of Air Force officers. Part I: Design of the study and description of the variables. Lackland Air Force Base, Texas: Personnel Laboratory, Wright Air Development Center, April, 1958. (*Technical Report* WADC-TR-58-91 (I), ASTIA Document No. AD 151 040.)

Maltzman, I., Simon, S., Raskin, D., & Licht, L. Experimental studies in the training of originality. *Psychol. Monogr.*, 1960, 74, 6, 1–23.

Maritain, J. *Creative intuition in art and poetry.* New York: Meridian Books, 1955.

Murphy, G. *Human potentialities.* New York: Basic Books, 1958.

Murray, H. A. *Thematic Apperception Test manual.* Cambridge: Harvard Univ. Printing Office, 1943.

Parnes, S. J. *Compendium of research on creative imagination.* Buffalo, N.Y.: Creative Educ. Found., 1960.

Poincaré, H. *Science and method.* (Trans. F. Maitland.) New York: Dover, 1952.

Rorschach, H. *Psychodiagnostics.* Bern: Huber (Grune & Stratton, New York, distributors), 1942.

Squier, L. H. Personality dimensions: a cluster analysis of ratings. Unpublished doctoral dissertation, Univ. of California, Berkeley, 1953.

Stein, M. I., & Heinze, Shirley J. *Creativity and the individual.* Glencoe: Free Press, 1960.

Strong, E. K., Jr. *Vocational interest blank for men.* Palo Alto: Stanford Univ. Press, 1938.

Taylor, C. W., et al. *The 1955 University of Utah research conference on the identification of creative scientific talent.* Salt Lake City: Univ. of Utah Press, 1956.

Taylor, C. W., et al. *The second (1957) University of Utah research conference on the identification of creative scientific talent.* Salt Lake City: Univ. of Utah Press, 1958.

Taylor, C. W., et al. *The third (1959) University of Utah research conference on the identification of creative scientific talent.* Salt Lake City: Univ. of Utah Press, 1959.

Taylor, D. W. Thinking and creativity. *Ann. N.Y. Acad. Sci.*, 1960, 91, 108–127.

Taylor, D. W., & McNemar, O. W. Problem solving and thinking. *Annu. Rev. Psychol.*, 1955, 6, 455–482.

Terman, L. M., & Oden, M. H. *The gifted child grows up.* Palo Alto: Stanford Univ. Press, 1947.

Torrance, E. P. *Sex role identification and creativity: an exploratory study.* Minneapolis: Bureau of Educ. Research, Univ. of Minnesota, 1959.

Torrance, E. P. Mental health problems of highly creative individuals. Paper read at Amer. Psychol. Assn., New York, August, 1961.

Torrance, E. P., Bowers, J. E., Radig, H. J., Palamutlu, N., & Krishnaiah, P. R. *Explorations in creative thinking in the early school years: I–XII.* Minneapolis: Bureau of Educ. Research, Univ. of Minnesota, 1959.

Usher, A. P. *A history of mechanical inventions.* (Rev. ed.) Cambridge: Harvard Univ. Press, 1954.

Welsh, G. S. A projective figure-preference test for diagnosis of psychopathology: 1. A preliminary investigation. Unpublished doctoral dissertation, Univ. of Minnesota, 1949.

Welsh, G. S. An anxiety index and an internalization ratio for the MMPI. *J. consult. Psychol.*, 1952, 16, 65–72.

Welsh, G. S., & Dahlstrom, W. G. (Eds.) *Basic readings in the MMPI in psychology and medicine.* Minneapolis: Univ. of Minnesota Press, 1957.

Wertheimer, M. *Productive thinking.* New York: Harper, 1945.

Wesman, A. G. *Personnel classification test.* New York: Psychological Corp., 1947.

White, R. Motivation reconsidered: the concept of competence. *Psychol. Rev.*, 1959, 66, 297–333.

Whiting, C. S. *Creative thinking.* New York: Reinhold, 1958.

Williams, H. L., & Lawrence, J. F. Comparison of the Rorschach and MMPI by means of factor analysis. *J. consult. Psychol.*, 1954, 18, 193–197.

Witkin, H. A. *Personality through perception.* New York: Harper, 1953.

Yamamoto, K. *Creativity and intellect: review of current research and projection.* Minneapolis: Bureau of Educ. Research, Univ. of Minnesota, 1961.

Index

DATE DUE

3 day reserve			
AUG 6			
OCT 2 2 1982			
JAN 1 9 1983			
NOV. 1 9 1984			
JAN. 2 5 1985			
SEP 2 7 1985			
JE 24 '87			
10/6/99			
AUG 2 2 2001			
GAYLORD			PRINTED IN U.S.A.